Endoluminal
Vascular Prostheses

Endoluminal Vascular Prostheses

Timothy A.M. Chuter, M.D.
Assistant Professor of Surgery, Columbia University College of
Physicians and Surgeons; Assistant Attending Surgeon,
Columbia-Presbyterian Medical Center, New York

Carlos E. Donayre, M.D.
Assistant Professor of Surgery, University of California,
Los Angeles, UCLA School of Medicine, Los Angeles;
Chief, Division of Vascular Surgery, Wadsworth Veterans
Administration Medical Center, Los Angeles; Division of
Vascular Surgery, Harbor-UCLA Medical Center, Torrance,
California

Rodney A. White, M.D.
Professor of Surgery, University of California, Los Angeles,
UCLA School of Medicine, Los Angeles; Chief, Division of
Vascular Surgery, and Associate Chairman, Department of
Surgery, Harbor-UCLA Medical Center, Torrance, California

Little, Brown and Company
Boston New York Toronto London

Library of Congress Cataloging-in-Publication Data

Endoluminal vascular prostheses / Timothy A.M. Chuter, Carlos E.
    Donayre, Rodney A. White [editors].
        p.   cm.
    Includes bibliographical references and index.
    ISBN 0-316-14373-1
    1. Blood vessel prosthesis. 2. Blood-vessels--Endoscopic surgery.
  I. Chuter, Timothy A.M. II. Donayre, Carlos E.
    [DNLM: 1. Blood Vessel Prosthesis--methods. 2. Blood Vessel
  Prosthesis--instrumentation. 3. Vascular Diseases--surgery.
  4. Endoscopy. WG 170 E557 1995]
  RD598.55.E52 1995
  617.4'130592—dc20
  DNLM/DLC
  for Library of Congress   94-32997
                                                                    CIP

Printed in the United States of America

MV-NY

Editorial: Nancy E. Chorpenning
Production Editor: Marie A. Salter
Copyeditor: Elizabeth Willingham
Indexer: Sharon Cloud Hogan
Production Supervisor/Designer: Cate Rickard
Cover Designer: Steve Webster
Composition and Production: Silverchair Science + Communications

To James A. Deweese, whose leadership, knowledge, and expertise have guided our vascular surgery careers

Contents

Preface

As recently as 1991, transluminal therapy of vascular lesions was limited to the treatment of disease with percutaneous techniques applied primarily by radiologists. Now, use of endovascular stents and stent-graft prostheses to treat vascular lesions has heightened the interest of vascular surgeons and other interventionalists in endovascular therapy. The potential to treat major vascular lesions, such as aneurysms, without conventional surgical procedures has stimulated tremendous interest and dramatic advances in this novel therapeutic approach. The importance of endoluminal methods has been acknowledged by many vascular specialists, and potential applications for endoluminal graft therapy are presently being evaluated in many areas of vascular surgery.

Developments in endoluminal therapy are occurring at a rapid rate, and with the numerous new experimental devices and techniques currently under investigation, it is difficult to obtain an up-to-date and accurate overview of advances and potential developments in the field. This text brings together current information from most of the major groups working in the field, in an attempt to provide a broad understanding of how endoluminal devices were developed, how they work, how they compare, what they are capable of, and what their future impact might be. The devices are described by their inventors, and their applications are detailed by investigators directly involved in the clinical studies. We must emphasize that these technologies are experimental and unapproved

and that long-term efficacy and safety have yet to be demonstrated.

The early results achieved with endoluminal vascular repair are
promising and suggest that this form of therapy may be an important new method in the effective treatment of vascular diseases. We
hope *Endoluminal Vascular Prostheses* will serve as a valuable
introduction to the field.

T.A.M.C.
C.E.D.
R.A.W.

Acknowledgments

We acknowledge the support and commitment of Little, Brown and Company in the timely preparation and publication of this text. In particular, we appreciate the work of Executive Editor Nancy Chorpenning, who kept us organized and focused to meet a demanding timetable. We also thank Suzanne Brendle for her editorial assistance, as well as Marie Salter and many others on the production staff.

We also recognize Elizabeth Willingham of Silverchair Science + Communications for completing the final production of this project.

Contributing Authors

Timothy A.M. Chuter, M.D.
Assistant Professor of Surgery, Columbia University College of Physicians and Surgeons; Assistant Attending Surgeon, Columbia-Presbyterian Medical Center, New York

Michael D. Dake, M.D.
Assistant Professor of Radiology and Medicine, Stanford University School of Medicine; Chief, Cardiovascular and Interventional Radiology, Stanford University Hospital, Stanford, California

Edward B. Diethrich, M.D.
Medical Director, Arizona Heart Institute, Phoenix

Carlos E. Donayre, M.D.
Assistant Professor of Surgery, University of California, Los
Angeles, UCLA School of Medicine, Los Angeles; Chief, Division
of Vascular Surgery, Wadsworth Veterans Administration Medical
Center, Los Angeles; Division of Vascular Surgery, Harbor-UCLA
Medical Center, Torrance, California
10. *Applications in Peripheral Vascular Surgery: Traumatic
    Arteriovenous Fistulas and Pseudoaneurysms*
11. *Applications in Peripheral Vascular Surgery: Femoropopliteal
    Disease*
12. *Patient Selection and Preoperative Assessment*
13. *Intraoperative Imaging System Requirements*

Krassi Ivancev, M.D.
Associate Professor of Diagnostic Radiology, University of Lund;
Head, Angiographic and Interventional Section, Malmö General
Hospital, Malmö, Sweden
12. *Patient Selection and Preoperative Assessment*

Harrison M. Lazarus, M.D.
Clinical Associate Professor of Surgery, University of Utah School
of Medicine; Staff Surgeon, FHP Healthcare, Salt Lake City, Utah
5. *The EVT Endoluminal Prosthesis: Developmental Concepts
    and Design*

James May, M.S.
Bosch Professor of Surgery, University of Sydney; Head, Division
of Surgery, Royal Prince Alfred Hospital, Sydney, Australia
7. *Stented and Nonstented Endoluminal Grafts for Aneurysmal
    Disease: The Australian Experience*

Juan C. Parodi, M.D.
Adjunct Professor of Surgery, Bowman Gray School of Medicine
of Wake Forest University, Winston-Salem, North Carolina;
Director, Instituto Cardiovascular de Buenos Aires, Buenos Aires,
Argentina
3. *Endovascular Repair of Abdominal Aortic Aneurysms*

William J. Quiñones-Baldrich, M.D.
Associate Professor of Surgery, University of California, Los
Angeles, UCLA School of Medicine; Attending Surgeon, UCLA
Medical Center, Los Angeles
  6. *The EVT Endoluminal Prosthesis: Clinical Experience and
     Results*

Marco Scoccianti, M.D.
Vascular Surgeon, Harbor-UCLA Medical Center, Torrance,
California
10. *Applications in Peripheral Vascular Surgery: Traumatic
    Arteriovenous Fistulas and Pseudoaneurysms*
11. *Applications in Peripheral Vascular Surgery: Femoropopliteal
    Disease*

Charles P. Semba, M.D.
Assistant Professor of Cardiovascular and Interventional
Radiology, Stanford University School of Medicine and Stanford
University Medical Center, Stanford, California
  8. *Endoluminal Stent-Grafting in the Thoracic Aorta*

Geoffrey H. White, M.D.
Associate Professor of Surgery, University of Sydney; Vascular
Surgeon, Department of Vascular Surgery, Royal Prince Alfred
Hospital, Sydney, Australia
  7. *Stented and Nonstented Endoluminal Grafts for Aneurysmal
     Disease: The Australian Experience*
13. *Intraoperative Imaging System Requirements*

Rodney A. White, M.D.
Professor of Surgery, University of California, Los Angeles, UCLA
School of Medicine, Los Angeles; Chief, Division of Vascular
Surgery, and Associate Chairman, Department of Surgery, Harbor-
UCLA Medical Center, Torrance California
12. *Patient Selection and Preoperative Assessment*
13. *Intraoperative Imaging System Requirements*
14. *The Utility and Development of Endovascular Prostheses*

Weiyun Yu, B.Sc.(Med), M.B., B.S.
Endovascular Research Fellow, Department of Surgery, University of Sydney; Surgical Registrar, Royal Prince Alfred Hospital, Sydney, Australia

Historical
Perspectives

I

Notice

The technologies discussed herein are experimental and unapproved. Clinical trials are ongoing, and long-term efficacy and safety have yet to be demonstrated.

The indications and dosages of all drugs in this book have been recommended in the medical literature and conform to the practices of the general medical community. The medications do not necessarily have specific approval by the Food and Drug Administration for use in the diseases and dosages for which they are recommended. The package insert for each drug should be consulted for use and dosage as approved by the FDA. Because standards for usage change, it is advisable to keep abreast of revised recommendations, particularly those concerning new drugs.

Endovascular Grafts: History of Minimally Invasive Treatment of Vascular Disease

1

Timothy A.M. Chuter

Potential applications of endovascular grafts have been found in all areas of vascular surgery, but their use for aortic aneurysms was the first to be explored. Current surgical treatment of aortic aneurysms is effective and relatively safe, but it engenders considerable morbidity, debility, and expense [1]. Because many of the patients with aortic aneurysm are elderly and frail, less invasive procedures are appealing.

These less invasive therapies follow a trend that has produced profound changes in all fields of surgery. Stent placement, angioplasty, and the various procedures performed using the laparoscope, thoracoscope, arthroscope, and endoscope are all distinguished by the indirect nature of the intervention. These techniques enable the surgeon to avoid making a large incision by operating through long narrow instruments from remote sites. When we view the development of endovascular treatment of aortic aneurysm in this broad context, we can learn from the lessons of some of the other procedures, such as laparoscopic cholecystectomy.

Minimally invasive treatment of aortic aneurysm actually has a much longer history than many of these other techniques. Many alternative approaches to the prevention of aneurysm rupture preceded the development of endovascular grafting, such as operations to induce aneurysm thrombosis and modifications of open surgical repair.

Induced Thrombosis

The common goal of many of the less invasive treatments of aortic aneurysm was aneurysm thrombosis. One method of inducing thrombosis was to introduce great lengths of wire into the aneurysm through the femoral artery. The thrombotic effect of the wire was later augmented by the application of electric current [2]. Despite the potential for aneurysm rupture and embolism during the introduction of wire, sporadic use of aneurysm wiring persisted into the mid-1970s.

Ligation or balloon occlusion of the arterial outflow was also introduced as a means of inducing thrombosis. The extent of aneurysm thrombosis was variable and sometimes difficult to assess [3]. Complete thrombosis occurred in approximately 30 percent of patients. In an attempt to induce complete thrombosis in the remainder, distal ligation was augmented by transcatheter introduction of bucrylate [4] and thrombin. In theory, these methods of inducing aneurysm thrombosis carried the risk of renal artery embolism, although deterioration in renal function was rarely seen.

Aneurysm Exclusion

The main limitation of induced thrombosis as a method of treating aortic aneurysm is its failure to prevent aneurysm rupture [3, 5]. To isolate the aneurysm from the circulation more completely, proximal ligation, or stapling, was added to distal occlusion and combined with a local arterial bypass [6]. The low rate of aneurysm rupture observed following this procedure has important implications for endovascular aneurysm repair, because both external and internal methods of aneurysm isolation leave the lumbar and inferior mesenteric branches as a potential source of collateral flow into the aneurysm.

Advances in Open Surgical Technique

In addition to these thrombus-inducing procedures, several modifications in the technique of open surgical repair can be viewed as steps toward endovascular grafting. The first was the substitution of aneurysm repair from within for aneurysm resection [7]. The second was the development of sutureless grafts.

Implantation of the "ring graft" was accomplished by tying the aorta around a rigid segment at the end of the graft [8]. The main advantages of this procedure were speed and low blood loss. The main problems have been degeneration of the aorta around the ring, size mismatch, and stenosis. Matsumae et al. [9] went one step further by using a self-expanding ring, which eliminated the need for periaortic dissection. Implantation into the descending thoracic aorta of nine dogs was accomplished rapidly with little blood loss and no migration, leakage, or aortic degeneration during follow-up extending to a maximum of 150 days. Although this sutureless graft was designed to be inserted into the surgically exposed artery, its method of attachment was clearly analogous to the function of the stent in endovascular repair.

The external wrap procedure of Robicsek et al. [10], although regarded as a lesser operation, actually represented a step away from endovascular repair. This kind of procedure required extensive surgical exposure and often failed to prevent aneurysm rupture.

Endovascular Grafting

A study of the patent literature reveals that the idea of endovascular grafting for aneurysm repair is far from new [11–14]. Why, then, has this approach taken so long to become a realistic proposition?

5

Although imaging systems have improved in recent years, the lack of suitable imaging was not the primary reason for the delay. As Parodi has demonstrated, relatively simple fluoroscopic equipment is adequate for accurate placement of an aortic prosthesis. The one missing element in all these early systems was a reliable means of graft attachment. Stapling alone was neither sufficiently secure nor sufficiently hemostatic. A better seal resulted when the graft was pressed against the aortic wall by a stent—hence the rapid progress in endovascular grafting for aneurysm repair following the development of arterial stents. The importance of arterial stents in the development of endovascular grafting is illustrated by the evolution of the Lazarus device from a reliance on staples [13] to the use of a self-expanding stent [14].

All current systems of endovascular grafting rely on some form of arterial stent for graft attachment. Even systems described as "stentless" rely on the incorporation of stentlike structural characteristics into the graft itself [15, 16]. So important is stent function to endovascular grafting that the differences between systems are largely attributable to the differences in the characteristics of their stents. The broad categorization of stents into self-expanding and balloon-expanded can therefore be equally well applied to endovascular grafts.

Self-Expanding Stents

Much of the original work with intra-arterial manipulation of catheters and guidewires is attributable to Charles Dotter and his collaborators in Portland, Oregon. Dotter can also be credited with the development of the first arterial stent for insertion through a remote artery [17]. The original Dotter stent (Fig. 1-1) was plagued by low expansion ratios and episodes of thrombosis, especially when coated with silicone.

The function of a simple coil stent was somewhat improved by taking advantage of the special thermal properties of nitinol [18]. The nitinol stent was introduced in a cooled system as a straight wire. Once in the bloodstream it warmed and expanded to its preformed diameter. A tightly wound version of this stent was found to limit the extravasation of blood enough to permit healing of an

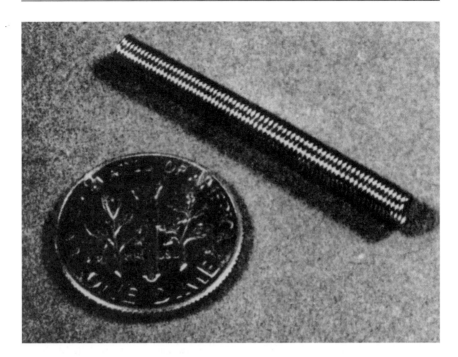

Fig. 1-1. Tubular coilspring endovascular prosthesis. (From CT Dotter. Transluminally-placed coilspring endarterial tube grafts. Long-term patency in canine popliteal artery. *Invest Radiol* 1969;4:329–332.)

experimental traumatic aneurysm in a dog. This is the first case of endoluminal aneurysm repair from a remote site [18]. On the basis of these acute experiments, it was suggested that tightly wound spiral stents could be used clinically to reinforce injured or aneurysmal vessels. However, this form of arterial repair has had very limited application and only recently has the nitinol coil stent been re-examined as a possible means of graft attachment.

Another helical stent, the double helix of Maas (Fig. 1-2), had several interesting features, chief of which was the capability of expansion to aortic diameters [19]. Maas successfully implanted helical stents in 65 dogs and five calves. This 1984 paper is also notable for its idea that a stent could be combined with microporous synthetics to serve a barrier function. The implication, through a reference to Cragg's work, was that such a stent-graft combination could be used for arterial repair.

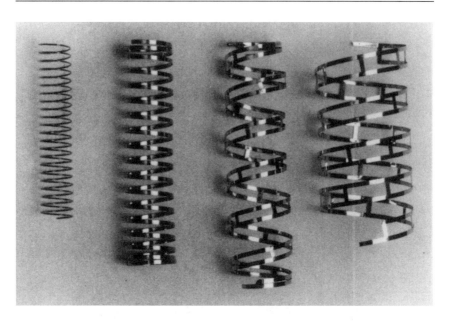

Fig. 1-2. Various types of implanted spiral springs, including two double-helix spirals. (From D Maas et al. Radiological follow-up of transluminally inserted vascular endoprosthesis: An experimental study using expanding spirals. *Radiology* 1984;152:659–663.)

Balko et al. can probably be credited with the first reported experimental use of a stent-graft combination for the treatment of artificial aneurysms [20]. In these experiments, a novel form of nitinol Z stent was combined with a sleeve of polyurethane (Fig. 1-3) and tested in a sheep model of aortic aneurysm. Although these experiments demonstrated the feasibility of inserting such devices transfemorally, placement was actually guided by direct aortic palpation, not fluoroscopy.

The first radiographically guided aortic graft implantations were reported by Lawrence et al. in 1987 [21]. They used a chain of Gianturco Z stents (Fig. 1-4) within a tube of woven polyester (Dacron). This stent-graft combination was implanted in the abdominal aorta of six dogs and thoracic aorta of another three. At follow-up, after seven to 35 weeks, all but one graft remained patent, although two had developed stenosis. The occurrence of graft stenosis and occlusion was thought to be largely due to folding

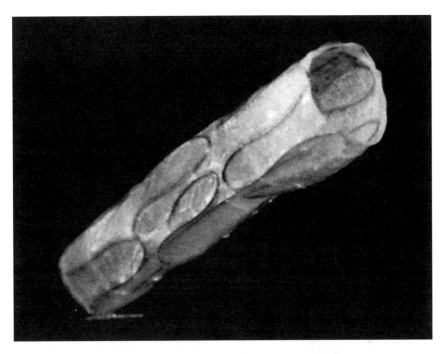

Fig. 1-3. The intraluminal polyurethane prosthesis of Balko. (From A Balko et al. Transfemoral placement of intraluminal polyurethane prosthesis for abdominal aortic aneurysm. *J Surg Res* 1986;40:305–309.)

and kinking of the inelastic Dacron fabric. There was no evidence of stent migration or strut rupture. Two stents implanted in the thoracic aorta were found to have penetrated the wall, but no extravasation was seen on angiography and neither dog suffered any apparent ill effects. Upon explantation, all grafts were found to be lined by a layer of endothelial cells and incorporated into the surrounding arteries by varying degrees of fibrosis.

In an effort to avoid graft stenosis and occlusion, a knitted nylon-Lycra combination was substituted for the woven polyester (Dacron) graft of the earlier experiments. The new prosthesis was implanted transfemorally using percutaneous technique in both the normal canine aorta [22] and a canine model of aortic aneurysm [23]. All but one of the grafts in the latter series remained patent at six months, but so did the adjacent side branches, due to the porosity of the knitted fabric. Only one prosthesis carried barbs. The oth-

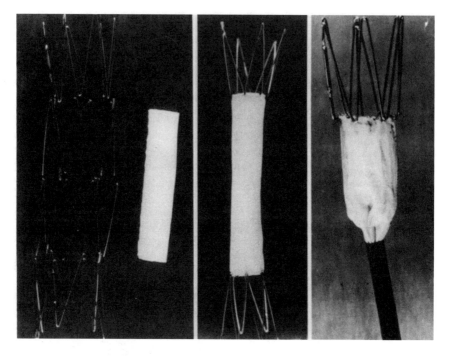

Fig. 1-4. The percutaneous endovascular graft of Lawrence. (From DD Lawrence Jr et al. Percutaneous endovascular graft: Experimental evaluation. *Radiology* 1987;163:357–360.)

ers had an entire stent protruding from the proximal end of the graft to act as an anchor. The single case of migration occurred with an unbarbed prosthesis. An interesting finding was the proliferation of granulation and connective tissue between the endovascular graft and the aortic wall.

Although these experiments did not proceed to clinical work, this system is a direct ancestor of several others, which are currently in clinical trials around the world. The closest relative is the system used by Dake et al. [24] to treat thoracic aortic aneurysms (see Chapter 8). In Dake's system a self-expanding endoskeleton was made by linking Gianturco Z stents to one another with loops of suture, whereas Mirich et al. had joined their stents with metal struts. The methods of graft delivery and extrusion were the same.

Chuter et al. used a rather different system to implant straight and bifurcated grafts for aortic aneurysm repair (see Chapter 4).

Stents were attached only to the graft orifices and not to each other. Therefore the graft had no column strength, necessitating fundamental changes in the delivery system. Eliminating the chain of stents was necessary to increase the flexibility of the prosthesis, which was essential for the development of a bifurcated graft. Transfemoral insertion of a bifurcated graft in dogs was first reported in 1992 [25]. Clinical trials of both the straight and bifurcated systems are proceeding, but to date only the bifurcated form has been used in patients [26], due to the more restrictive requirements for use of a straight graft [27].

Ivaneu et al. have repaired aortic aneurysms with straight aortic and aortoiliac grafts, using a system originally designed for the insertion of covered stents into the esophagus. This system also used a central carrier to pull the graft from the delivery system. A single loop of suture attached the graft to the button at the proximal end of the carrier. The suture loop traversed the carrier through its central lumen to the outer end, where it could be cut to release the graft.

Another system that relies on self-expanding Z stents appears to have been developed quite independently in Russia [28]. Straight and bifurcated forms of this prosthesis have been inserted in large numbers of patients. In the majority of cases, the prosthesis was placed directly into the artery following conventional surgical exposure and control. However, the Russian prosthesis has also been inserted into the infrarenal aorta under fluoroscopic control, using a novel combined axillary and femoral approach.

The early history of the Lazarus device (manufactured by EndoVascular Technologies) is documented only in the patent literature (see Chapter 5). The original version relied on balloon-driven stapling [13], whereas the device currently in clinical trials incorporates a self-expanding Z stent at each graft orifice [29]. A balloon is used to augment barb implantation, but only when the stent has already expanded.

The Wallstent already has a role in the treatment of arterial occlusive disease due to its low profile and flexibility. It is actually a form of spiral stent, in which several spirals are braided together to enhance the resistance to compression, improve expansion ratios, and reduce shortening. A version of the Wallstent with a high wire density and lower porosity has been studied in animal models of aortic aneurysm [30]. Coated Wallstents have also been studied in animals, but none of these modified Wallstents have been used clinically to treat aneurysms.

Balloon-Expanded Stents

The first balloon-expanded stent, described by Palmaz in 1985, was a tubular wire mesh. This stent lacked radial compliance and accumulated thrombus. For these reasons Palmaz soon substituted a lath design [31]. Extensive experience has established a role for the Palmaz stent in the treatment of peripheral vascular occlusive disease. Its role as a means of securing endovascular grafts was first explored by Parodi and Palmaz in a large number of canine insertions, culminating in the series of six canine aortic aneurysm repairs reported to the Radiology Society of North America in 1990 [32]. All six of these grafts were still patent six months later. In contrast, Laborde et al. [33] noted graft thrombosis shortly following two of eight canine aneurysm repairs, using the same method and the same model. Moreover, four other grafts developed kinks. The occlusions were attributed to twists in the graft and the kinks to shortening of the aneurysm.

Interestingly, the autopsy findings in these two studies were very similar. The interval between the aneurysm wall and the graft was found to be filled with thrombus, and the adjacent graft lacked intima. The tissue ingrowth and neointima deposition observed by Mirich et al. [23] probably reflects the different model of aortic aneurysm. The Palmaz-Parodi aneurysm was constructed of Dacron, whereas that used by Mirich et al. was a balloon-dilated artery.

The study reported by Boudghene et al. [34] is most notable for the creation of an aneurysm by the instillation of elastase into an isolated segment of aorta. Aneurysm repair was accomplished successfully in all eight dogs using a thin-wall graft mounted on Palmaz stents. The lack of kinking in these studies provides support for the suggestion that the kinks seen by Laborde et al. were due to shrinkage of their prosthetic aneurysms.

The first six cases of human endoaortic graft insertion were performed by Parodi in Argentina and described in his landmark 1991 paper [35]. One graft was inserted for aortic dissection; the other five patients had abdominal aortic aneurysms. Parodi has since gained enormous experience with this technique for treatment of aortic aneurysm and a variety of other applications (see Chapter 3).

Many other balloon-expanded systems are currently under development, several of which integrate the structural properties of the stent into components of the graft.

De Vries et al. [15] have developed a double-walled polyurethane tube that becomes rigid when a layer of acrylate between its walls polymerizes on exposure to ultraviolet light. The system developed by White et al. [16] has crowns of malleable wire sewn into the wall of the graft throughout its length. These "graft attachment devices," as they are called by the team in Sydney, retain their balloon-expanded configuration, thereby keeping the graft pressed against the artery.

Strecker stents have been manufactured in a double-knit structure to reduce porosity, in the hope that the stent alone will limit the extravasation of blood enough to permit aneurysm thrombosis and healing. Strecker stents have also been used experimentally in conjunction with polytetrafluorethylene (PTFE) membrane [36], although perhaps the most promising approach has been to co-knit Dacron fabric into the walls of the stent [37]. The co-knit Strecker stent has been used for aneurysm repair in a small number of patients, with mixed results. Multiple overlapping stents were implanted sequentially to achieve the desired length. This method of varying the length of the final combined prosthesis eliminated some of the problems with exact sizing that are commonly encountered using straight aorto-aortic grafts.

In addition to gaining extensive experience with aneurysms, Parodi has adapted his technique for use in the treatment of false aneurysms and arteriovenous fistulas (see Chapter 10). The Parodi system has also been used to treat arterial occlusive disease, mainly in the iliac arteries [38]. In this technique, long segments of graft extend between the anchoring stents, which are located only at the graft orifices.

The first use of an endovascular graft as an adjunct to balloon angioplasty was probably by Cragg et al. [39], whose system combines a novel serpentine nitinol stent with expanded PTFE grafts. This system is now commercially available in Europe, and clinical experience is accumulating rapidly.

Palmaz has adopted yet another approach to the use of endovascular graft-stent combinations for the treatment of occlusive disease that takes advantage of the elastic properties of ePTFE by expanding both the graft and the stent with a balloon [40]. This helps minimize the volume of the delivery system.

References

1. Breckwoldt WL, Mackey WC, O'Donnell TF Jr. The economic implications of high-risk abdominal aortic aneurysms. *J Vasc Surg* 1991;13:798–804.

2. Blakemore A. Progressive, constrictive occlusion of the abdominal aorta with wiring and electrothermic coagulation: One-stage operation for arteriosclerotic aneurysm of the abdominal aorta. *Ann Surg* 1951;133:447–462.

3. Karmody AM et al. The current position of nonresective treatment for abdominal aortic aneurysm. *Surgery* 1983;94:591–597.

4. Goldman ML et al. Bucrylate embolization of abdominal aortic aneurysms: An adjunct to nonresective therapy. *AJR Am J Roentgenol* 1980;135:1195–1200.

5. Schanzer H, Papa MC, Miller CM. Rupture of surgically thrombosed abdominal aortic aneurysm. *J Vasc Surg* 1985;2:278.

6. Shah DM et al. Treatment of abdominal aortic aneurysm by exclusion and bypass: An analysis of outcome. *J Vasc Surg* 1991;13:15–22.

7. Creech O Jr. Endoaneurysmorrhaphy and treatment of aortic aneurysm. *Ann Surg* 1966;164:935–946.

8. Oz MC et al. Replacement of the abdominal aorta with a sutureless intraluminal ringed prosthesis. *Am J Surg* 1989;158:121–126.

9. Matsumae M, Uchida H, Teramoto S. An experimental study of a new sutureless intraluminal graft with an elastic ring that can attach itself to the vessel wall. *J Vasc Surg* 1988;8:38–44.

10. Robicsek F, Daugherth HK, Mullen DC. External grafting of aortic aneurysms. *J Thorac Cardiovasc Surg* 1971;61:131–134.

14

11. Ersek RA. Method for fixing prosthetic implants in a living body. US Patent Number 3,657,744, 1972.

12. Choudhury MH. Method for performing aneurysm repair. US Patent Number 4,140,126, 1979.

13. Lazarus HM. Intraluminal graft device: System and method. US Patent Number 4,787,799, 1988.

14. Lazarus HM. Artificial graft and implantation method. US Patent Number 5,104,399, 1992.

15. de Vries J. Instant tubular prosthesis. Presented at Workshop on Transluminal Treatment of Aneurysms, Symposium on Endovascular Procedures. January 28, 1994, Utrecht, Netherlands.

16. White GH et al. A new non-stented balloon-expandable graft for either straight or bifurcated endoluminal bypass. Presented at VII International Congress on Endovascular Interventions. February 14, 1994, Scottsdale, AZ.

17. Dotter CT. Transluminally-placed coilspring endarterial tube grafts. Long-term patency in canine popliteal artery. *Invest Radiol* 1969;4:329–332.

18. Cragg A et al. Nonsurgical placement of arterial endoprostheses: A new technique using nitinol wire. *Radiology* 1983;147:261–263.

19. Maas D et al. Radiological follow-up of transluminally inserted vascular endoprosthesis: An experimental study using expanding spirals. *Radiology* 1984;152:659–663.

20. Balko A et al. Transfemoral placement of intraluminal polyurethane prosthesis for abdominal aortic aneurysm. *J Surg Res* 1986;40:305–309.

21. Lawrence DD Jr et al. Percutaneous endovascular graft: Experimental evaluation. *Radiology* 1987;163:357–360.

22. Yoshioka T et al. Self-expanding endovascular graft: An experimental study in dogs. *AJR Am J Roentgenol* 1988;151:673–676.

23. Mirich D et al. Percutaneously placed endovascular grafts for aortic aneurysms: Feasibility study. *Radiology* 1989;170:1033–1037.

24. Semba CP et al. Endovascular grafting for the treatment of thoracic aortic aneurysms: Preliminary experience at Stanford University Medical Center [abstract]. Presented at VII International Congress on Endovascular Interventions. February 1994, Scottsdale, AZ.

25. Chuter TAM et al. Transfemoral endovascular aortic graft placement. *J Vasc Surg* 1993;18:185–197.

26. Scott RAP, Chuter TAM. Clinical endovascular placement of bifurcated graft in abdominal aortic aneurysm without laparotomy. *Lancet* 1994;343:413.

27. Chuter TAM et al. Infrarenal aortic aneurysm morphology: Implications for transfemoral repair. *J Vasc Surg* 1993;17:1120–1121.

28. Volodos NL et al. Clinical experience of the use of a self-fixing synthetic prosthesis for remote endoprosthetics of the thoracic and the abdominal aorta and iliac arteries through the femoral artery and as intraoperative endoprosthesis for aorta reconstruction. *Vasa* 1991;33(Supp):93–95.

29. Lazarus HM. Experience with endovascular abdominal aortic prosthetic grafting. Presented at VII International Congress on Endovascular Interventions. February 17, 1994, Scottsdale, AZ.

30. Hagen BH et al. Self-expanding macroporous nitinol stents for transfemoral exclusion of aortic aneurysms in dogs: Preliminary results. *Cardiovasc Intervent Radiol* 1993;16:339–342.

31. Palmaz JC et al. Expandable intraluminal vascular graft: A feasibility study. *Surgery* 1986;99:199–205.

32. Palmaz JC et al. Transluminal bypass of experimental abdominal aortic aneurysm. *Radiology* 1990;177(Supp):202.

33. Laborde JC et al. Intraluminal bypass of abdominal aortic aneurysm: Feasibility study. *Radiology* 1992;184:184–190.

34. Boudghene FP et al. New model of abdominal aortic aneurysms: Treatment with an endoprosthesis through a femoral approach. *Radiology* 1992;185(Supp):162.

35. Parodi JC, Palmaz JC, Barone HD. Transfemoral intraluminal graft implantation for abdominal aortic aneurysms. *Ann Vasc Surg* 1991;5:491–499.

36. Valbracht C, et al. New PTFE closed stent: First experimental results. *Radiology* 1990;181(Supp):161.

37. Piquet P, et al. Tantalum Dacron co-knit stent for endovascular treatment of aortoiliac aneurysms: Experimental study and early clinical experience. Presented at VII International Congress on Endovascular Interventions. February 17, 1994, Scottsdale, AZ.

38. Veith F. Endovascular graft repair for aneurysm, trauma and occlusive lesions. Presented at Symposium on Endovascular Procedures. January 29, 1994, Utrecht, Netherlands.

39. Cragg AH, Dake MD. Percutaneous femoropopliteal graft placement. *Radiology* 1993;187:643–648.

40. Palmaz JC. Balloon expandable graft combinations. Presented at Western Angiographic and Interventional Society. October 1, 1993, Portland, Oregon.

Applications to Aortic Disease

II

Anatomy of the Infrarenal Aortic Aneurysm

2

Timothy A.M. Chuter

It is customary to describe the anatomy of the infrarenal aortic aneurysm in terms of a single variable—its diameter. This belies a great variability in the shape of the aneurysm, its length, and its relation to the major branches of the distal aorta. With the advent of endovascular aneurysm repair, these details of variant anatomy have become more important. The techniques of endovascular grafting may be less invasive than conventional surgical techniques, but they are also less versatile. The feasibility of endovascular repair is often limited by arterial anatomy, just as the feasibility of conventional repair is limited by the patient's ability to withstand operation. Thus, arterial anatomy now determines not only the need for repair but also the method. Variations in arterial anatomy must be anticipated through appropriate imaging to permit proper system design, patient selection, and graft sizing.

For successful endovascular aneurysm repair, the graft must be delivered through the distal vasculature and implanted securely in the nondilated artery at both ends of the aneurysm. No system of endovascular aneurysm repair will be very useful unless it can accomplish these goals in the presence of the anatomic variants that frequently accompany aortic aneurysm. Given information on the behavior of the system and the frequency of the most limiting anatomic features, it should be possible to predict the number of suitable candidates. However, a great amount of experience in a wide range of human patients is needed to define the performance of any particular system. This kind of information is not yet available on any of the current systems, nor is it likely to emerge soon, as the early clinical studies include only the easier cases to ensure good results. Moreover, the functional limits are likely to change rapidly as these systems evolve and other systems emerge.

Imaging of Aneurysm Anatomy

Information about aneurysm anatomy can be obtained through a variety of imaging modalities. Multiplane arteriography gives an accurate representation of luminal shape, size, and direction but rarely shows the aneurysm wall due to the presence of mural thrombus. A graft implanted in thrombus will not provide adequate protection from risk of aneurysm rupture. Therefore suitability for graft implantation must be based on studies that show the anatomy of the arterial wall, not just the lumen.

Conventional cross-sectional computed tomography (CT) images display the dimensions of the arterial wall but only in a transverse plane. Pearce et al. [1] have used conventional CT scanning and angiography to study arterial diameters in a variety of patients with and without aneurysms. They have also used CT scans to study mural thrombus within aneurysms.

Processing CT data to give a three-dimensional reconstruction provides additional information on the shape, direction, and length of arterial segments. Three-dimensional reconstruction of CT data was therefore used as the basis for a study of the aortoiliac anatomy found in a series of 22 aneurysm patients [2]. In this study, dynamic contrast CT scans were performed in all patients who presented to Strong Memorial Hospital in Rochester, New York, for aortic aneurysm repair between June 1991 and December 1992. Only patients who had a CT scan from another institution were excluded. Images were recorded at 3-mm intervals in the region of the renal arteries and 5-mm intervals down to the mid-pelvis. These images were examined and the profile of the aorta, the renal arteries, the iliac arteries, and the mesenteric arteries were outlined manually. The data points from each outline were stored and stacked by a visual data processing unit (ISG Technologies, Inc., Ontario, Canada) to form a three-dimensional virtual object, which could be viewed and printed from any angle. Lateral views were then used to calculate dimensions and deviations in a sagittal (anteroposterior) plane. Anterior views were used to calculate dimensions and deviations in a coronal (transverse) plane. All diameters were measured at right angles to the long axis of the vessel.

The major limitation of this method was the lack of an outside standard for calibration of measurements. However, the two independent methods of calibration that were used produced very similar results. One was based on the transverse diameter measured by conventional CT scanning; the other was based on a computer-generated measurement of aneurysm neck length, as shown in Figure 2-1.

Another potential source of error in this study was the apparent shortening that occurred between points outside the same coronal plane. For example, an aorta that had a long axis at 60 degrees to the sagittal plane would appear to be only half its true length on the anterior view. Of course, this would be revealed when the segment was inspected on the lateral view, but unfortunately most cases combined angulation in one plane with angulation in the other.

Aneurysm Neck

Secure, accurate, hemostatic implantation of the proximal end of the graft in the segment of nondilated aorta between the renal arteries and the aneurysm (the neck) is critical to graft function. Leakage and displacement are likely to occur if the graft is not closely applied to the aorta at this point, due to the primary direction of blood flow from proximal to distal.

The prerequisites for adequate proximal graft implantation vary among systems. In most, the proximal graft attachment component (usually a stent) conforms best to the inner surface of an aortic segment that is straight and roughly cylindrical. Because the aortic profile was

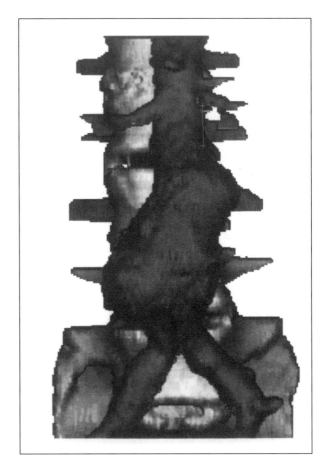

Fig. 2-1. Three-dimensional reconstruction of an aneurysm, showing computer-generated measurement of neck length. (From TA Chuter. Infrarenal aortic aneurysm structure: Implications for transfemoral repair. *J Vasc Surg* 1994;20:44–50.)

thought to have a significant effect on the feasibility of stent implantation, the extent of the proximal neck was defined more by the rate of change of aortic diameter than by the absolute diameter. The proximal end of the neck was bounded by the lower of the renal arteries.

The length of the proximal neck is probably the most important parameter measured. It determines the suitability for endovascular repair through its effects on the security of stent implantation, the area of contact between the graft and the aorta, and the leeway for variation in stent position. Out of 22 patients, the proximal neck

Table 2-1. Length of the proximal neck and distal cuff in 22 aortic aneurysms by three-dimensional reconstruction of CT data

	≤10 mm	10.1–20.0 mm	>20 mm
Neck	4	4	14
Cuff	18	3	1

was longer than 20 mm in 14 and more than 10 mm in 18 (Table 2-1), with a mean length of 26.7 ± 4.1 mm (Fig. 2-2). The similarity between the mean diameter of the neck just below the renal arteries (24.9 ± 1.4 mm) and the mean diameter at the proximal end of the aneurysm (27.1 ± 1.5 mm) confirmed that the segments designated as aneurysm neck were indeed cylindrical.

Any system incapable of implanting the proximal end of an endovascular graft in a patient with a proximal neck shorter than 10 mm would have excluded 18 percent of patients, based on this criterion alone. A more conservative approach (or a less versatile system) would have excluded 46 percent of cases by requiring that the neck be longer than 20 mm.

The lower limit of required neck length can be reduced by increasing the accuracy of graft placement—to a point. A zone of apposition is still needed to prevent leakage between the graft and the aorta. A segment of nondilated aorta is also needed for secure stent implantation. Some authors have suggested that the latter requirement can be reduced by implanting the stent over the renal orifices. There is anecdotal evidence that this entails little risk of renal artery occlusion, at least in the short term. The long-term effects on patency and the risk of damage from a barbed stent are unknown.

Distal Cuff

The distal cuff is the segment of nondilated aorta between the aneurysm and the origins of the common iliac arteries. It is important as the distal implantation site for straight aorto-aortic grafts. The

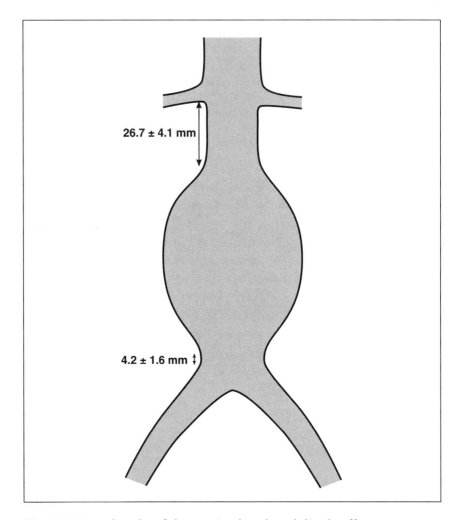

Fig. 2-2. Mean lengths of the proximal neck and distal cuff.

potential for leakage and graft displacement is less than at the prox-imal orifice. However, most groups with clinical experience of straight graft insertion agree that a stent is also required at the distal end of a straight graft to prevent retrograde flow into the aneurysm. Therefore the distal cuff is also defined, by its suitability for stent implantation, as a straight segment with roughly parallel walls.

In this series [2], the mean length of the distal cuff was 4.2 ± 1.6 mm (see Fig. 2-2). Only one patient had a distal cuff longer than 20

26

mm, only four had a cuff longer than 10 mm, and 14 had no measurable distal cuff at all (see Table 2-1). Based on this information, the distal cuff would rarely be long enough for endovascular insertion of an aorto-aortic graft, even applying the most optimistic estimates of the current systems' functional limitations. Angiographic information would tend to inflate the number of suitable cases by displaying an apparent cuff composed of mural thrombus.

Another, less insurmountable obstacle to the use of straight grafts is the frequent disparity between the aortic diameters proximal and distal to the aneurysm. The difference between the diameter of the cuff and the diameter of the neck was more than 5 mm in nine cases and more than 10 mm in four. These would require elastic or tapered grafts for straight graft repair.

Iliac Aneurysm

The maximum diameter of each common iliac artery was measured perpendicular to the long axis of the vessel. The large (5-mm) interval between the lower slices on the original CT scans represented a potential source of inaccuracy, particularly when the measured vessel traversed the body perpendicular to the long axis of the scan, as the iliac arteries sometimes did. Iliac arteries were considered to be aneurysmal if their maximum external diameter was greater than 20 mm or was more than twice the minimum diameter.

Common iliac artery aneurysms always contraindicate straight graft repair, but they only become an impediment to bifurcated graft repair when they extend to within 2 cm of the common iliac bifurcation. Extending the graft into the external iliac artery was not considered a viable option, because the internal iliac artery is deprived of prograde flow. Another risk is that the internal iliac artery, bypassed in this way, might expose the aneurysm to continued risk of rupture from retrograde perfusion through pelvic collaterals.

Seven patients (32 percent) had 11 common iliac artery aneurysms. This rate was similar to previously reported figures based on angiography [3], and conventional CT [4]. In most cases the distal common iliac artery was unaffected. Three of the seven patients had segments of distal common iliac artery suitable for implantation of a bifurcated graft on both sides. In the other four it would not have been feasible to preserve prograde flow to both internal iliac arteries and exclude all aneurysms. The external and internal iliac arteries were not studied. It is possible that the number of unsuitable patients would also have been augmented by the presence of aneurysms at these locations.

It is unclear whether both the right and left internal iliac systems need to be perfused. Endovascular aneurysm repair does not afford the opportunity to inspect the colon intraoperatively and reimplant the inferior mesenteric artery, if necessary. Therefore, I favor a conservative approach and avoid cases in which pelvic blood flow might be compromised by the presence of iliac artery aneurysms. It may be possible to be more aggressive and exclude one or the other internal iliac artery if rectal ischemia proves to be a rare complication.

The importance of a patent inferior mesenteric artery on preoperative angiograms is also unclear. I currently regard it as a contraindication to endovascular repair if the vessel is large or if there is other evidence that inferior mesenteric artery blood flow is indispensable, such as large collaterals or stenosis of other mesenteric arteries.

Aneurysm Dimensions

The aneurysms in this study were relatively small (mean transverse diameter 56.4 ± 3.3 mm). The frequent disparity between the transverse diameter of the aneurysm and corresponding anteroposterior diameter (mean difference 5.1 ± 1.09 mm) may reflect the asymmetric bulging seen in many cases (Fig. 2-3). In this study, the diameters were measured at right angles to the axis of the aneurysm, which eliminated one potential source of inaccuracy. Measurements that are not perpendicular to the axis of aorta can be falsely magnified. The measurement of diameter most affected is the one in the same plane as maximum deviation in the axis. This effect is difficult to eliminate when examining the cross-sectional images generated by conventional CT scanning [5].

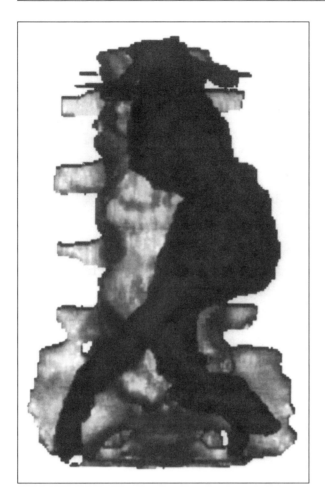

Fig. 2-3. Three-dimensional reconstruction of an aneurysm, showing asymmetric enlargement and twisting of the aneurysm. (From TA Chuter. Infrarenal aortic aneurysm structure: Implications for transfemoral repair. *J Vasc Surg* 1994;20:44–50.)

The correlation between aneurysm diameter and common iliac artery diameter was relatively weak ($r = 0.43$ on the right, $r = 0.48$ on the left) throughout the range of aneurysm dimensions. Patients with large aortic aneurysms were no more likely to be excluded from endovascular repair on the basis of iliac artery aneurysm than those with small aortic aneurysms.

For aortic aneurysms smaller than 60 mm in diameter, the diameter of the aneurysm bore no relation to the length of the neck. The neck was longer than 20 mm in 71 percent of these cases. However, aneurysms larger than 60 mm in diameter were associated with shorter necks. Only 38 percent of these aneurysms had necks longer than 20 mm. This is unfortunate because it means that the very patients who might benefit the most from the less invasive nature of endovascular repair are more likely to be excluded for lack of a suitable proximal implantation site. These patients are often referred for endovascular repair because they are at high risk from conventional repair due to poor general health and at high risk for rupture of their large aneurysms.

The observation that large aneurysms have short necks suggests that as aneurysms grow they encroach on the previously nondilated segments of aorta. This concept is consistent with the strong positive correlation between aneurysm diameter and aneurysm length ($r = 0.79$, $p < .001$). In addition, dilatation of the aneurysm neck has been noted on serial follow-up of patients with small aneurysms [1], and the aneurysm neck is sometimes the site of recurrence many years after an original conventional aneurysm repair. It is hoped that the presence of an endovascular graft and stent will help prevent dilatation of the neck of the aneurysm. If not, the proximal end of the prosthesis must be designed to expand with the aorta; otherwise leakage and dislocation will occur. A recent case of proximal stent dislocation, three years after endovascular graft implantation, may be a manifestation of this process [6].

Angulation of the Aorta

Angulation of the aorta might conceivably cause difficulty inserting the delivery system and ensuring accurate placement of the prosthesis. In this study the degree of aortic angulation was measured at three points:

1. Between the axis of the suprarenal aorta and the aneurysm neck
2. Between the neck and the aneurysm
3. Between the aneurysm and the distal cuff (when there was one)

30

The most common form of aortic angulation was anterior deviation of the neck at or immediately above the renal arteries. All cases in which there was a measurable neck showed at least 10 degrees of anterior deviation between the proximal aorta and the neck of the aneurysm. The mean was 23.1 ± 3.0 degrees. Lateral angulation was also common (mean 22.5 ± 4.6 degrees). Taking the greater of the two angulations in each case, the overall mean was 31.1 ± 19.3 degrees. Angulation was rarely as severe as that depicted in Figure 2-4. In only four cases did the aorta deviate by more than 45 degrees in any direction.

It is unlikely that the relatively mild deviation seen in this study would preclude insertion of the delivery system. Of greater concern is the potential for difficulty in ensuring accurate graft placement. Most delivery systems induce some straightening of the aorta, which can be associated with movement of the aneurysm neck. Placing the graft by referring to an angiogram that was recorded before insertion of the delivery system can lead to malposition. Therefore it is wise to repeat the angiogram with the delivery system in place if intraoperative angiography shows aortic tortuosity in the region of the renal arteries.

Aortic angulation between the proximal neck and the aneurysm itself is less important as a potential cause of proximal stent malposition but may cause inaccuracy in preoperative measurements of graft length if these are based largely on conventional CT data or if a calibrated wire in the angulated segment is used to calibrate angiographic measurements.

Iliac Artery Tortuosity

In my experience, iliac tortuosity has not impeded delivery system insertion, once guidewires are in place. A more important concern has been the effect of a localized kink in the proximal common iliac artery on the patency of the underlying limb of a bifurcated graft. Therefore this study focused on the angle between the proximal common iliac artery and the distal aneurysm or cuff, which was the most consistent site for a change in the arterial axis.

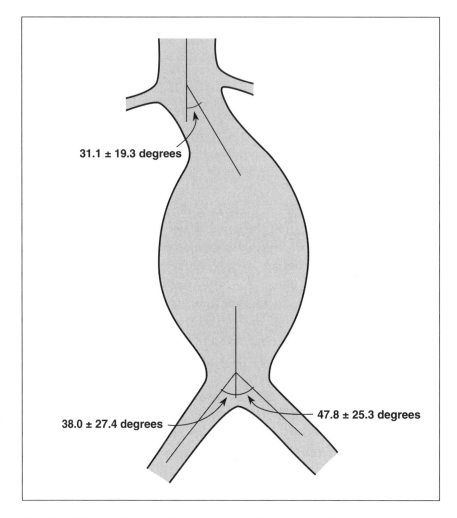

Fig. 2-4. Mean values for the maximum observed angulation between the proximal aorta and the neck, and between the infrarenal aorta and the common iliac arteries.

The proximal common iliac arteries showed some degree of posterior and lateral deviation in all cases. Taking the maximum deviation in either direction for each iliac artery, the overall mean values were 38.0 ± 27 degrees on the right and 47.8 ± 25.3 degrees on the left. More than 45 degrees of deviation was seen in seven cases on the right and nine cases on the left. However, pronounced angulation (more than 90 degrees) at this point was seen only in one patient.

Those who find iliac tortuosity to be a significant impediment to delivery system insertion will not find information on common iliac artery angulation to be particularly helpful, because the junction between the common iliac artery and the aorta is not likely to be the site of obstruction. Instrumentation of a tortuous artery is usually arrested when the instrument meets the arterial wall just beyond a kink. There is no such obstruction immediately proximal to the common iliac artery orifice. Bends in the distal common iliac and external iliac arteries are more likely to impede delivery system insertion, particularly in view of the smaller external iliac artery diameter. Unfortunately, only the proximal iliac arteries were studied due to the limited extent of the CT scans, nor did we study the incidence of iliac stenosis.

Probably the most important feature of a delivery system that affects its insertion is the size of the outer sheath. Some are as large as 29 French. Larger systems are generally less flexible and allow no latitude for deviation of the artery from the shape of the delivery system, thus limiting their ability to negotiate tortuous iliac arteries.

Given the positive correlation between aneurysm diameter and aneurysm length, it was surprising to find no correlation between the diameter of the aneurysm and the degree of aortic or iliac angulation. Perhaps these processes are not as closely linked as commonly believed.

Other Morphologic Features Warranting Study

Most aneurysms contain mural thrombus; the quantity and consistency of the thrombus vary widely. It may not be as crumbly as it seems in the operating room, but fatal instances of microembolism have been reported following endovascular aneurysm repair in which there was extensive aortic instrumentation [6]. The preoperative images must be reviewed in all such cases to help identify patients at high risk of this complication. Pearce et al. [1] have identified several CT scan findings that are associated with embolism as a presenting symptom of abdominal aortic aneurysm. These include irregularity of the lumen, multiple lumens, and heterogeneity of mural thrombus. Such findings may indicate an increased risk for embolism at the time of endovascular repair and may be relative contraindications.

Calcification of the aneurysm neck impedes conventional repair through its effects on clamping and suture penetration. It is unclear whether this will influence proximal stent implantation. Only the Lazarus (EVT) system depends heavily on barb implantation. Of course, aortic clamping is not part of endovascular technique, but the possible effects of aortic calcification should be considered when the results of endovascular aneurysm repair are studied.

Predictions

It is difficult to use this anatomic information to predict the potential role of endovascular aneurysm repair, with so little information on the functional limits of the various systems. Clinical trials may show which anatomic features predict success and which predict failure for each system, but only if investigators adopt an aggressive approach to patient inclusion, which seems unlikely given the need to obtain uniform success for regulatory approval. Moreover, the capabilities of both the delivery systems and their users are likely to expand. Features that limit application now may be overcome as endovascular techniques mature. Despite these caveats, it is still instructive to apply the arbitrary cutoff points used in this study to the study population of 22 patients [2].

We found no patients who met the following criteria for straight graft repair: an aneurysm neck longer than 20 mm, no distal common iliac artery aneurysm, no iliac artery angulation more than 45 degrees from the long axis of the aorta, and a distal cuff longer than 20 mm. Even eliminating the need for a distal cuff by performing a bifurcated graft repair would have raised the proportion of suitable cases to only 32 percent. Reducing the required neck and cuff lengths to 10 mm and eliminating iliac angulation as a reason for exclusion make 9 percent eligible for straight graft repair and 58 percent eligible for repair with a bifurcated graft.

With regard to the proportion of patients suitable for straight graft repair, a similar result was obtained by researchers in Utrecht [7]. Three patients were selected for repair with the EndoVascular Technologies system from a group of 35 potential candidates, mainly on the basis of inadequate distal cuff. The selection criteria in the Dutch series were a little more stringent than those listed above, but the initial group of potential candidates had already been screened at other centers, thereby eliminating many unsuitable patients and increasing the apparent yield.

Conclusion

Three-dimensional reconstruction of CT data provided valuable information concerning the anatomy of the distal arterial tree in 22 patients with aortic aneurysm. Whether this kind of information is a necessary part of preoperative evaluation is unclear (see Chapter 12).

The most significant finding in the study of three-dimensional CT reconstructions was the paucity of the distal cuff, which was rarely long enough for endovascular aneurysm repair with a straight aorto-aortic graft using any of the current systems.

References

1. Pearce WH. Important vascular morphologic parameters. Presented at SVS/ISCVS/NIH Research Initiatives in Vascular Disease Symposium. March 26, 1994, Bethesda, MD.

2. Chuter TAM et al. Infrarenal aortic structure: Implications for transfemoral repair. *J Vasc Surg* 1994;20:44–50.

3. Kwaan JHM et al. The value of arteriography before abdominal aneurysmectomy. *Am J Surg* 1977;134:108–114.

4. Todd GJ et al. The accuracy of CT scanning in the diagnosis of abdominal and thoracoabdominal aortic aneurysms. *J Vasc Surg* 1991;13:302–310.

5. Ouriel K et al. An evaluation of new methods of expressing aortic aneurysm size: Relationship to rupture. *J Vasc Surg* 1992;15:12–20.

6. Barone HD. Endovascular prosthesis for aneurysm. Presented at Symposium on Endovascular Procedures. January 29, 1994, Utrecht, Netherlands.

7. Eikelboom BC. Endovascular repair of aortic aneurysm: Case demonstration. Presented at Workshop on Transluminal Treatment of Aneurysms. January 29, 1994, Utrecht, Netherlands.

Endovascular Repair of Abdominal Aortic Aneurysms

3

Juan C. Parodi

Attempts to decrease the risks and complications associated with standard operative repair of abdominal aortic aneurysms resulted in the development of various therapeutic modalities based on the concept of endoluminal aneurysm exclusion. However, our initial prototypes developed in 1976 were marked by a high failure rate [1].

The first was a thin fabric graft mounted on a metallic cagelike structure composed of a self-expandable mesh with a "zigzag" configuration. The apparatus was compressed inside a tubular sheath, which acted as a vessel introducer and carrier. Experiments in normal canine aortas lead to the abandonment of this prototype due to an inconsistent deployment of the metallic cage. The radial expansion properties of the cage were difficult to control and predict. Overexpansion resulted in aortic wall injury and subsequent rupture. Conversely, underexpansion lead to leakage of blood between the apparatus and the host aorta with subsequent device migration.

The next prototype involved a Dacron graft fitted on a Silastic bag with a cylindrical lumen, which could be distended by the injection of silicone into the bag. Unfortunately, this method was associated with prompt thrombosis of the aorta in all experimental animals.

No other devices were developed until 1988, when large-diameter balloon-expandable stents became available. The ends of a tubular thin wall graft could be attached to a proximal and distal stent and packed inside a catheter, and then the stent-graft combination deployed using balloon expansion (Fig. 3-1).

Feasibility Animal Studies

To test the concept of intraluminal graft implantation, a canine aneurysmal model was used. A 6-cm segment of the infrarenal aorta was resected and replaced with a fusiform conduit made of crimped woven Dacron, measuring 8 cm in length (Fig. 3-2). Histologic studies demonstrated endothelium graft coverage of the experimental aneurysm neck, coupled with mural thrombus formation in the body of the aneurysm. Both of these changes were regularly encountered within a month after implantation of the aneurysmal graft. Six weeks later the aneurysms were bypassed using endoluminal graft deployment techniques. A noncrimped knitted Dacron tube of an appropriate diameter and length was attached to carefully selected stents (Palmaz; Johnson & Johnson Interventional Systems). Two-thirds of each stent were covered by graft material, but one-third of the stent was left exposed to anchor the graft to the aortic wall. The graft was folded clockwise in two folds, mounted on a balloon catheter, placed over a guidewire, and loaded into a 14 French Teflon sheath. The right femoral artery was chosen for vascular access. Under fluoroscopy guidance the leading stent was advanced over the guidewire into the neck of the aneurysm, below the renal orifices and above the body of the aneurysm. Following the proper positioning of the device, the introducer sheath was withdrawn and balloon inflation used to secure the graft by deploying either one or two stents. In one group of dogs only a proximal stent was used, but in a second, larger group a distal stent was added to achieve total aneurysm exclusion. Angiography was then used to confirm correct stent-graft deployment and verify that the aneurysm was successfully bypassed (Fig. 3-3) [2, 3].

38

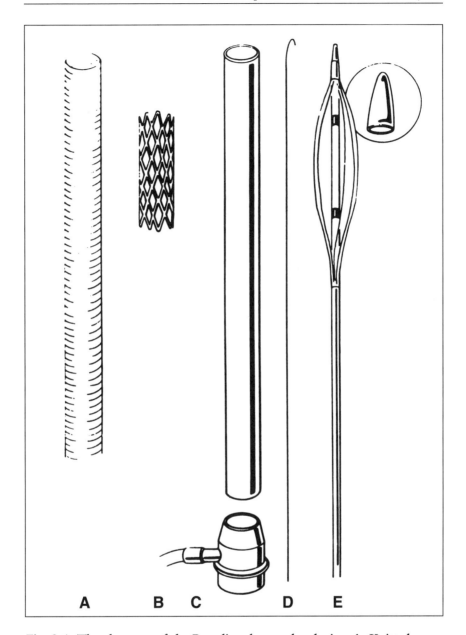

Fig. 3-1. The elements of the Parodi endovascular device. A. Knitted Dacron graft. B. Large, balloon-expandable Palmaz stent. C. Teflon sheath. D. Stiff guidewire. E. Balloon catheter. (From JC Parodi. Endovascular repair of abdominal aortic aneurysms. *Adv Vasc Surg* 1993;1:87.)

Fig. 3-2. Fusiform "artificial aneurysm" constructed using Dacron grafts and interposed into canine infrarenal aorta. (From JC Parodi. Endovascular repair of abdominal aortic aneurysms. *Adv Vasc Surg* 1993;1:88.)

Forty-three dogs were studied, mostly to evaluate and develop different models of experimental aneurysm, or to test the various components of our device, such as stents, balloons, and grafts. Six months after endoluminal bypass the dogs were evaluated by duplex ultrasound scans and/or angiography [4]. Complete pathologic studies were performed in all the explanted aortas and devices. The excluded aneurysm lumen underwent thrombosis, and there was a reduction in aneurysmal diameter. Histologic studies and scanning electron microscopy demonstrated that both ends of the stented grafts were covered by endothelium, with only a patchy coverage of the mid-graft portion. The number of monocytes attached to the unstented prosthetic graft surface, an indicator of thrombogenicity [5], was greater than the number of monocytes found covering the stent. The inner wall of the graft in the region of the experimental aneurysm was covered by a thick fibrin-platelet barrier.

The difficulties encountered with endoluminal aneurysm exclusion gave us insight into some of the problems that lay ahead with human atherosclerotic aneurysms. The large size of the introducer sheath caused spasm and occasional injury of the selected access

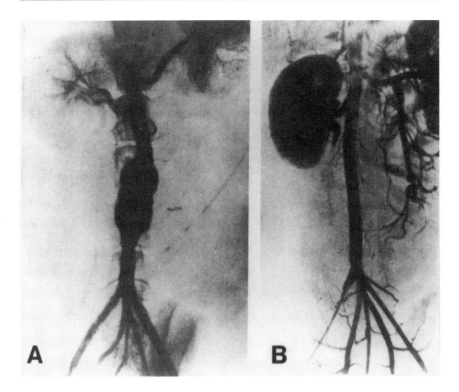

Fig. 3-3. A. Aortogram four weeks after the construction of an "artificial aneurysm" in canine aorta. B. Aortogram following the implantation of a stented graft through a right femoral artery approach in the same dog. (From JC Parodi. Endovascular repair of abdominal aortic aneurysms. *Adv Vasc Surg* 1993;1:89.)

artery. Until the device could be miniaturized, human candidates for endoluminal aneurysm repair had to have large and fairly straight iliac arteries. The presence of spiral folds on the completion arteriography was associated with graft torsion and early graft thrombosis. As a result a radiopaque, thin, gold wire was knitted into each graft. This permitted the rapid radiographic identification of both ends and sides of the graft to prevent and possibly correct torsion during implantation. A 10- to 15-percent balloon overexpansion of the aortic diameter at the time of stent deployment was found to correlate with adequate anchoring and low risk of stent-graft migration.

Clinical Experience

Once we were satisfied that a Dacron graft could be delivered through a catheter and firmly fixed in place by balloon-expandable stents, permission was obtained from the Institutional Ethical Committee to perform a pilot study with a small group of patients who were at high risk for operative aneurysmorrhaphy and were fully aware of the experimental nature of our work [1, 2].

The Graft-Stent Prosthesis

The first component of the device is a super-stiff guidewire with a diameter of 0.038 inches. It facilitates introduction of the device through tortuous iliac arteries, keeps the axis of our device parallel to that of the aorta, and, by minimizing manipulations, prevents disruption of laminated thrombus that lines atherosclerotic aneurysms.

The large-diameter balloon-expandable stent, 3.5 cm in length, is a cylindrical tube with longitudinal slots that adapt to a diamond shape when expanded. This design, initially described by Palmaz [1], permits the stent to expand from a diameter of only 5 mm when collapsed to a diameter of more than 30 mm when expanded.

A knitted, crimped, Dacron graft with a wall thickness of 0.2 mm and tensile and bursting strengths comparable to those of commercially available grafts has to be securely sutured to the stents and placed to overlap one-third of the length of the stent. The diameter and length of each graft has to be tailored to fit the individual patient, but the grafts we have used most often are 18 to 20 mm in diameter and 8 to 12 cm in length.

The balloon catheters have a shaft constructed of polyvinyl chloride with a 9 French diameter and contain either two or three lumens depending on the number of polyethylene balloons affixed to them. When two balloons are used, the caudal one has a cylindrical configuration with a 30-degree angle to the catheter shaft immediately below it to allow simultaneous balloon inflation and secure anchoring of the prosthetic graft. The last piece of the device is a Teflon sheath with a 21 French diameter and a hemostatic valve at the proximal end.

Patient Selection

Patients considered potential candidates for endoluminal aneurysm bypass have to be evaluated as if they were going to undergo conventional operative repair. A contrast computed tomography (CT) scan of the abdominal aorta is performed at 1-cm intervals, with added views across the proximal and distal ends of the aneurysm. The CT scan can give an estimate of the proximal neck, the distance between the renal arteries and the beginning of the body of the aneurysm, and the diameter of the aorta at the upper and lower ends of the aortic aneurysm. Also, the distance from the renal arteries to the aortic bifurcation can be calculated and used to predict the graft length that will be needed. In addition, a biplanar abdominal aortogram is obtained in every patient, since it provides further detail concerning the visceral branches, the patency of the inferior mesenteric and lumbar arteries, and the course and diameter of the iliac arteries. Angiography is performed using a pigtail catheter having gold calibrations at 2-cm intervals and with a radiopaque ruler positioned vertically behind the patient to obtain the most accurate measurements.

Both the angiographic features and the CT data should complement each other. If substantial differences are encountered the data must be reviewed prior to device assembly. Minor differences are not uncommon, with the CT scan sometimes overestimating the intraluminal diameter of the aorta by a factor of 1 to 4 mm, since coronal views make the aneurysm lumen appear oval rather than circular. Once all dimensions have been determined and agreed on, the implantation device can be designed.

Procedure

The patient must be prepared and draped as if conventional aortic aneurysm repair were being performed. Using either local anesthesia or epidural regional anesthesia, the common femoral artery is exposed through a standard groin incision ipsilateral to the iliac artery with the largest diameter and least tortuosity. After sodium heparin (5,000 IU) is administered intravenously, a number 18 Cournand needle is inserted under direct control into the common femoral artery. A soft-tip (0.038-inch) guidewire is advanced cephalad through the needle into the distal thoracic aorta, and a 5 French pigtail angiographic catheter is introduced over it. The catheter is positioned in the visceral segment of the abdominal aorta, the wire is removed, and preprocedural angiography is performed. This specially designed pigtail catheter has radiopaque calibrations at 20-mm intervals. A radiopaque ruler is placed behind the patient parallel to the axis of the aorta, and measurements are again taken and compared to those previously collected. It is only now that construction of the appropriate endoluminal graft is undertaken.

The graft must overlap the proximal stent by approximately two-thirds. It is then attached to the stent using two synthetic sutures on each side and placed 180 degrees from each other. After mounting the stent(s) over the balloon(s), the graft is folded and the entire assembly is introduced into a 21 French Teflon sheath. The assembled device is advanced over a super-stiff (Amplatz) wire to the level of the proximal neck of the aneurysm. The sheath is now removed, leaving the graft, stent(s), and balloon(s) in the aortic lumen (Fig. 3-4). To prevent distal migration during inflation of the proximal balloon, an intravenous infusion of nitroglycerin is started to lower the mean systemic blood pressure below 80 mm Hg. The proximal balloon is inflated for one minute with whatever volume is necessary to attain the proper diameter for that particular patient. To distend the stent in a perfectly cylindrical shape, the balloon may be reinflated in both ends of the stent.

After the proximal stent has been deployed, the balloon is inflated along the shaft of the graft to distend it under low pressure. Provided all previous measurements were correct, the distal radiopaque calibrations on the graft should be flush to the aortic bifurcation at the conclusion of the procedure. A completion aortogram is then obtained (Figs. 3-5 and 3-6). In the past, a second stent was deployed if the aortogram demonstrated reflux around the distal end of the graft into the aneurysm sac, but this approach was abandoned due to distal neck dilatation in single-stented grafts. Now we always use a proximal and distal stent [1]. Specially

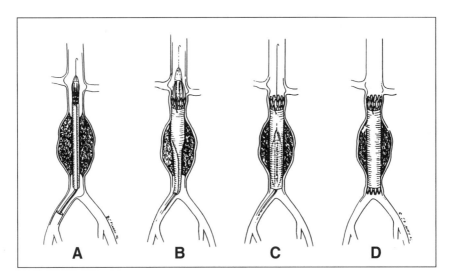

Fig. 3-4. Schematic illustration of the endovascular treatment of abdominal aortic aneurysms using the Parodi device. A. Device properly positioned following removal of delivery sheath. B. Proximal stent deployed by balloon expansion, under nitroglycerin-induced hypotension. C. Balloon-assisted graft distention. D. Final result after deployment of distal stent. (From JC Parodi. Endovascular repair of abdominal aortic aneurysms. *Adv Vasc Surg* 1993;1:93.)

designed balloons must be used to deploy the second stent, since the distal neck of the aortic aneurysm is usually short and the angle at the origin of the common iliac artery is at 30 degrees. The arteriotomy is then closed after flushing the iliac artery to vent any aneurysmal debris that might have been loosened during the procedure. The patient is transferred to an intensive care unit for the next 24 hours and usually spends two additional days on a regular nursing floor before being discharged from the hospital.

Clinical Results

As stated before, initially only those patients with serious comorbidities, implying a high surgical risk with conventional repair, were selected for endoluminal bypass. After initial clinical success, few

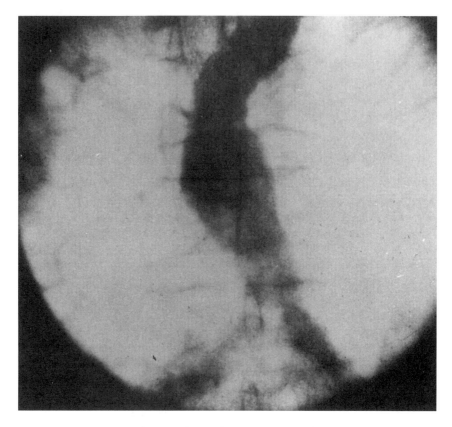

Fig. 3-5. Aortogram showing large iliac vessels and long distal neck. (From JC Parodi, JC Palmaz, HD Barone. Transfemoral intraluminal graft implantation for abdominal aortic aneurysms. *Ann Vasc Surg* 1991;5:496.)

volunteers considered candidates for standard operative repair have been treated by endoluminal bypass. The following anatomic criteria are desirable for the endoluminal placement of an aorto-aortic tube graft:

1. Both the proximal and distal necks of the aortic aneurysm had to measure at least 2 cm in length.
2. At least one of the iliac arteries had to be patent and sufficiently straight to allow delivery of the device and carrier. An external iliac diameter of at least 7 mm is desirable for a common femoral approach.

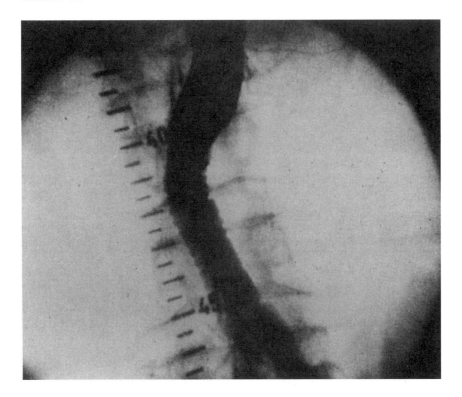

Fig. 3-6. Aortogram following deployment of endovascular graft. (From JC Parodi, JC Palmaz, HD Barone. Transfemoral intraluminal graft implantation for abdominal aortic aneurysms. *Ann Vasc Surg* 1991;5:497.)

A short segment of iliac stenosis, which can be successfully corrected by a percutaneous transluminal angioplasty (PTA) in order to accept the delivery carrier, is not considered a contraindication to endoluminal stent-graft bypass.

Patients with patent inferior mesenteric and/or lumbar arteries have been excluded, but with these exceptions, approximately half of all candidates evaluated have met anatomic criteria for endoluminal repair. Placement of aortoiliac bifurcation grafts through both common femoral arteries using a modification of our endoluminal approach will increase the percentage of patients in whom abdominal aortic aneurysms could be treated without standard techniques.

Table 3-1. Comorbid factors in patients treated with an endoluminal stent-graft

Comorbid factors	Number (n = 40)	Percentage
Severe coronary heart disease	26	65.0
Pulmonary insufficiency	20*	50.0
Pulmonary edema	1	2.5
Acute myocardial infarction	1	2.5
Renal insufficiency	4	10.0
Cirrhosis/ascites	1	2.5
Cerebrovascular accident	1	2.5
Hostile abdomen	1	2.5

*Home oxygen (n = 3).

Since September 6, 1990, 40 patients have been treated with an endoluminal stent-graft [1, 8]. The greater male incidence of aortic aneurysmal disease, as well as the requirement of larger iliac vessels for delivery of the device, are reflected in our series, which includes 38 men and 2 women. They range in age from 62 to 83 years (mean: 71 years), with five patients over 80 years of age. Their follow-up periods extend from 3 to 23 months (mean: 10 months). The incidence of comorbid factors in this population has been high and includes recent myocardial infarction, severe coronary artery disease, pulmonary edema, hemorrhagic brain infarction, chronic renal failure, pulmonary insufficiency, and a hostile abdomen (Table 3-1).

Transfemoral access from either side was obtained in the majority of patients. If the external iliac artery could not accept the introducer sheath, the common iliac artery was approached through a short extraperitoneal incision and anastomosed to a temporary 10-mm, straight Dacron graft to allow delivery of the device. Tortuous iliac vessels were handled by a circumferential dissection and division of the minor branches of the external iliac and common femoral arteries at the level of the inguinal ligament and gently pulling down on the femoral artery, which "straightens" the proximal segment of the access vessel, allowing device delivery.

When proximal and distal necks were of adequate length (20 patients), an aorto-aortic tube graft was deployed, using a proximal

Table 3-2. Types of endoluminal tube grafts used for aneurysm repair

Stent location	N	Successes	Failures	Failure rate (%)
Aorto-aortic				
Proximal stent only	8	6	2	25
Proximal and distal stent	20	18	2	10
Aorto-iliac	12	8	4	33

Table 3-3. Nonfatal complications experienced in patients treated with endoluminal stent-graft repair

Complications	Number (n = 40)	Percentage
Immediate		
Groin hematoma	2	5.0
Macro- and microembolization	3	7.5
Detachment of proximal stent	1	2.5
Distal leak	2	5.0
Stent migration	1	2.5
External iliac artery injury	1	2.5
Procedure-related death	2	5.0
Corrected deployment errors	3	7.5
Proximal leak		
Inadequate length		
Graft torsion		
Late		
Distal reflux or expansion		

and distal stent in 12 and only a proximal stent in eight. If the distal neck was less than 2 cm in length or nonexistent, an aorto-iliac tube graft was used and supplemented with a crossed femoral-femoral graft (12 patients) (Table 3-2). In these cases balloon occlusion of the contralateral iliac limb was performed to prevent aneurysm formation of the common iliac artery due to retrograde blood flow.

Morbidity and Mortality

A variety of nonfatal complications have been encountered in one-third of the patients treated with endoluminal stent-graft repair (Table 3-3) [6, 8, 9]:

1. *Inguinal hematoma.* This complication occurred in the first patient treated and was probably related to systemic heparinization not reversed with protamine sulfate after the procedure. It has occurred only once since then.

2. *Malpositioning of the proximal stent.* In the second patient treated, an accidental misplacement of the marking ruler lead to the deployment of the stent 3 cm distal to the selected target. As a result the distal graft laid in the right common iliac artery and excluded the contralateral iliac artery from the circulation. Standard operative aneurysm repair was undertaken uneventfully. At operation the implanted stent was firmly attached and partial aortic resection was required.

3. *Proximal stent migration.* Initially, the graft was secured to its stent with only two sutures positioned 180 degrees apart. In one case, a suture loosened, allowing graft migration to occur distally on that side. This problem was handled by successfully deploying another stented Dacron graft within the lumen of the displaced graft. Further complications of this kind have been avoided by using four sutures (two on each side) to securely attach the graft to the selected stent.

4. *Distal graft leak, reflux, or dilatation.* If the graft implanted is too short to reach the distal neck of the aortic aneurysm, a distal leak will occur. Deployment of a second stented graft of appropriate length within the lumen of the original graft solves this problem. Reflux of blood into the aneurysm sac at the distal end of the implanted graft also requires deployment of an additional stent. Also, if the stent deployed is only in contact with laminated mural thrombus, not the true aortic wall, further dilatation of the distal aorta will occur. Operative replacement of the distal end with a new Dacron graft at the level of the aortic bifurcation corrects this complication (Fig. 3-7).

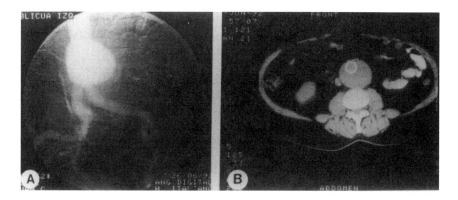

Fig. 3-7. Progressive dilatation of distal aortic aneurysm following endovascular repair. A. Aortogram 18 months after deployment of stented graft of inadequate length. Aortic dilatation occurred despite placement of distal stent. B. CT scan showing distal stent deployment into mural thrombus, not aortic neck. (From JC Parodi. Endovascular repair of abdominal aortic aneurysms. *Adv Vasc Surg* 1993;1:98–99.)

Micro- and macroembolization were seen in three patients, and unfortunately they lead to two fatalities. Such a disastrous complication is probably related to prolonged catheter manipulation at the time of graft deployment. Increased risk of embolization may be predicted by the luminal appearance of the aortic aneurysm in the preoperative contrast CT scan. The presence of an irregular, stellate-shaped lumen, multiple lumens, or a heterogeneous thrombus may require control of both common femoral arteries prior to catheter manipulation within the aneurysm [1]. There have been two late deaths not related to the endoluminal procedure. One patient died secondary to colon cancer (13 months) and the other due to cardiorespiratory failure (eight months).

Two-thirds of the patients have been free of complications and have patent grafts during a follow-up period ranging from one to 35 months (mean: 16 months). In five patients the renal artery orifices were bridged by a portion of the uncovered stent, due to the presence of a short proximal neck [1]. No loss of renal function has been noted.

Patients have been followed at regular intervals with both color duplex and CT scanning, and on occasion aortography. Since the color duplex has been just as accurate as CT scanning in this group of patients, it may suffice for long-term surveillance.

If the late results of stented grafts for the treatment of aortic aneurysms prove to be successful, because of their cost-effectiveness and low morbidity, the future indications for endovascular management undoubtedly will be extended to include low surgical risk patients and patients with smaller aneurysms. Prospectively randomized studies of endovascular treatment versus operative repair will no doubt be undertaken to find if endovascular treatment represents an efficient compromise from the standpoints of both patient safety and health care expenditures.

References

1. Parodi JC. Endovascular repair of abdominal aortic aneurysms. *Adv Vasc Surg* 1993;1:85–106.

2. Parodi JC et al. Tratamiento endoluminal de los aneurismos de la aorta abdominal. Presented at II Convencion de Cirujanos Vasculares de Habla Hispana. October 1990, Buenos Aires, Argentina. Summary, page 122. Edicto: JM Capedevila, Barcelona, Spain.

3. Laborde CL et al. Intraluminal bypass of abdominal aortic aneurysm: Feasibility study. *Radiology* 1992;184:185–190.

4. Parodi JC. Transluminal aneurysm bypass: Experimental observations and preliminary clinical experience. Presented at IV International Congress on Endovascular Therapy in Vascular Disease. February 1991, Scottsdale, AZ.

5. Kottke-Marchant K et al. Vascular graft associated complement activation and leukocyte adhesion in an artificial circulation. *J Biomed Mater Res* 1987;21:379–397.

6. Parodi JC, Palmaz JC, Barone HD. Transfemoral intraluminal graft implantation for abdominal aortic aneurysms. *Ann Vasc Surg* 1991;5:491–499.

7. Palmaz JC et al. Intraluminal stents in atherosclerotic iliac artery stenosis: Preliminary report of multicenter study. *Radiology* 1988;168:727–731.

8. Parodi JC. Endovascular treatment of abdominal aortic aneurysms. Presented at VII International Congress on Endovascular Interventions: On the Cutting Edge. February 1994, Scottsdale, AZ.

9. Schonholz C, Parodi JC. Transfemoral intraluminal bypass grafting of abdominal aortic aneurysms: Development and clinical experience. Presented at Endovascular Symposium 1993: Endoluminal Aneurysm Grafting, Stent Application, and Endovascular Interventions. November 1993, Sydney, Australia.

10. Parodi JC. Abdominal aortic aneurysms. Presented at the 1994 Research Initiatives in Vascular Disease, symposium on transluminally placed endovascular prostheses. March 1994, Bethesda, MD.

11. Goldstone J et al. Endoluminal stents and grafts for abdominal aortic aneurysms. *Perspect Vasc Surg* 1993;6:41–55.

Straight and Bifurcated Endovascular Grafts for Infrarenal Aortic Aneurysm Repair

4

Timothy A.M. Chuter

The anatomic considerations of endovascular grafts, described in Chapter 2, dictate that endovascular aneurysm repair will be feasible in only a small number of patients if it is confined to the insertion of a straight graft. The main limitation is the paucity of the distal cuff.

One solution is to develop an endovascular system for bifurcated graft insertion. Bifurcated graft repair moves the distal implantation site out of the aorta into the common iliac arteries. The longer distal target zone expands the number of suitable candidates and facilitates graft sizing.

Apparatus Design

Endovascular aneurysm repair differs from conventional repair in two ways: (1) the graft is attached by stents, not sutures, and (2) the graft is introduced into the aorta through the distal arterial tree, not the abdominal cavity. Therefore, in addition to the graft, the basic apparatus for endovascular aneurysm includes stents, some means of controlling stent implantation, and a system of catheters or sheaths for graft delivery.

In the Chuter-Gianturco system [1], graft attachment relies on self-expanding Gianturco Z-stents. These barbed crowns of springy stainless steel have a resting diameter that is larger than the aorta and the graft. When deployed the stents exert an outward force, which presses the graft against the surrounding vessel wall.

Straight Grafts

The straight graft has two stents, one inside each orifice. The stent-graft combination (prosthesis) is mounted on a carrier system of coaxial catheters. Attachment to this carrier relies on the presence of the innermost catheter. When this is removed, the prosthesis is released from the carrier.

The upstream end of the carrier has an olive-shaped tip that engages the upstream margin of the introducer sheath, closing the delivery system. The result is a smooth outer profile, capable of traversing the tortuous iliac arteries without catching on the arterial wall or mural thrombus. A single-sheath delivery system is one of the distinguishing features of this apparatus, the main advantage being a lower overall volume than that of a comparable double-sheath system.

Bifurcated Grafts

In straight graft repair, all the graft implantation sites lie along the line of graft insertion. Bifurcated graft repair is more complicated, because one of the limbs must be implanted in an artery remote from the line of primary graft insertion. Assuming, for the purposes of discussion, that the primary site of insertion is the right femoral artery, there are a relatively limited number of options for deployment of the left graft limb:

1. The left limb can be inserted through the left femoral artery and, together with a separately inserted right limb, attached to the aorta.

2. The left limb can be inserted through the left femoral artery and somehow joined to the main trunk of the graft, which has been inserted separately through the right femoral artery.
3. The left limb can be attached to the rest of the graft before insertion and pulled from the aorta into the left iliac artery using a snare or a basket.
4. An already attached left limb can be pulled into position by a catheter or suture, which is accessible at the femoral level after the graft has been inserted.

Clinical application of the first alternative has been explored by Palmaz, without success. One problem with this approach lies in the need to join two stents to the inner wall of the aorta or a stent implanted in the aortic wall. These stents all tend to expand to form cylinders. Even if the stents mold to one another, a leak is still likely. The second and third alternatives entail intra-arterial manipulations that risk dislocation of the already deployed graft. Therefore, I favor approach number four. Animal experiments [2] and early clinical trials [3] have shown this method to be effective.

The catheter attached to the left limb of the graft (left-limb catheter) is accessible only when the introducer sheath has been withdrawn, and then it is to be found next to the central catheter at the right groin (Fig. 4-1). To be useful in pulling the left limb of the graft into the left iliac artery, the left-limb catheter must be pulled through the distal arterial tree, from the right femoral artery to the left. This is accomplished by attaching it to a second (cross-femoral) catheter, which runs around the distal arterial tree from one femoral arteriotomy to the other. These catheters were the main addition to the original straight graft system and accompany its adaptation for bifurcated graft insertion. Other important additions were the two small sheaths, which maintain the distal stents in their compressed state until left-limb translocation has been completed.

Patient Selection

At the time of this writing, bifurcated graft insertion has been performed in 15 patients as part of phase 1 clinical trials. An important

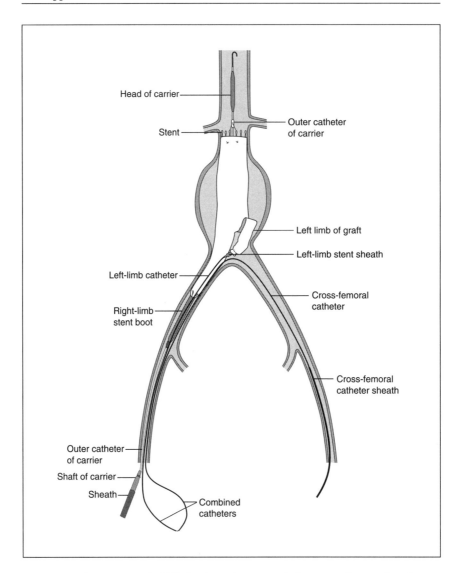

Head of carrier

Stent

Outer catheter
of carrier

Left limb of graft

Left-limb stent sheath

Left-limb catheter

Cross-femoral
catheter

Right-limb
stent boot

Cross-femoral
catheter sheath

Outer catheter
of carrier

Shaft of carrier

Sheath

Combined
catheters

Fig. 4-1. The carrier, the left-limb catheter, and the cross-femoral catheter are all exposed at the right groin by removal of the sheath.

goal of phase 1 trials was to refine selection criteria, which have become progressively less exclusive. Current requirements are:

1. A proximal neck longer than 10 mm that deviates from the axis of the suprarenal aorta by no more than 60 degrees.

2. No iliac artery aneurysm.
3. External iliac artery diameter greater than 6 mm with or without balloon dilatation.
4. Common iliac artery diameter greater than 8 mm.
5. No large inferior mesenteric artery.
6. Distal cuff longer than 15 mm (straight graft insertion only).

We have taken the position that it is not safe to explore the functional limitations of a system in patients too ill for conventional surgery. The early cases, in which the performance was entirely unknown, were confined to patients in relatively good general health with clearly suitable arterial anatomy. After the system had been shown to be effective, these selection criteria were relaxed. Some insertions were performed in patients whose arterial anatomy was outside the range already tried. Others had severe cardiac or pulmonary disease that would have precluded abdominal operation. But we did not relax both physiologic and anatomic criteria in the same patients. We felt that sick patients needed to be assured of successful endovascular graft insertion by favorable arterial anatomy.

Technique of Graft Insertion

Straight Grafts

Straight graft insertion can be performed entirely through one femoral artery, although bilateral control, either surgically or with an occluding balloon, is probably advisable to minimize the risk of embolism.

The procedure of straight graft insertion is theoretically rather simple. An angiogram is performed to localize the implantation sites proximally and distally. The angiographic catheter is replaced over a guidewire for the delivery system. Correct graft position is maintained by manipulation of the central carrier, as the introducer sheath is withdrawn. The stents expand spontaneously as soon as they leave the confines of the introducer sheath. The graft is released from the carrier by removal of the inner catheter, permitting removal of the delivery system.

In practice, straight graft insertion is complicated by the usual paucity of the distal implantation site (the distal cuff). It can be difficult to find suitable patients for straight graft repair. Indeed, after 26 bifurcated insertions, I have only encountered four patients with an adequate distal cuff who would have been adequate for straight graft repair. Therefore, the procedure of straight graft insertion will not be described further.

Bifurcated Grafts

The steps in bifurcated graft insertion are as follows:

1. It is usually performed in the operating room, with an anesthesiologist present.

2. The patient must be positioned on a radiolucent operating table to permit fluoroscopic visualization of the aorta to the diaphragm.

3. A radiopaque ruler down the patient's back provides a fixed frame of reference, which allows angiographic landmarks to be located even when the fluoroscopy unit or the patient has been moved.

4. Antibiotics with a broad spectrum of activity against gram-positive organisms are administered intravenously before the procedure.

5. The patient is prepared and draped for conventional aortic surgery.

6. Anesthesia may be general, regional, or local depending on the patient's general health and ability to withstand two hours of immobility.

7. Throughout the following description it will be assumed that the graft is delivered from the right, only because this is slightly easier for a right-handed surgeon. The system need only be rotated 180 degrees about its long axis to bring the graft into the correct orientation for insertion from the left groin. (This has not been necessary in any of the 15 insertions performed to date.)

8. Current practice is to expose both common femoral arteries. Hemostatic loops are passed around the artery just proximal and distal to the origin of the inferior epigastric artery. The two loops can be alternately relaxed and tightened for hemostasis during the introduction of catheters and sheaths.

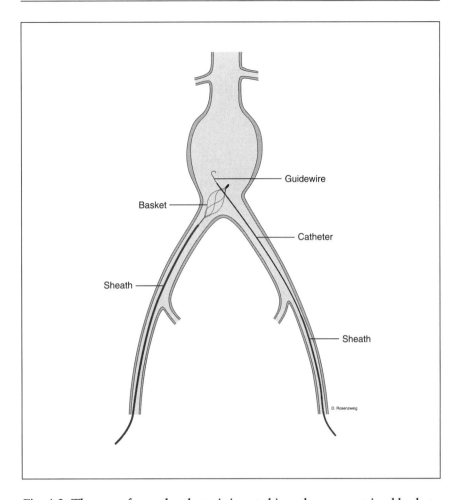

Fig. 4-2. The cross-femoral catheter is inserted into the stone retrieval basket.

9. Heparin (10,000 units) is administered intravenously three minutes before arterial clamping.

10. The common femoral arteries are incised transversely. The right-sided arteriotomy is a little longer than the left, to permit introduction of the 18 French delivery system.

11. The cross-femoral catheter is inserted through the left iliac artery into a waiting stone retrieval basket (Fig. 4-2) and pulled down the right iliac artery to the right groin (Fig. 4-3). Insertion of the stone retrieval basket and catheter is seldom accomplished without preliminary insertion of a guidewire, due to the tortuosity of the

61

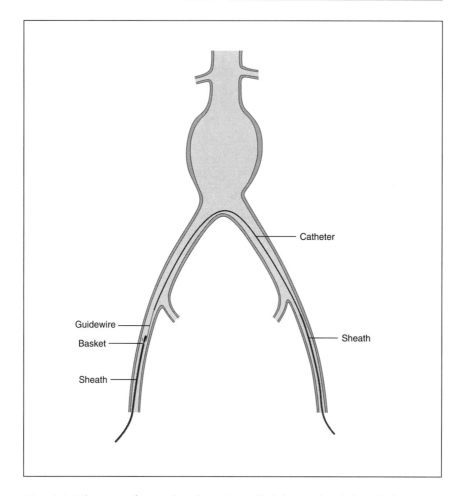

Fig. 4-3. The cross-femoral catheter is pulled down the right side by the stone retrieval basket.

iliac arteries. In difficult cases, a slippery (hydrophilic-coated) guidewire with a long, soft tip can be quite effective, in conjunction with a slightly angulated angiographic catheter. A J-tip wire may be less likely to cause dissection but is sometimes more difficult to pass. "Road mapping" permits real-time fluoroscopy to be superimposed on an angiographic image of the arterial tree. The composite image is useful as a guide to manipulation of the catheter and wire.

12. The right-sided end of the cross-femoral catheter is passed through the central lumen of a double-lumen dilator (Fig. 4-4). When

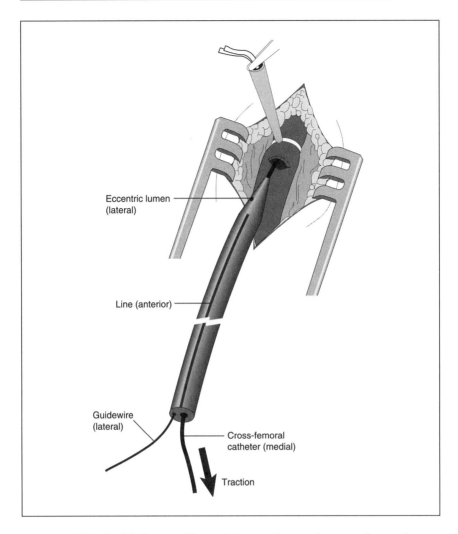

Eccentric lumen
(lateral)

Line (anterior)

Guidewire
(lateral)

Cross-femoral
catheter (medial)

Traction

Fig. 4-4. The double-lumen dilator is inserted over the cross-femoral catheter.

the line on this dilator is anterior, the eccentric lumen is to the patient's right. A soft-tip, 35-gauge guidewire is advanced halfway into the dilator through the eccentric lumen. The dilator is then inserted into the right femoral artery and advanced up to the aorta, keeping the line always in view on the anterior surface. Passage of the dilator is enhanced by maintaining traction on both ends of the cross-femoral catheter. Once the dilator is at the bifurcation, the guidewire

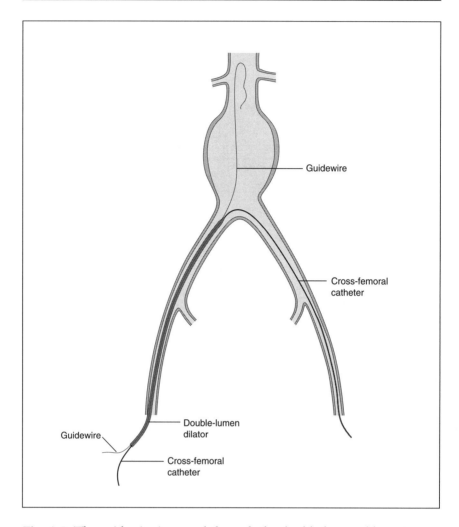

Fig. 4-5. The guidewire is passed through the double-lumen dilator into the proximal aorta.

can be advanced through the aneurysm into the proximal aorta (Fig. 4-5). As the dilator is removed it is important to ensure that the line remains oriented anteriorly and that the guidewire remains in the proximal aorta. The dilator leaves the femoral artery with its eccentric lumen always to the right of the central lumen. Therefore, the guidewire always emerges from the dilator to the right of the cross-femoral catheter, and the two are not twisted around one another.

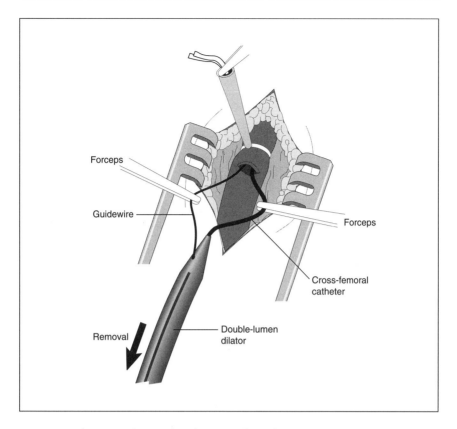

Fig. 4-6. The cross-femoral catheter and guidewire are separated on removal of the double-lumen catheter.

The catheter and wire are then separated at the femoral arteriotomy to ensure that this orientation is maintained (Fig. 4-6).

13. The right-sided end of the cross-femoral catheter is trimmed back to remove any portions that have been clamped. A 6-0 Prolene suture is passed through the cut end of the cross-femoral catheter so that both ends of the suture emerge from the orifice (Fig. 4-7).

14. An angiographic catheter is inserted over the guidewire. Brief flushes of dye help locate the neck of the aneurysm. The imaging system is positioned so that the aneurysm neck is in the center of the screen and the catheter tip is immediately above the renal arteries.

15. The imaging system is fixed in position. The markings on the ruler are traced onto a tape stuck on the screen. As long as the tape marks remain superimposed on the image of the ruler, the surgeon

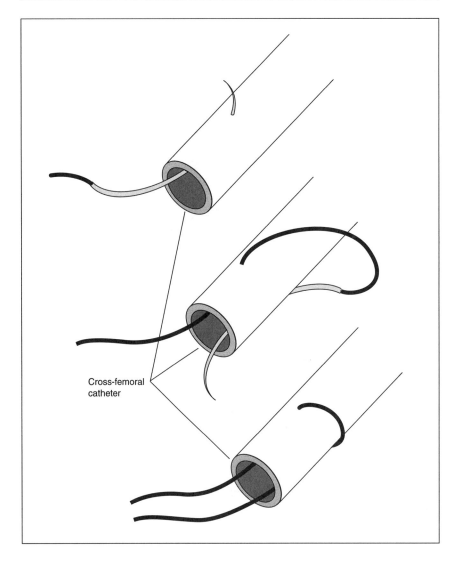

Cross-femoral
catheter

Fig. 4-7. A suture is passed through the end of the cross-femoral catheter.

can be reasonably sure that the relative positions of the patient and the fluoroscopy are the same as they were when the tape was placed. This precaution is important because any movement invalidates angiographic localization.

16. Angiograms are performed by the intra-aortic injection of 10 to 30 ml of dye at the level of the renal arteries. A power injector is

66

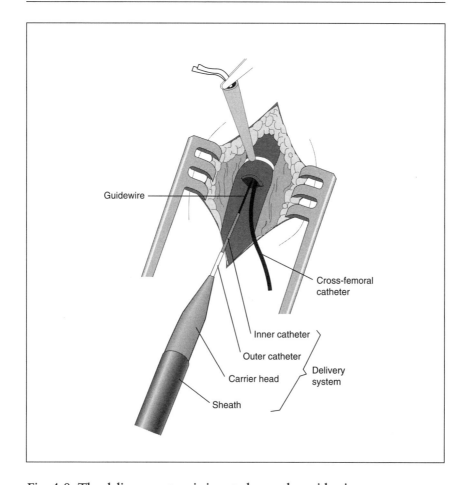

Fig. 4-8. The delivery system is inserted over the guidewire.

useful but not essential. Angiography is performed mainly to locate the renal arteries. The distal implantation site rarely has to be located, because the common iliac arteries allow some leeway in positioning. Indeed, the exact position of distal stent implantation is determined mainly by the length of the graft. The operator's main goal should be accurate proximal stent implantation.

17. The angiography catheter is exchanged over a stiff 35-gauge wire for the delivery system (Fig. 4-8). Markers on the anterior aspect of the delivery system help ensure that proper orientation is maintained. Radiopaque markers on the proximal stent perform the

same function. The delivery system can be rocked back and forth a little to facilitate insertion, but the correct orientation should be disturbed as little as possible.

18. In cases where the aortic neck is markedly (more than 30 degrees) angulated, the straightening induced by the delivery system can alter the position of the renal artery orifices. Under these circumstances it is prudent to perform a second angiogram using a catheter from the left groin to inject dye (Fig. 4-9). If tortuous left iliac arteries impede insertion of this catheter, the double-lumen dilator can be inserted over the cross-femoral catheter and its second lumen used as a conduit for a guidewire. With the guidewire in position, catheter insertion is relatively simple.

19. A lock at the outer end of the sheath must be released before the graft can be extruded. The position of the graft is maintained during extrusion by manipulation of the shaft of the delivery system. The sheath is radiopaque, and its progress from the tip of the delivery system can be followed on fluoroscopy. The proximal stent dilates spontaneously when it is released from the confines of the sheath. The partially expanded stent has a conical shape (Fig. 4-10). This appearance is a cue for final adjustments in stent position before further sheath removal permits complete expansion of the proximal stent.

20. The sheath is then withdrawn to its fullest extent, exposing the catheters of the delivery system in the right groin (see Fig. 4-1). It should be remembered that the graft is still attached to the delivery system, and the barbs are oriented to resist only caudal displacement. Heavy-handed movements of the delivery system at this point could theoretically displace the graft proximally, although this has yet to happen in practice.

21. The small left-limb catheter is disconnected from the main stem of the delivery system by cutting the fine blue suture loop. The green suture loop is used to tie the left-limb catheter to the end of the cross-femoral catheter.

22. A small (3.5 French) sheath is advanced from the left groin over the cross-femoral catheter to cover the sutured connection.

23. The conjoined catheter, comprising the cross-femoral catheter, the left-limb catheter, and the sheath, is withdrawn into the right femoral artery by applying traction at the left groin. The hemo-

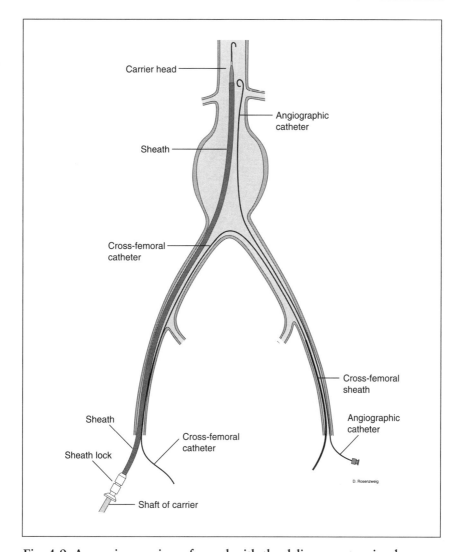

Fig. 4-9. An angiogram is performed with the delivery system in place.

static loops are relaxed a little on both sides to minimize the necessary force. On fluoroscopy, the conjoined catheter will be seen to roll out of the right iliac artery, straighten, and begin to pull the left-limb stent into the left iliac artery (Fig. 4-11). The left limb of the graft unfolds as the stent on the left limb of the graft descends to reach its final position in the left iliac artery, at approximately the same level as the stent on the right limb.

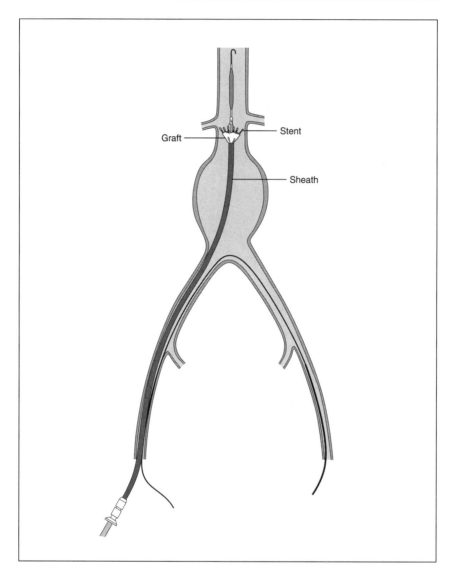

Fig. 4-10. The proximal stent assumes a conical shape as it starts to leave the delivery system.

24. The guidewire is withdrawn to the tip of the delivery system. A Luer-Lok at the outer end of the delivery system is released, permitting the inner catheter to be removed. The position of the inner catheter can be followed on fluoroscopy by watching the progress of

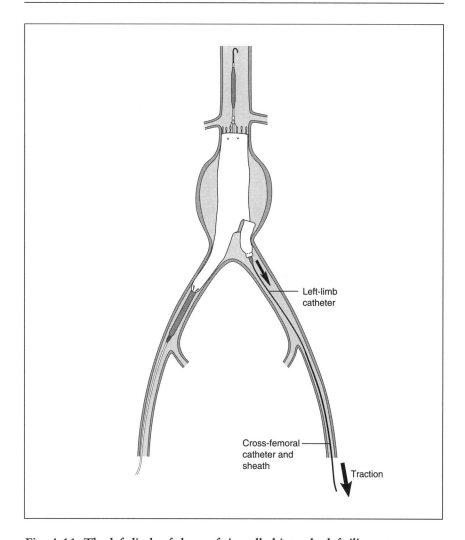

Fig. 4-11. The left limb of the graft is pulled into the left iliac artery.

the guidewire within. The proximal stent will be seen to move a little as the tip of the inner catheter passes and the stent's attachments
to the delivery system are released. Gentle traction on the delivery
system will now be transmitted to the graft only through the distal
stent. Thus, the graft is completely straightened before further withdrawal of the inner catheter also releases the distal stent.

25. The delivery system, freed of its attachments to the graft,
will slide out of the aorta and right iliac artery, taking the sheath

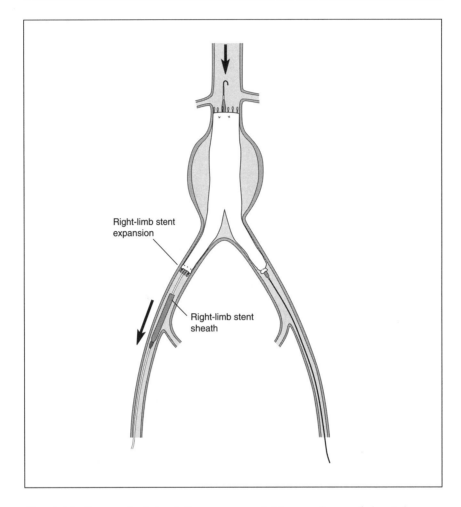

Right-limb stent
expansion

Right-limb stent
sheath

Fig. 4-12. Removal of the delivery system initiates release of the right-limb stent.

around the right-limb stent with it (Fig. 4-12). With the resultant expansion of the right-limb stent, the graft is now open into the right iliac artery, and a pulse can be felt at the right groin above the hemostatic loops.

26. The inner catheter can now be replaced and the guidewire advanced into the proximal aorta to provide access for completion angiography. Reinsertion of the inner catheter also helps with hemostasis during delivery system removal.

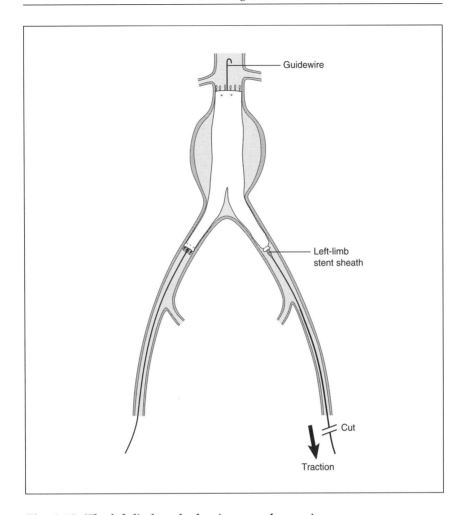

Fig. 4-13. The left-limb cathether is cut under tension.

27. Traction is applied to the left-limb catheter at two points, between which the catheter is transected (Fig. 4-13), cutting the suture loop within its lumen and freeing the stent (Fig. 4-14). As this is done the stent will be seen to spring from its sheath. The left-limb catheter and its sheath slide over the suture loop as they are removed from the femoral artery. A strong pulse should now be palpable at the left groin. The suture itself is not removed until a satisfactory result has been confirmed by completion angiography or intravascular ultrasound.

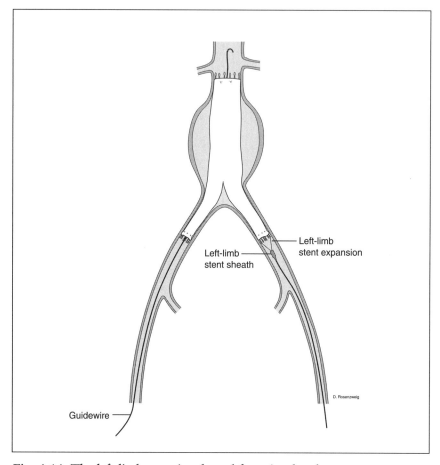

Fig. 4-14. The left-limb stent is released from its sheath.

28. The completion angiogram is usually performed by insertion of a catheter over the right-sided guidewire. Angiograms are performed to exclude renal artery occlusion, perigraft leakage, and kinking.

29. Kinking occurs when the graft is placed through an area of iliac stenosis of severe (greater than 80 degrees) angulation. The remedy is insertion of another stent. Whatever stent is used, care must be taken during insertion of the delivery system not to displace the distal limb stent. On the right, a guidewire is already in place. On the left, a guidewire has to be inserted before introduction of the delivery system. Traction on the remnant of the left-limb suture loop is a useful precaution against stent displacement.

30. The femoral arteries are flushed one more time before they are closed in the standard fashion. Flushing should be performed onto pads or gauze, which can be inspected for particles of thrombus. This is one reason for using open surgical access to the left femoral artery. Otherwise it would be relatively easy to perform all left-sided maneuvers percutaneously.

Lessons from Early Clinical Experience

At the time of writing, bifurcated graft insertion has been attempted in 23 patients, with success in 20. The first two failures resulted from the excessive force necessary to pull the left-limb distal stent sheath off the stent. This component has been modified and the problem has not recurred in the last seven insertions.

Securing the Proximal Stent

The method of attachment between the proximal end of the graft and the neck of the aneurysm, with a barbed Gianturco stent, has proved to be both hemostatic and secure. No evidence of stent migration has been seen on serial abdominal radiographs with follow-up extending up to six months from insertion. It is not clear what role the barbs played in securing the position of the proximal stent. Although stents now carry eight barbs, earlier versions had only two in case some problem with graft placement required operative correction. Moreover, these barbs were designed to be retractile. Very little radial force was transmitted to the barb tips from the stent. Instead, they were angulated caudally to penetrate the aortic wall and act as anchors, only if the open stent started to move downstream.

Kinking

We found that iliac limbs constructed of conventional graft material (Cooley Verisoft) were prone to kinking. This material was rather stiff and became even stiffer when it was ironed to remove crimps. Implantation of additional stents (Wallstent) was found to be a very effective remedy for this problem. The presence of a Wallstent straightened the artery and flattened irregularities in the graft. Completion angiography and intravascular ultrasound after stenting showed no signs of residual kinking in the region of the stent. So effective has stenting been in the prevention of kinking and thrombosis that we have adopted a policy of routine Wallstent insertion whenever conventional graft material is used. As a result, there have been no instances of graft thrombosis in the last 15 cases.

Another way to prevent kinking is by using kink-resistant graft material. Some of the newly available thin-wall grafts have proven to be much more pliant and less prone to kinking (Fig. 4-15).

These findings highlight the importance of high-quality completion angiography or even intravascular ultrasound (see Chapter 13) to permit the early detection and correction of such problems.

Infection

Many patients developed fevers in the immediate postoperative period, which persisted for up to a week. None have subsequently developed signs of graft infection. The Argentinian and Australian groups have also reported self-limited febrile responses following endovascular aneurysm repair of large aneurysms. This effect may be attributable to the deposition of large quantities of thrombus within the aneurysm following graft insertion, although the mechanism remains obscure.

The potential for infection is of particular concern following endovascular graft insertion, because cultures of mural thrombus removed at operation have shown high rates of bacterial contamination. My current practice is to administer broad-spectrum cephalosporins immediately before endovascular aneurysm repair, although vancomycin might be indicated in light of the increasing prevalence of multiresistant, coagulase-negative *Staphylococcus*.

Tortuosity

The sometimes severe iliac artery tortuosity seen in these cases (Fig. 4-16) never prevented delivery system insertion. One stenotic exter-

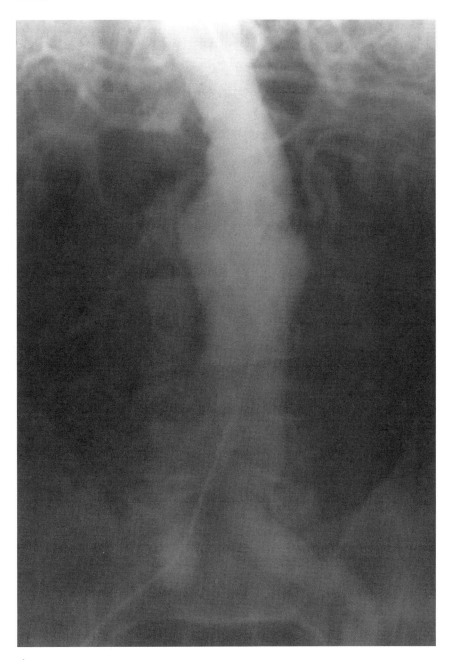

A

Fig. 4-15. Preoperative (A) and postoperative (B) angiograms: endovascular aneurysm repair using a thin-wall bifurcated graft.

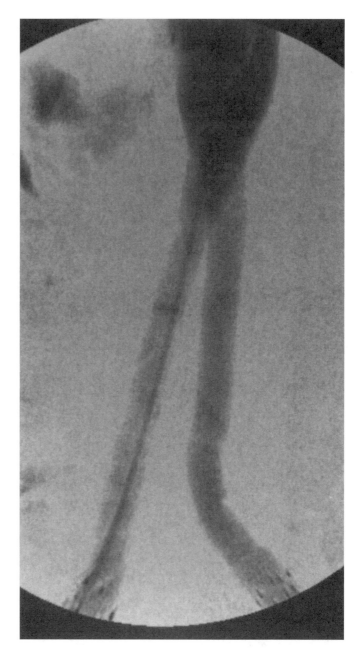

B

Fig. 4-15 *(continued)*

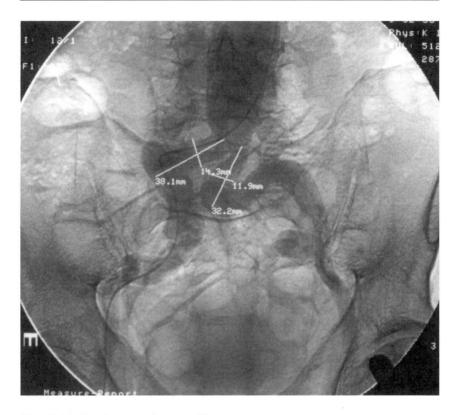

Fig. 4-16. Angiogram showing iliac artery tortuosity.

nal iliac artery required balloon dilatation and another required balloon dilatation and stenting. One patient required bilateral common iliac dilatations.

I found the iliac arteries to be surprisingly mobile. Acute angulations sometimes straightened completely when the delivery system was inserted over a rigid guidewire. However, it is possible that the insertion of a larger, less flexible delivery system might not have been accomplished so easily.

Conclusion

The apparent simplicity of straight-graft insertion is misleading. Although bifurcated graft insertion has many steps, none can com-

79

pare in difficulty with the task of simultaneously positioning both ends of a straight graft, especially if the length is not quite right.

Despite the apparent complexities of bifurcated graft insertion, the advantages are now widely recognized. These include a greater number of suitable candidates and easier graft sizing. All groups evaluating systems for abdominal aortic aneurysm repair are attempting to adapt to bifurcated graft insertion, although the only clinical successes have been with the system described in this chapter.

References

1. Chuter TAM et al. Transfemoral endovascular aortic graft placement. *J Vasc Surg* 1992;18:185–197.

2. Chuter TAM et al. Transfemoral aortic aneurysm repair: Straight and bifurcated grafts in dogs. *J Vasc Surg* 1993;17:233.

3. Chuter TAM, Donayre C. Bifurcated endoluminal grafts: Experimental studies and initial clinical experience. Presented at Endovascular Symposium. November 27, 1993, Royal Prince Alfred Hospital, Sydney, Australia.

The EVT Endoluminal Prosthesis: Developmental Concepts and Design

5

Harrison M. Lazarus

The early systems designed for the endovascular repair of aortic aneurysms were hampered by limitations of the devices that were used to attach and anchor the graft to the aortic wall. An example is the device patented by Choudhury in 1979 [1].

Later, improvements in angioplasty balloons provided a new means of graft attachment. These balloons could be used to drive hooks into the aorta. I tested this method in a series of experiments performed in the mid-1980s. Early experiments used only one set of hooks to attach the proximal end of the graft [2]. Based on the results of these experiments, it was apparent that it would be necessary to attach the other end of the graft to the aorta distal to the aneurysm [3].

After meeting the goals of developing a system for endovascular aortic aneurysm repair and testing the system in animals, clinical

testing was begun at several centers around the world. The accumulating clinical experience has been the basis for several minor
changes in the system, but the basic elements remain the same [4].

Device Development and Description

Goals

The delivery system must be able to traverse the iliac arteries from
the groin and seat the graft securely in the aorta. This requirement
has several implications for the functional characteristics of the
delivery system, the graft, and the means of attachment. Desirable
features of the delivery system include:

1. Small diameter—to permit transfemoral insertion.
2. Flexibility—to negotiate the often tortuous iliac arteries.
3. A capsule that is impervious to the hooks of the attachment—
   to maintain the graft in a compressed state during delivery.
4. A pusher rod assembly—to extrude the graft from the capsule.
5. A guidewire—to lead the delivery system through the distal
   arterial tree and prevent trauma due to impingement of the
   upstream end against the vessel walls or their lining of
   thrombus.

Desirable features of the graft include:

1. Construction from standard graft materials known to be
   biocompatible and durable.
2. Construction that encourages incorporation into surrounding tissues.

Desirable features of the attachment system include:

1. Control of deployment from a remote site via a catheter.
2. Compressibility to permit catheter-based delivery.
3. Secure hemostatic apposition of the graft to the aorta.

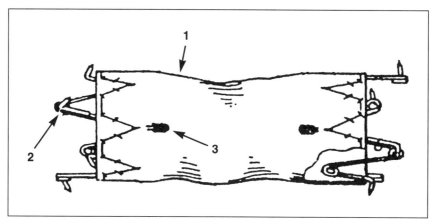

Fig. 5-1. Graft to be implanted. 1. Graft material. 2. Hooks of attachment. 3. Radiopaque markers for alignment of graft. (From HM Lazarus. Intraluminal graft device: System and method. US Patent Number 4,787,799, 1988.)

Concept

The above goals were met by mounting a tube graft on two self-expanding attachment means (Fig. 5-1), which carried small hooks. Balloon-driven (Fig. 5-2) implantation of these hooks was used to ensure secure attachment. The prosthesis was delivered in a compressed state within a flexible, metal-wrapped capsule (Fig. 5-3) at the end of a catheter (Fig. 5-4). A pusher rod (Fig. 5-5) within the capsular catheter was used to extrude the prosthesis from the capsule. Following graft deployment the capsule, the balloon catheter, and the pusher rod were all removed (Fig. 5-6).

Capsule

The endovascular grafting system requires a device to contain the graft and navigate the course of the femoral and iliac arteries to the aorta (see Fig. 5-3). The device consists of a capsule supported on the end of a nylon catheter from 40 to 100 cm in length (see Fig. 5-3, number 3). To make this nylon tube radiopaque it is loaded with bismuth subcarbonate or barium sulfate.

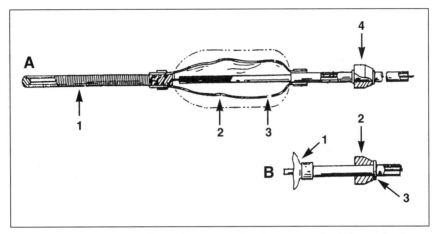

Fig. 5-2. Angioplasty balloon for setting hooks. A: 1. Flexible guidewire. 2. Balloon. 3. Injection tube. 4. Pusher button. B: 1. End of balloon. 2. Movable pusher button. 3. Stop for pusher button. (From HM Lazarus. Intraluminal graft device: System and method. US Patent Number 4,787,799, 1988.)

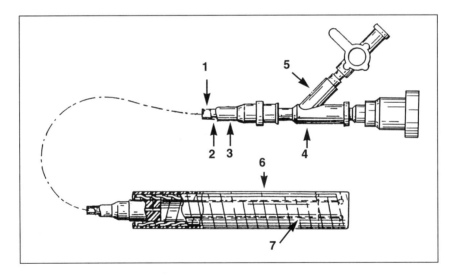

Fig. 5-3. Delivery component of the endovascular grafting system. 1. Lumen of liner. 2. Lubricous liner. 3. Capsular tubing. 4. Wye adapter. 5. Side arm. 6. Capsule for graft. 7. Kevlar strands. (From HM Lazarus. Intraluminal graft device: System and method. US Patent Number 4,787,799, 1988.)

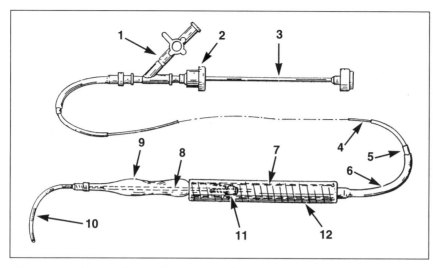

Fig. 5-4. Endovascular grafting system for aortic grafting. 1. Side arm for injection of contrast with attachment. 2. Touhy-Borst adapter. 3. Pusher rod. 4. Pusher tube and wire. 5. Lubricous liner. 6. Capsular tubing. 7. Kevlar strands. 8. Injection tube. 9. Angioplasty balloon. 10. Flexible guidewire. 11. Pusher button. 12. Capsule containing graft. (From HM Lazarus. Intraluminal graft device: System and method. US Patent Number 4,787,799, 1988.)

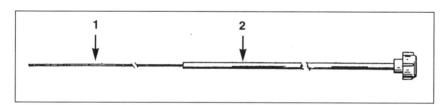

Fig. 5-5. Pusher rod for ejection of graft from delivery capsule. 1. Pusher tube. 2. Pusher wire. (From HM Lazarus. Intraluminal graft device: System and method. US Patent Number 4,787,799, 1988.)

An inner liner (see Fig. 5-3, number 2) is made for the nylon tube of a lubricous material such as Tefzel (ethylene tetrafluoroethylene) or Teflon FEP (fluorinated ethylene polypropylene), both of which are radiation-sterilizable. The pusher rod passes through the lumen of the liner (see Fig. 5-3, number 1).

An adapter (see Fig. 5-3, number 4) is secured to the proximal end of this catheter component. The side arm (see Fig. 5-3, number

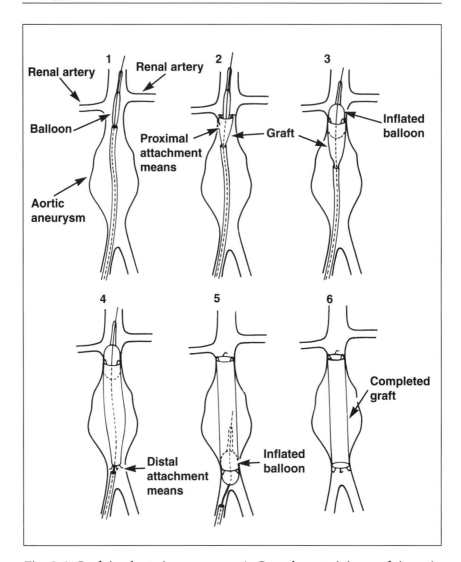

Fig. 5-6. Graft implantation sequence. 1. Capsule containing graft is positioned distal to the renal artery. 2. Capsule is withdrawn, freeing proximal attachment means with hooks. 3. Angioplasty balloon is brought into the attachment. 4. Capsule is removed, freeing the distal attachment means. 5. Balloon is moved to the distal attachment means and inflated to seat the hooks. 6. Graft is attached distal to the renal arteries and proximal to the iliac bifurcation, excluding the abdominal aortic aneurysm.

5) of the adapter has a three-way stopcock with a Luer-Lok fitting for injection of angiographic contrast or vasodilating medications. The center arm of this adapter is connected to a Touhy-Borst fitting, which carries an adjustable O-ring to create a hemostatic seal.

The capsule is a composite structure with an inner layer of stainless steel ribbon and an outer layer of heat-shrinkable polyethylene (see Fig. 5-3, number 6). The ribbon is spiral-wound on a mandrel so that each wrap overlaps the preceding wrap by approximately 30 to 50 percent and the ribbon's edges (on the inner aspect) face in the same direction as the graft extrusion. Snagging of the graft on the ribbon is further minimized by polishing the inner surface of the capsule. The ends of the ribbon are bonded together by tin-silver solder.

To prevent elongation of the capsule and separation of the wraps, four strands of Kevlar are glued to the outer aspect of the metal ribbon (see Figure 5-3, number 7). The outer layer of polyethylene overlies both the Kevlar strands and the steel ribbon wrap. The Kevlar and polyethylene permit some movement between adjacent winds of the steel ribbon, which lends the capsule enough flexibility to bend 70 to 120 degrees, depending on its length. The three layers of the capsule have a combined thickness of 0.012 inches.

Balloon

The central balloon catheter carries not only the balloon used to augment hook implantation but also the pusher button used in the graft (see Figs. 5-2 and 5-4). The balloon, measuring from 12 to 35 mm in diameter, is inflated by injecting dilute contrast material through an inflation lumen in the central balloon catheter. In addition to the appearance of the contrast within the balloon, the position of the balloon can be readily detected on fluoroscopy by its location between the radiopaque pusher button and the guidewire.

The pusher button is initially located on the balloon catheter shaft 2 to 3 cm proximal to the balloon, although it is actually movable between the proximal end of the balloon (see Fig. 5-6, number 1) and a stopper annular bulb (see Fig. 5-6, number 3), which is formed by heating a localized area of the balloon shaft. The pusher button (see Figs. 5-2A, number 4; 5-2B, number 2; and 5-4, number 11;) is made from 300 series stainless steel with a diameter ranging from 0.12 to 0.2 inches. The steel makes the pusher button radiopaque.

A very flexible guidewire is secured at the distal end of the balloon catheter (see Figs. 5-4, number 10, and 5-6, number 1). Alternatively, the guidewire can pass through the length of the balloon catheter within a second lumen, which permits insertion of the delivery system over a preinserted guidewire.

Pusher Rod

The balloon inflation lumen of the balloon catheter can also serve as a conduit for the insertion of a pusher rod, consisting of a thin-walled stainless steel tube (see Figs. 5-4, number 4, and 5-5). The lumen of the pusher tube contains an elongated, flexible, solid wire (see Fig. 5-5, numbers 1 and 2). The wire is long enough to extend through the balloon shaft and engage a plug at the distal end of the balloon. This pusher rod assembly stabilizes the pusher button while the capsule is retracted by turning a knob on the handle.

Graft

The graft can be made from any of the fabrics used for conventional grafts. One material found to be satisfactory is the woven uncrimped Dacron vascular prosthesis, manufactured by United States Catheter Industry (Billerica, MA). When this textile is used, the ends of the graft are heat-sealed to prevent fraying of the woven fabric.

The dimensions of the graft depend on the length of the aneurysm and the diameter of the segments of aorta proximal and distal to the aneurysm, where the graft is attached. The length of the graft should allow at least a 1-cm zone of approximation between the end of the graft and the aortic implantation site, both proximally and distally. Thus, the graft is at least 2 cm longer than the aneurysm.

Coils of platinum wire are sutured at the graft in pairs as radiopaque markers. These permit the detection of graft twisting in the carrier or at the time of deployment.

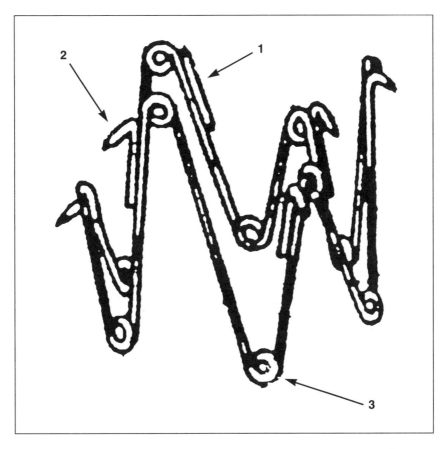

Fig. 5-7. Attachment means of graft. 1. Vs joined together. 2. Hooks. 3. Helical coils. (From HM Lazarus. Intraluminal graft device: System and method. US Patent Number 4,787,799, 1988.)

Attachment Spring Means

The attachment spring means (Fig. 5-7; see Fig. 5-1, number 2) are sewn inside the proximal and distal ends of the graft. Their function is to urge the graft from a compressed state to an expanded state, and to attach the graft to the aorta through a system of hooks.

The attachment spring means (see Fig. 5-7, number 1) are formed from a series of V-shaped metal wires, which are laser-welded to one another to form a zigzag ring or crown. The point of each V-shaped element is wound, forming a coil similar to the bend in a safety pin (see Fig. 5-7, number 3), which allows the angle between adjacent straight segments to open and close. The resting position is with the angles open and the spring attachment means expanded. Compressing the spring attachment means closes the angles and stores energy within the coils. This energy provides the force for graft expansion when the prosthesis is subsequently released from the confines of the capsule (see Fig. 5-6, number 2).

Hooks

The spring attachment means contains sharp metal (Elgiloy) hooks, which project outward beyond the proximal and distal ends of the graft. The proximal hooks are angulated slightly in the direction of blood flow. The distal hooks are angulated in the opposite direction. The proximal attachment prevents distal displacement; the distal attachment prevents proximal displacement. The graft is thereby stretched between its proximal and distal attachments.

Method of Graft Deployment

Figure 5-4 shows the endovascular grafting apparatus assembled for use. It is intended that the graft be loaded into the delivery system in the central manufacturing facility. To do so the graft is compressed, squeezed onto the balloon catheter, and positioned within the capsule. The pusher button (see Fig. 5-4, number 11) is positioned immediately behind the proximal attachment means.

At the time of implantation, an expandable sheath is placed through an oblique arteriotomy in the common femoral artery and advanced up the iliac artery to the aorta. The dilator is then removed, permitting the sheath to be used as a conduit for the main delivery system. A system of valves provides hemostasis following removal of the dilator.

The delivery system is advanced into the neck of the aorta under fluoroscopic guidance. When the capsule reaches the desired position, the pusher rod is used to stabilize the position of the proximal graft attachment means as the capsule is withdrawn (see Fig. 5-6, number 2). Once the proximal attachment means is outside the confines of the capsule, it expands outwardly to engage the vessel wall.

Inflation of the balloon with dilute contrast forces the hooks of the attachment means into the arterial wall (see Fig. 5-6, number 3).

When the proximal stent has been seated in this way, the capsule is further withdrawn over the graft and the distal attachment means by applying traction. The balloon is kept inflated during this phase of graft extrusion to stabilize the position of the proximal attachment means. The balloon is then deflated and pulled into the distal attachment means, where it is inflated again (see Fig. 5-6, number 5). Finally, the balloon is deflated and removed from the arterial tree along with the other elements of the delivery system, leaving only the graft attached to the aorta (see Fig. 5-6, number 6). Completion angiography is used to confirm correct placement of the graft and look for perigraft leakage.

Summary

This description of a system for endovascular aneurysm repair is only a snapshot of an evolving process. The early clinical experience has already lead to changes in the apparatus and its method of insertion, which soon will be entering phase 2 trials. Perhaps the most significant change is the development of a method of bifurcated delivery. The goal of these improvements is to broaden the range of suitable patients.

References

1. Choudhury MH. Method for performing aneurysm repair. US Patent Number 4,140,126, 1979.

2. Lazarus HM. Intraluminal graft device: System and method. US Patent Number 4,787,799, 1988.

3. Lazarus HM. Artificial graft implantation method. US Patent Number 5,104,399, 1992.

4. Lazarus HM, Williams RG, Sterman WD. Endovascular grafting apparatus: System, method, and devices for use therewith. US Patent Number 5,265,622, 1994.

The EVT Endoluminal Prosthesis: Clinical Experience and Results

6

William J. Quiñones-Baldrich

Lazarus's concept of a self-expanding attachment device with fixation pins to be driven into the wall of the abdominal aorta by using a balloon angioplasty to produce graft fixation was further developed and patented by EndoVascular Technologies (EVT), Inc. Several groups have been developing techniques for the endovascular repair of abdominal aortic aneurysms and associated conditions. There are at least four patents listed for grafts with various attachment systems to accomplish transfemoral remote placement of endovascular grafts [1–5].

Currently, the EVT prosthesis is the only device that has received U.S. Food and Drug Administration approval for initial clinical investigation in the United States. Selected sites for phase 1 clinical trials in the United States include the University of California at San Francisco, the University of California at Los Angeles (UCLA), and Stanford University. Clinical investigation is also occurring at international sites, with the largest experience coming from the group at the Royal Prince Alfred Hospital in Sydney, Australia (see Chapter 7).

Clinical Experience

The first implantation of the EVT endoluminal prosthesis occurred at the UCLA Medical Center on February 10, 1993. Further clinical experience has been accumulated in all three centers, with the largest experience at the UCLA Medical Center, consisting of 12 patients at the time of this writing (April 1994). The experience gained in the selection, evaluation, and management of these patients has given us an opportunity to further refine both the clinical and technical aspects of this procedure.

Patient selection for the currently available device (tube graft) requires the use of computed tomography and arteriography. In all patients, magnetic resonance imaging has also been of value in making precise measurements to determine if the proximal and distal necks are suitable for endovascular graft repair with current technology. A patient must have a demonstrable aneurysm neck (5 mm) below the renal arteries, an aneurysm neck proximal to the bifurcation of the iliac arteries, and no evidence of dependence of the inferior mesenteric artery to supply flow to the bowel. Presence of other anomalous arteries, such as polar renal arteries, would also contraindicate endovascular repair. Using these studies, the graft diameter and length are selected for each individual patient. By and large, using a slightly oversized graft for the determined diameter has proven to be safe and preferable. As already described, the graft itself has a fixation device placed at each end that is essentially a self-expanding attachment system, with pins placed around the circumference that will engage the aorta at an approximate 80-degree angle proximally and 85-degree angle distally (Fig. 6-1). The graft is compressed into a small capsule that is attached to a catheter delivery system. The system encloses a balloon angioplasty catheter (Fig. 6-2). The original design has been modified so that the present system is an over-the-wire device, thus preventing subintimal placement.

Patients currently receive general anesthesia, mainly because under phase 1 clinical trials, the rate of conversion to standard surgical repair was unknown. Based on the experience to date, however, it is anticipated that either regional or even local anesthesia will be feasible in most patients. We feel strongly that an operating room environment is

94

Fig. 6-1. End view of graft with attachment system. Note that the directions of the hooks of the attachment system are variable, as well as the location of the pins in the circumference of the vessel.

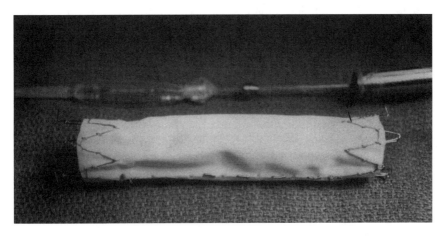

Fig. 6-2. Endovascular tube graft with attachment systems. Carrier system is shown above the graft and includes the capsule, guidewire, and implantation balloon.

preferable to carry out endovascular aneurysm repair, given that, on occasion, urgent conversion to transabdominal or retroperitoneal abdominal aortic aneurysm repair may be necessary, and the time necessary to move the patient to an operating room could be detrimental. The patient is prepared and draped for transabdominal repair in all instances so that the procedure can be quickly aborted and standard surgical repair carried out with minimal additional risk.

Selection of the access site is of utmost importance. Factors to consider include the diameter of the proximal iliac artery, the presence or absence of occlusive disease, and tortuosity. The selected femoral artery is then exposed through a standard surgical approach, maintaining the exposure relatively high, slightly above the inguinal ligament. In most instances, partial division of the inguinal ligament is helpful, especially if the artery needs to be pulled down to correct tortuosity. We routinely will ligate the circumflex iliac and circumflex pudendal arteries to accomplish adequate mobilization. Initially, a small introducer sheath is inserted, followed by a guidewire and a pigtail multihole angiogram catheter with centimeter marks. An aortogram is obtained, preferably with road map capabilities, so that final measurements can be confirmed, especially in relation to the length of the prosthesis needed. The small sheath is then removed, the patient fully heparinized, and a special large 20 French introducer sheath is placed through an oblique femoral arteriotomy. This is inserted through the iliac system under fluoroscopic control over a stiff guidewire. Once the sheath is in place, an internal obturator is advanced to obtain uniform expansion of the sheath. The obturator is then removed.

The device, with its special catheter containing the graft, is then introduced over the guidewire and advanced under fluoroscopic control until adequate positioning of the proximal attachment system is evident (Fig. 6-3). This is a critical step in the placement of this prosthesis. A special radiopaque marking system is extremely helpful in ensuring no twists in the prosthesis. Once the ideal position is verified, the capsule is remotely advanced by manipulating the control knob in the handle of the catheter system. This will allow the self-expanding attachment system to deploy. Minor adjustments are made throughout this process to ensure that the attachment system is deployed at the exact desired location. It must be recognized that once the proximal attachment system is deployed, only minor adjustments in the distal attachment system loca-

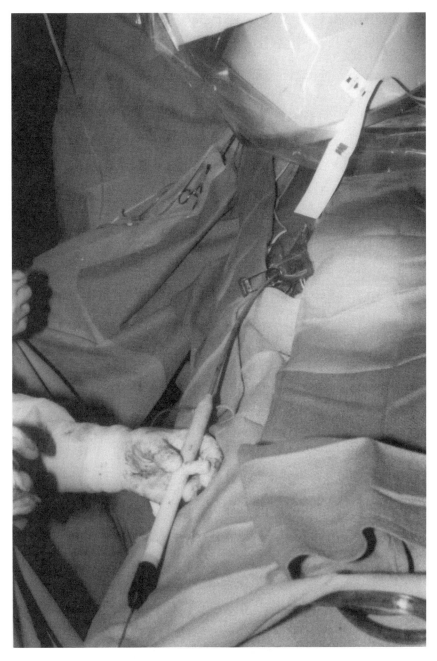

Fig. 6-3. Transfemoral placement of EVT device. Long handle contains a control knob for proximal detachment system. Note fluoroscopy unit used to guide the catheter system to its proper location.

tion are possible. Once the self-expanding system is deployed proximally, the implantation balloon is advanced to the proper location. This is
identified by a marker in the balloon system that will allow the balloon
to be centered in the area of the attachment system. The balloon is
inflated to 2 atm (Fig. 6-4), deflated, rotated 180 degrees, and reinflated. With the proximal balloon inflated, the remainder of the enclosing
capsule is withdrawn, thus exposing the distal attachment system. The
location of the distal attachment system is then verified under fluoroscopy with additional angiographic contrast injection made through
the capsule, if necessary. The locking push system for the distal attachment is then advanced to the location and the capsule enclosing the
attachment system is withdrawn, again making final minor adjustments
as necessary. The distal attachment system is then deployed, the balloon
withdrawn to its proper location, and the distal attachment system
secured with, again, two inflations of the balloon, rotating the balloon
prior to the second inflation. On occasion, a second balloon catheter
system is introduced through the contralateral groin to improve the
deployment of the distal attachment system with the use of the kissing-
balloon technique. A completion angiogram is then performed, after
withdrawal of the entire system, to document the presence or absence
of proximal or distal graft leaks (Fig. 6-5). The introducer sheath is then
withdrawn and the femoral arteriotomy closed. The groin is then closed
with standard surgical technique and the patient is allowed to recover
from the anesthetic and returned to his or her room following a short
stay in the recovery room. The following day, a CT scan and an ultrasound of the abdomen are performed to document any evidence of leak,
thrombosis, or changes in the aneurysm.

UCLA Results

To date, 12 patients have been found candidates for endovascular
grafting of infrarenal abdominal aortic aneurysms using the currently approved device. It must be emphasized that these 12 patients
came from a large pool of patients (greater than 70) referred to our
institution for consideration of the endovascular graft. The most
common reasons for rejection were the absence of a distal neck suitable for tube graft repair and involvement of the iliac arteries with

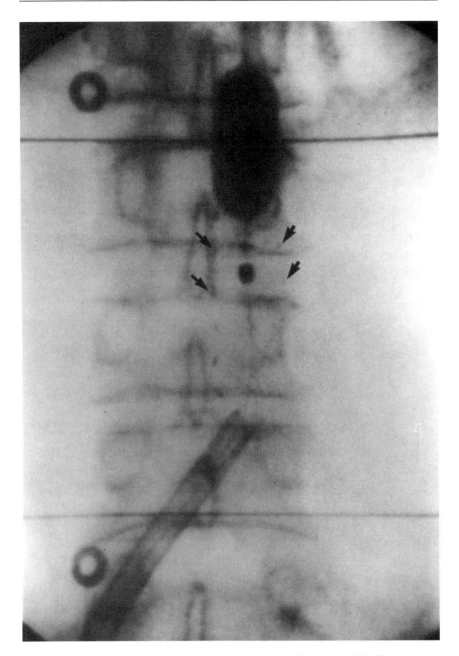

Fig. 6-4. Fluoroscopy view of implanted device after second balloon dilatation and deployment of the endovascular graft. Note retracted capsule in right iliac system and radiographic markers (arrows) to document the absence of twists by parallel location.

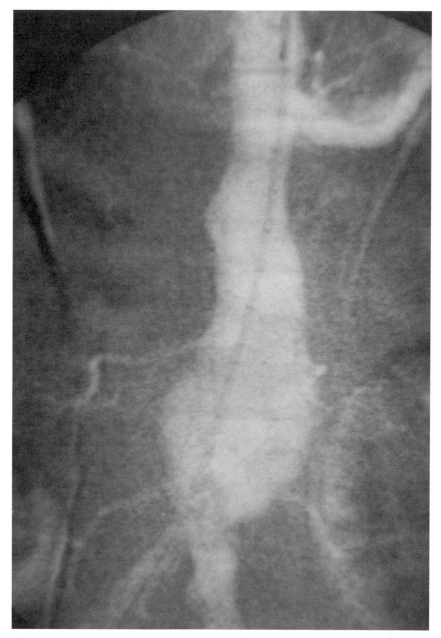

A

Fig. 6-5. A. Intraoperative angiogram of aneurysm prior to endovascular repair. B. Completion angiogram following endovascular repair. Note absence of leaks, with unimpeded flow to iliac arteries.

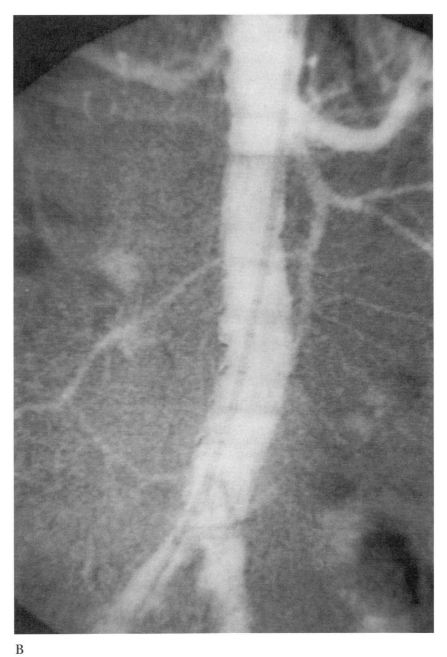

B

aneurysmal disease requiring a bifurcated graft repair. The latter underscores the need for a bifurcated endovascular graft, which is currently under development.

Of the initial 12 patients, two required conversion to standard surgical repair. The first patient underwent endovascular graft placement, at which time some difficulty negotiating tortuosity of the aneurysm was encountered. This prosthesis was inadvertently placed in a subintimal position. The patient required standard surgical reconstruction 48 hours after the initial attempt at endovascular repair. After this case, the device was redesigned as an over-the-wire system, without any subsequent difficulties with subintimal placement. The second conversion occurred in a patient who had an extremely tortuous (90 degrees) proximal neck that could not be negotiated with the device. Standard surgical repair was carried out at the time of attempted endovascular graft placement. The other 10 patients had successful implantation of the endovascular graft. In four instances, leaks around the graft were evident, with two of them obviously from the proximal or distal attachment location and the other two without a recognized site for perigraft blood flow. These leaks have spontaneously sealed in two of these patients, as documented by subsequent CT scan and duplex scan. Two remaining patients were followed closely and required repeat balloon angioplasty to seal a leak. In no instance, however, has there been any evidence of growth of the aneurysm, although follow-up is very limited (ranging from one month to one year).

At this point, phase 1 clinical trials of the EVT device have been completed and phase 2 is about to be launched. Phase 2 trials will consist of a randomized, prospective study in which patients will be allocated to either conventional or endovascular repair. It is the consensus among investigators that this is the only way to properly evaluate this new technology.

Further Considerations

Before transfemoral endovascular grafting can be recommended for routine clinical use, several important issues must be resolved:

1. *Security of fixation.* Since fixation of this device depends on radial forces exerted by the attachment system, there is concern that continued expansion of the neck of the aneurysm will lead to either growth of the aneurysm and failure of the fixation or perianastomotic leaks that certainly would be expected to increase the risk of aneurysm rupture. Initial experimental data would suggest some degree of pannus ingrowth; however, the amount of protection that this will offer in securing the attachment system to the aortic wall is unknown. In addition, the behavior of this prosthesis in animals cannot be fully applied to the expected behavior of the prosthesis in humans. Only prospective, carefully designed clinical trials will be able to answer this most important question.

2. *Risk of aneurysm rupture.* The purpose of intervention in the presence of an infrarenal abdominal aortic aneurysm is to eliminate or reduce the risk of rupture. In most instances, infrarenal abdominal aortic aneurysms are asymptomatic lesions, and the only recognized benefit to the patient is the reduction of risk of sudden death. The fact that blood flow around the graft may continue from collateral circulation due to either patent lumbar arteries and/or inferior mesenteric arteries may represent a continued risk of aneurysm expansion and rupture in patients in whom perigraft flow is evident. In our limited experience, this is likely to occur in a minority of patients and will be self-limited and temporary in some. Nevertheless, it will be important to identify such patients so that, if necessary and after a period of observation, these leaks can be corrected. Most important will be identifying those factors that will suggest this possibility occurring after endovascular repair, so that preintervention occlusion of these collateral vessels can be considered. This issue will be an important factor to study during upcoming clinical trials.

3. *Induction of mesenteric ischemia.* When conventional abdominal aortic aneurysm repair is carried out, in most instances the inferior mesenteric artery is either thrombosed or ligated at the time of repair without consequence. A small number of patients, however, will develop significant mesenteric ischemia following ligation of a patent inferior mesenteric artery. During conventional repair, direct visual evaluation of the sigmoid colon allows the surgeon to reimplant the artery when deemed necessary. Other maneuvers include evaluation of the back-bleeding, or even back pressure measurements of the

stump of the inferior mesenteric artery. Colon ischemia following conventional aneurysm repair is a rare complication, mostly because it can be prevented by careful surgical technique. On the other hand, with endovascular grafting, the opportunity to directly evaluate for this possibility is not present. It is not known whether the risk of mesenteric ischemia is increased by endovascular repair. Patients in whom a patent inferior mesenteric artery is being excluded from circulation with endovascular graft repair should be monitored closely, perhaps even with prophylactic sigmoidoscopy or rectal pH monitoring, to identify this process without delay. Certainly, careful physical examination of the abdomen following endovascular repair should be carried out, considering that tenderness in the left-lower quadrant would have implications, given the absence of a laparotomy.

4. *Need for bifurcated prosthesis.* One of the lessons that has been learned during recent experience with endovascular grafting and screening for this procedure has been the clear need for bifurcated repair in most patients with infrarenal abdominal aortic aneurysm. Whereas with direct surgical repair a tube graft may be placed in the absence of a distal neck by surgically recreating a neck and sewing the graft to the actual bifurcation, with endovascular technique, the presence of a normal diameter segment of aorta is imperative for tube graft repair. Thus, when endovascular technique is considered, bifurcated repair will be the most commonly needed configuration. Several groups are currently evaluating the feasibility of bifurcated endovascular grafts. Our own efforts have been successful in the laboratory and are currently awaiting the start of phase 1 clinical trials.

Endovascular Graft Training

The necessary training for physicians caring for patients with abdominal aortic aneurysm is critically important. At present, endovascular grafts must be placed only by surgeons skilled in the management of patients with abdominal aortic aneurysms. The complications of this procedure are likely to require prompt surgical intervention, and therefore the surgeon is in the best position to make a decision about when to abort a transfemoral deployment or when to convert the operation to conventional graft repair. Perioperative complications of abdominal aortic aneurysm repair are well known to vascular surgeons treating these patients. They are thus in the best position to identify these complications and treat them without delay. Surgical skills necessary for conventional repair, however, are not sufficient to provide the necessary skills for endovascular graft placement. The surgeon must be familiar with fluoroscopy, angiography, and arterial catheter and guidewire manipulation. These skills may be acquired by the surgeon who practices deployment of devices either in the currently clinical area or by using experimental and/or animal models. Involvement from colleagues in interventional radiology as a team approach may be desirable, depending on the local circumstances of the individual surgeon. The patient must remain under the care of the surgeon, however, who is the only appropriate physician who can care for the potential complications following intervention.

It is imperative that companies developing these devices ascertain the competence of the individuals who are to use it. Marketing the device without this assurance will lead to inappropriate deployment and use of these devices and therefore will only increase the morbidity, mortality, and delay in gaining the necessary knowledge about the safety and efficacy of this new technology.

References

1. Lazarus HM. Endovascular Grafting for Repair of Abdominal Aortic Aneurysms. In SS Ahn, WS Moore (eds), *Endovascular Surgery* (2nd ed). Philadelphia: Saunders, 1992. Pp. 532–534.

2. Choudhury MH. Method for performing aneurysm repair. US Patent Number 4,140,126, 1979.

3. Kornberg E. Aortic graft device and method for performing an intraluminal abdominal aortic aneurysm repair. US Patent Number 4,562,596, 1986.

4. Kornberg E. Device and method for performing an intraluminal abdominal aortic aneurysm repair. US Patent Number 4,617,932, 1986.

5. Lazarus HM. Intraluminal graft device, system and method. US Patent Number 4,787,899, 1988.

Stented and Nonstented Endoluminal Grafts for Aneurysmal Disease: The Australian Experience

7

Geoffrey H. White
James May
Weiyun Yu

The vascular surgery unit at the Royal Prince Alfred Hospital, at the University of Sydney in Sydney, Australia, has had active interest and participation in angioplasty and percutaneous recanalization procedures for many years, and in more complex endovascular techniques including vascular stenting since 1989. From this involvement grew an interest in the concept and application of coated stents and endoluminal bypass grafts in the management of a range of arterial disease states.

Initial studies in bench models, excised vessels, and experimental animals led to numerous developments and improvements in design that eventually allowed safe progression to the use of

107

Table 7-1. Severe medical comorbidities in 16 of 41 patients undergoing endoluminal repair of aneurysms

Comorbidity	Number of patients
Poor cardiac function	8
Renal impairment	3
Chronic obstructive airway disease (on oxygen 16 hours per day)	1
Chronic liver disease (hepatitis C) with thrombocytopenia	1
Hostile abdomen	3
Total	16

endoluminal grafts in humans. Endovascular repair of aneurysms has been approved by the Institutional Review Board at our hospital, and informed consent was obtained from each participating patient. As of April 1994, we have performed more than 40 clinical cases of endoluminal graft implantations in patients with varying medical conditions (Table 7-1).

Our initial human clinical experience was with coated stents (conventional Palmaz arterial stents coated with thin-walled polytetrafluoroethylene (PTFE) graft material) [1, 2] and with Parodi stent-graft devices in several configurations [3–7]. Subsequently, we have also gained experience with the EVT device (EndoVascular Technologies, Menlo Park, CA), the Chuter bifurcated graft [8], and with the Sydney Endovascular Graft (Table 7-2).

The design features of our own endovascular graft (the Sydney Endovascular GAD Graft, or White-Yu Endograft) were originally conceived in 1989 and have evolved considerably since that time. This graft, which does not require the use of any of the arterial stents used in other endografts, first underwent clinical trial in June 1993 for the successful management of a symptomatic abdominal aortic aneurysm in a 73-year-old patient with severe cardiac disease [9].

This chapter describes our experience and results with each of these grafts, particularly the pitfalls and complications of various techniques of endoluminal grafting we have encountered. The graft devices used are catagorized as either stented or nonstented designs.

Table 7-2. Configuration of endoluminal grafts used in 41 patients

	Graft configuration			
	Tube	Tapered Aortoiliac Aortofemoral	Bifurcated	Peripheral
Coated stent	—	—	—	1 (subclavian)
Parodi	3	6	1	—
White-Yu	11	6	1	3 (iliac)
EVT	8	—	—	—
Chuter	—	—	1	—

Stented Endoluminal Grafts

Coated Stents

Vascular stents have become well-established in the management of stenotic or occlusive disease of the iliac arteries and aorta but are limited by a high rate of restenosis in the femoral position. Future improvement and development of stent techniques will most likely include the frequent use of stents lined or coated with prosthetic vascular graft materials to halt the restenosis process.

Model Studies

Stent-graft combinations were prepared by wrapping a thin-walled prosthetic graft around the unexpanded stent, with two sutures used to provide safe attachment of the components [2]. PTFE materials were used for most of these studies (Fig. 7-1). A sheet of thin-walled PTFE was trimmed to size and wrapped around the unexpanded stent after the inner aspect of the wrap had been sutured to the stent. The devices were deployed in transparent plastic tubing (Fig. 7-2). These studies allowed calculation of degrees of overlap that would be required to create an effective seal; mechanisms of combining balloon, endoluminal graft, and access sheaths; and observations of the balloon strength required to expand the stent and graft.

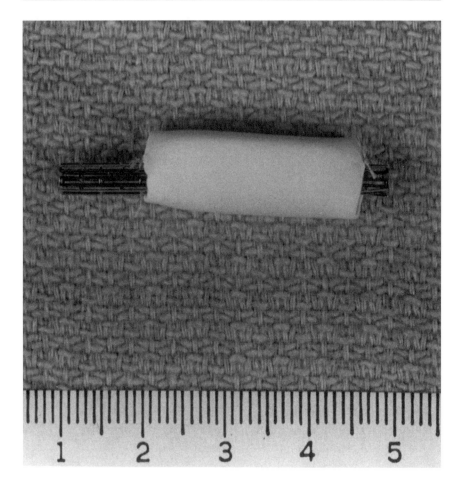

Fig. 7-1. Stent-graft (PTFE) combination for endoluminal grafting.

We concluded from these studies that balloon-expandable and self-expanding intraluminal grafts each have identifiable advantages and disadvantages when used in conjunction with prosthetic vascular graft materials. Balloon-expandable stents within a graft are more bulky than self-expandable designs, but controlled expansion and positioning are easier. It may also be simpler to align the graft walls with the internal vascular lumen. There is a tendency, however, for the graft material to be dislodged from the stent during passage to the site of deployment, unless the graft has been firmly attached to the stent by suturing or glueing. This tendency can be

110

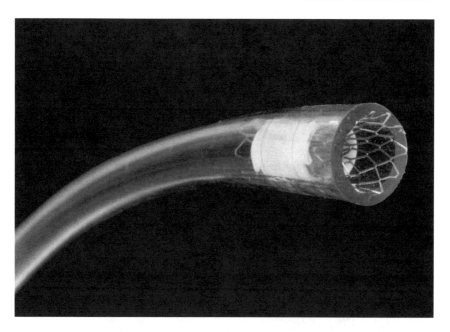

Fig. 7-2. Stent-graft (PTFE) implanted in plastic tubing model. The graft effectively forms a coating to the implanted stent.

especially problematic when passing the graft-stent combination through an access sheath during percutaneous implantation.

Balloon rupture during expansion may also be a problem and is caused by constriction of the prosthetic material around the stent, requiring excessive pressure for inflation, or by perforation of the thin-walled balloon by metallic struts of the stent.

Animal Studies

Experimental Dacron- and PTFE-covered stents were developed and deployed successfully in excised arterial segments and in vivo in the aorta and iliac and femoral arteries of dogs. Fluoroscopy, angioscopy, and intravascular ultrasound (IVUS) were compared for precision of control of the implantation process and monitoring expansion of the prosthesis. The interactions of the prosthetic devices in zones of overlap with the arterial wall at the ends of the graft, and in the surface internally lined by the graft, were examined. Satisfactory implantation and early patency were achieved in the animal studies, and required improvements were identified for the access sheaths, further miniaturization of the devices, and deployment techniques. Comparative studies to nonstented endografts are described below.

The Parodi Graft

Great interest in endoluminal repair of aortic aneurysms was generated by the first report of the use of this technique in humans by Parodi [10]. Following very helpful consultation with Dr. Parodi and his team, we commenced our program of endoluminal grafting of aortic aneurysms in May 1992. We have previously presented our early clinical experience with this technique and documented some of the problems encountered [2–7, 11].

Materials and Methods

Endoluminal repair with modifications of the Parodi graft has been attempted to date in 10 patients with abdominal aortic aneurysms. The patients were all male, with an average age of 72 years. Four were considered fit for standard open repair of the aneurysm while the remaining six had been rejected for open repair at other medical centers.

The morphology of the aneurysms allowed the patients to be divided into two groups. In one group of three patients the aneurysms were confined to the aorta and had proximal and distal necks making them suitable for repair with an endoluminal tube graft. In the other group of seven patients there were no distal necks to the aneurysms, and the common iliac arteries were either ectatic or frankly aneurysmal. These patients were treated by an endoluminal aortofemoral or aortoiliac graft technique as described below.

Technique of Endoluminal Repair

A balloon-expandable stainless steel stent was used in combination with a PTFE or Dacron graft in these 10 patients. The grafts were delivered into the aorta through a sheath introduced through the femoral or iliac arteries and anchored proximally with a stainless steel stent under radiographic control, in the manner described by Parodi [10]. In three instances the graft was a tubular one confined to the aorta. In the remaining seven instances a tapered aortoiliac or aortofemoral graft was used, either in combination with a femoro-femoral crossover graft and contralateral iliac artery interruption as described by May et al. [4] (Fig. 7-3), or an endoluminal aortoiliac graft combined with an extraluminal distal graft [6] or a bifurcated graft was inserted.

Results

In five of the 10 patients in which this method was used, the endoluminal procedure was converted immediately to standard open repair. (One additional patient required open revision operation at three weeks following the endoluminal implantation, due to displacement of the stent from the aortic neck.) The causes of failure leading to open repair were access problems in two patients and occurred early in our experience. Balloon malfunction occurred in another patient; the balloon inflated preferentially at the upper end and forced the stent distally from its correct place at the neck into the body of the aneurysm. The most frustrating complication was that of stent dislodgment, which occurred in three patients. The stent with its attached aortoiliac graft was satisfactorily deployed immediately below the renal arteries. It was not possible, however, to withdraw the balloon catheter without placing traction on the tapered distal end of the graft. This restriction was due to the poor profile of the balloon following deflation. Although there was a good profile of 4.5 mm in diameter before inflation, the "wings" of the deflated balloon could not be reduced to less than 10 to 12 mm in diameter. This resulted in the balloon producing traction on the graft sufficient to cause dislodgment of the stent.

There has been no perioperative loss of life or limb during any of the endoluminal or open operations. However, there have been two cardiac deaths, and one death associated with liver failure and a bleeding peptic ulcer in long-term follow-up.

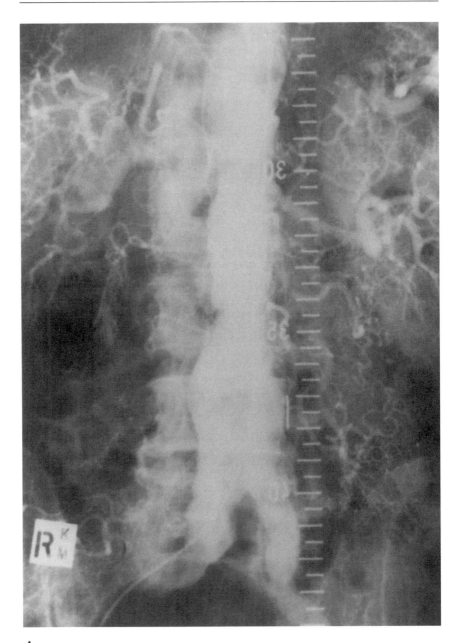

A

Fig. 7-3. Iliac artery approach for endoluminal repair of complex infrarenal abdominal aortic aneurysm combined with extraluminal bifurcated iliac graft placement. A. Preoperative angiogram (anteroposterior view) demonstrating infrarenal abdominal aortic aneurysm that extends to

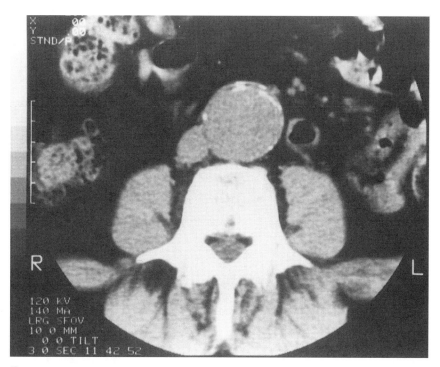

B

the aortic bifurcation and is therefore not suitable for endoluminal tube graft. B. Preoperative CT scan (contrast enhanced) of the aorta at a level just above the bifurcation, showing that the aortic diameter at this point is approximately 4 cm. C. Postoperative angiogram (anteroposterior view) demonstrating the endoluminal aortic graft that has been implanted via a retroperitoneal access to the right iliac artery. D. Postoperative angiogram (anteroposterior view) demonstrating the runoff via a retroperitoneal, extraluminal, bifurcated graft with limbs anastomosed distally to the external iliac artery on each side. The anastomosis of the endoluminal graft to the extraluminal graft is indicated (arrow). E. Postoperative digital subtraction angiogram showing the limbs of the bifurcated graft running distally to the external iliac artery on each side, with retrograde filling of the internal iliac artery on the right side. Both common iliac arteries were ligated via the original retroperitoneal incision to prevent back-filling of the aortic aneurysm sac.

115

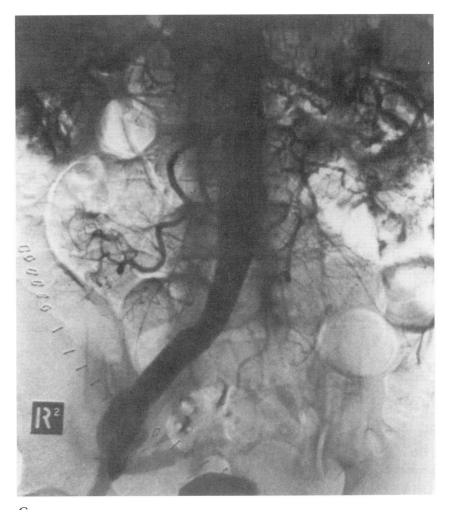

C

Fig. 7-3 *(continued)*

Complications

Complications that did not lead to conversion of the endoluminal repair to open repair occurred in three patients. In one of these, a leak from the lumen of the aorta into the aneurysmal sac at the superior end of the graft was sealed by introduction of a further covered stent, which was deployed 1 cm superior to the original stent. Two other patients developed stenosis in the midportion of their tapered

116

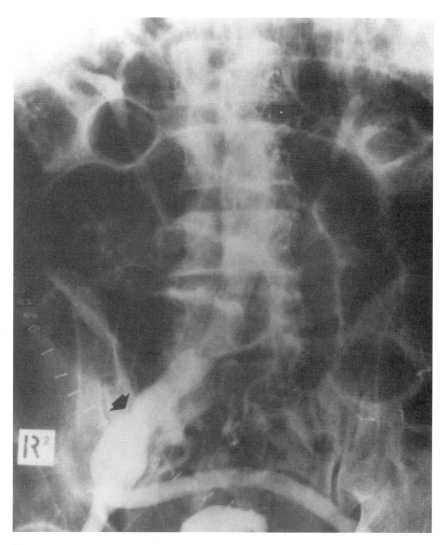

D

aortofemoral grafts. This was treated successfully by percutaneous balloon angioplasty in one and surgical revision of the distal portion of the graft in the other.

The complications listed above that led to abandonment of the endoluminal repair in favor of an open repair were access problems (2), balloon malfunction (1), and stent migration (3). These are further analyzed below.

117

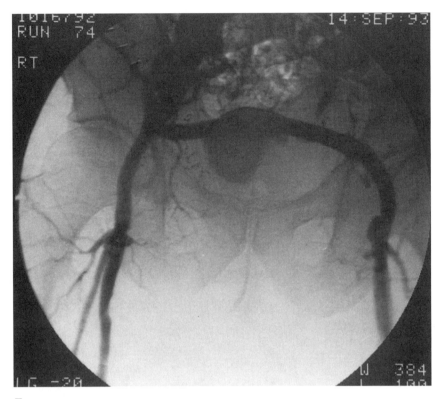

E

Fig. 7-3 (continued)

Access Problems

The delivery sheath introduced into the femoral artery for this graft was 29 French external diameter. This is almost 10 mm and was too large to be accepted by the 7-mm diameter external iliac artery in one patient. The disparity was known before operation, but we hoped the artery could be dilated. We avoided this problem subsequently by instituting a policy of not attempting sheath insertion into arteries less than 10 mm in diameter.

The second patient with an access problem readily accepted the introducing sheath into the aorta, but the bifurcated Dacron graft with balloon and stent could not be packaged in a sufficiently low profile to allow safe passage along the introducing sheath, once the

118

graft had been expanded in thickness by contact with blood. This problem should have been identified in the laboratory beforehand and was eliminated in all subsequent cases by trial package of the graft-stent device well before operation.

Balloon Malfunction

In one patient the graft-stent device was delivered without difficulty into the appropriate position below the renal arteries. It was also noted that the stent was centered correctly between the radiopaque markers of the 30-mm diameter balloon. Upon inflation, however, the balloon expanded preferentially at its upper end. Attempts to make the lower end of the balloon inflate were unsuccessful, with the result that the stent with its attached graft was pushed distally into the aneurysm. Attempts to retrieve the stent were unsuccessful, and the endoluminal repair was abandoned in favor of an open repair.

Stent Migration

Stent migration is a serious problem we have observed in three patients. Early in our experience, a graft-stent device was delivered into the appropriate position within the neck of the aneurysm. When the balloon was inflated, however, insufficient upward pressure was maintained on the shaft of the balloon, and successive cardiac contractions pushed the balloon with its trapped stent distally into the aneurysm (Fig. 7-4). This stent migration resulted in a leak at the upper end of the graft that did not seal off over a three-week period and required conversion to an open repair. This problem has been minimized but not entirely eliminated by reducing the systolic arterial pressure to 80 mm Hg prior to inflation of the balloon, combined with the application of firm upward pressure on the shaft of the balloon at the time of inflation.

Two further patients had successful placement of graft-stent devices in the correct position in the neck of the aneurysm. Problems were experienced, however, in removing the deflated balloon through the distal 10-mm diameter portion of the tapered graft in each case. Although the balloons had a low profile of 4.5 mm in diameter before inflation, the diameter of the wings of the

Fig. 7-4. Stent dislodged from balloon due to uneven expansion of the balloon. This endoluminal graft, removed at open repair of the abdominal aortic aneurysm, had been unsuccessfully deployed due to poorly controlled balloon expansion causing displacement of the graft from the neck of the aneurysm.

120

deflated balloon exceeded 10 mm. Attempts were made to reduce the diameter of the balloons by applying negative pressure, but without success. Unsuccessful attempts were also made to recover the balloons by withdrawing them into 21 French Teflon sheaths passed into the aorta through the Dacron grafts. The amount of force required to free the balloons in these two patients produced excessive traction on the grafts and dislodged the stents from the neck into the body of the aneurysm. Both required conversion to an open repair.

Conclusions From Early Experience

We concluded from this initial experience that endoluminal repair of aortic aneurysms is feasible. It was clear, however, that there is a long learning curve to be negotiated in acquiring the skills required for this technique of balloon expansion of a stent-graft device. Although complications reduced the overall success rate and required conversion of endoluminal repair to open repair in six of 10 patients, none appeared to have suffered any ill effects from the abandoned attempt. For those poor-risk patients with large aneurysms who had been rejected for operation at other centers, this approach seemed to be their only hope and was justified in all circumstances.

This experience also highlighted the liability for tapered or bifurcated grafts to be dislodged from position by other catheters (and particularly balloon catheters in these cases), catching against the tapered section during removal. A tendency for stenosis of the section of graft positioned within the iliac artery was also identified, due to external compression at the orifice of the common iliac artery. This tendency has important ramifications for any bifurcated graft implanted into nonaneurysmal iliac arteries.

These results should not be used as judgment of the Parodi technique in general, since we did not have available a good access system at this stage and attempted graft implantation in some patients who were not well-suited to an endoluminal approach. We identified the cause of failures to be inadequate equipment, particularly with respect to available balloons and access sheaths, and decided that the combination of a vascular stent and a graft was not the best technique for endoluminal grafting in our hands. This stimulated continued development of our own nonstented endoluminal grafting system, as described below.

EVT Endograft

The Royal Prince Alfred Hospital is one of six centers involved in a multicenter phase 1 study of the EndoVascular Technologies endoluminal grafting system (EVT) monitored by the U.S. Food and Drug Administration. The first clinical cases were performed in September 1993, after preliminary training on the calf model at the Biomedical Testing Laboratory in Salt Lake City, Utah.

To date, we have implanted an EVT endograft in eight patients. The protocol for inclusion in this study defines strict criteria for morphology of the aorta and iliac arteries (see Chapter 6). The length of the proximal neck of the aneurysm must be 2 cm or greater, and the distal neck 1.5 cm or greater. The minimum diameter of the iliac arteries must be 8 mm. The endograft used was tubular in all cases.

Results

The EVT endograft was implanted successfully in all eight of these carefully selected patients; there have been no failures requiring conversion to an open operation (Fig. 7-5). One patient, however, required access by retroperitoneal approach to the iliac artery after failed access via the femoral route. The introducing sheath was not able to be advanced beyond the iliac bifurcation due to severe calcification and tortuosity (Fig. 7-6). After the graft had been deployed, this patient also had evidence of incomplete seal of the distal end of the graft on the postoperative angiogram, with leak of contrast retrogradely around the graft into the distal aspect of the aorta. This leak is not palpable clinically as a pulsatile mass and is being observed by follow-up duplex ultrasound imaging and computed tomography (CT) scans for evidence of closure.

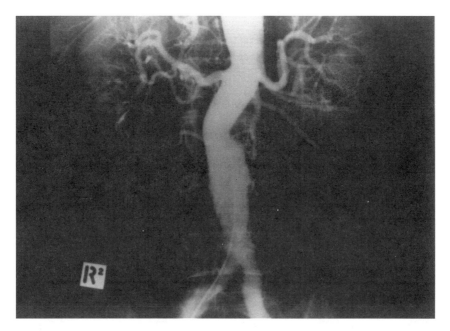

A

Fig. 7-5. EVT endograft of abdominal aortic aneurysm. A. Preoperative angiogram (anteroposterior view) demonstrating infrarenal abdominal aortic aneurysm, with approximately 3-cm length of proximal neck. This aneurysm was shown to be 5.5 cm in maximal diameter on CT scan. B. Preoperative angiogram (lateral view) demonstrating infrarenal aneurysm. Note the use of calibrated angiographic catheter with three radiopaque lines (at 1-cm intervals) at the distal end. C. Postoperative angiogram (anteroposterior view) following implantation of an EVT endograft. The metallic inserts in the walls of the graft can be seen external to the contrast within the graft lumen. D. Postoperative angiogram (lateral view) following implantation of EVT endograft. E. Postoperative plain abdominal x-ray (anteroposterior view) showing the metallic stents at each end of the graft and the interval metal markers in the wall of the graft. The graft follows the curvature of the aorta at the neck of the aneurysm.

123

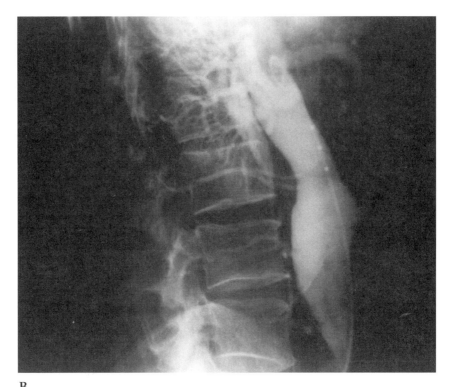

B

Fig. 7-5 *(continued)*

The only other complications that have occurred have been the development of atrial fibrillation in one patient, and postoperative urinary retention requiring transurethral prostatic resection in a second patient.

The EVT device appears to be a good technique for carefully selected patients who have early aneurysms with morphology suitable for tube graft implantation. Current evidence from angiogram and CT scan studies suggests that only 10 to 20 percent of patients with abdominal aortic aneurysms will meet these selection criteria. Use of a bifurcated design may extend the indications for patient selection in the future. The fact that the implantation procedure involves spikes or barbs that are pushed into the wall of the aorta raises the possibility of perforation of the wall and perhaps even damage to adjoining tissues; the possibility of late complications is being monitored by close follow-up studies.

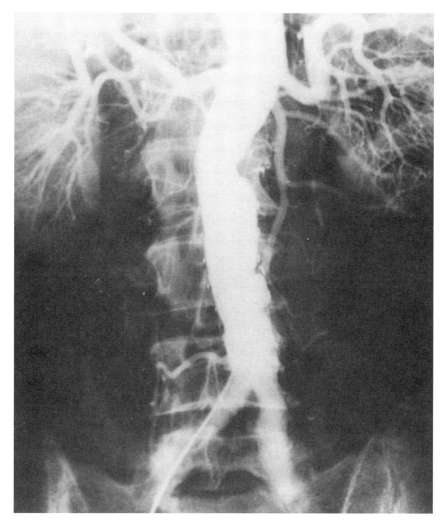

C

Nonstented Endoluminal Grafts

The Sydney Endograft

Concept and Development

After numerous bench studies of various combinations of arterial stents and vascular graft materials, we concluded that it would be

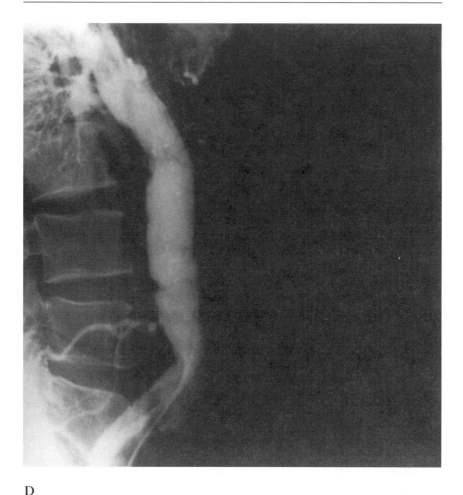

D

Fig. 7-5 *(continued)*

preferable to incorporate metallic supports into the material of the graft, rather than attach it to a stent. We regarded the metallic implants as graft attachment devices (GADs) that could be spaced at intervals suited to the particular application of the graft (aneurysm or occlusive disease), and perhaps to the morphology of particular aneurysms.

It seemed that a conventional arterial stent coated with a conventional or thin-walled graft might be ideal for very localized lesions in straight segments of artery but would not be appropriate for large aneurysms or those involving longer segments of aorta or peripheral vessels. The new balloon-expandable endoluminal graft

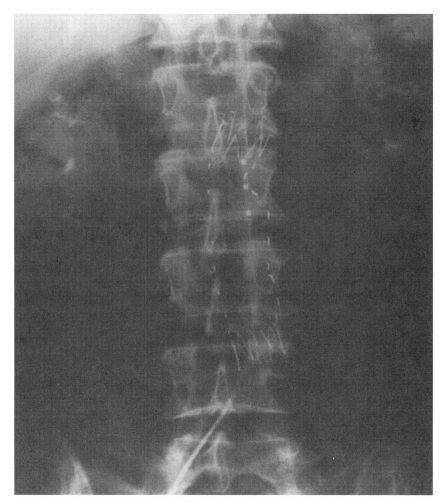

E

design we developed is applicable to endovascular grafting of occlusive arterial disease as well as aneurysms.

Implantation in Bench Models and Excised Vessels

Tensile strength measurements in tubular plastic models and in excised segments of aorta and iliac arteries demonstrated that greater attachment of the prosthesis to the vessel wall was achieved with a design that incorporated parts of the GAD into the graft

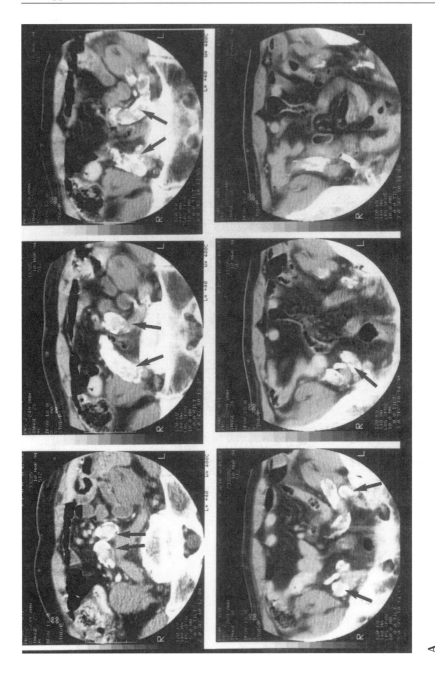

A

128

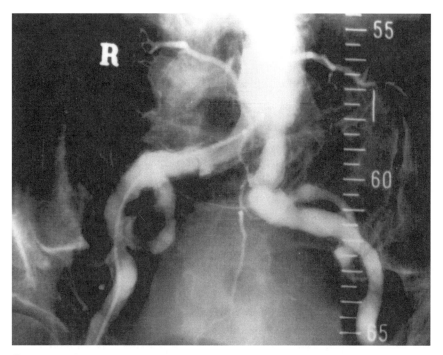

B

◄ Fig. 7-6. Problems in graft implantation. Severe calcification of the common iliac artery seen at preoperative radiologic studies. This renders the iliac artery less flexible for the passage of the large introduction sheath and increases the likelihood of iliac artery trauma or perforation.
A. On these CT scan images, the very tortuous, calcified iliac arteries are indicated by the arrows. B. Preoperative angiogram (anteroposterior view) of the same patient demonstrates iliac tortuosity and confirms the calcification of the arterial wall.

material. The force required to dislodge a GAD-graft combination was greater than double that required to completely remove a graft anchored within a similar conduit by a Palmaz stent.

In these studies we also found that GAD-grafts could be overlapped to provide a total longer length of endoluminal grafting and that the use of a noncompliant balloon was preferable to achieve complete expansion of the graft and to reduce the incidence of balloon rupture.

Animal Studies of Sydney Endovascular Graft

Prototype designs of the GAD-graft combination were implanted, under general anesthesia, into the aorta and iliac arteries of mongrel dogs in a study aimed at testing methods of deployment of endoluminal grafts and comparing several design variations. The devices were further studied by angiograms, angioscopy, and IVUS examinations obtained at the time of deployment and at harvest to monitor graft deployment and positioning. Implantation was via a small surgical cutdown to the common femoral arteries.

In one set of animal experiments, comparisons were made between two prosthetic grafts implanted into paired, normal iliac vessels [2]. A Palmaz stent coated with a 3-cm length of wrapped PTFE thin-wall graft (6 mm diameter) was mounted onto an 8-mm balloon catheter with 3.8 French shaft and compressed into a 14 French introducer catheter. The introducer catheter was advanced over a guidewire, through a small incision in the femoral artery, up to the common iliac artery and deployed by retraction of the sheath and inflation of the balloon. A GAD-graft of the same length and diameter was deployed by a similar-size sheath and balloon catheter into the contralateral common iliac artery. Two more devices were also implanted into the abdominal aorta. Fluoroscopic monitoring was used to guide positioning, inflation, and deployment of the endoluminal grafts. Angiographic and IVUS imaging of the grafts were performed.

Following initial exposure and access to each femoral artery, angiographic definition of the arterial anatomy of the aorta and iliac vessels was obtained. Next, a 5.0 French, 30-MHz IVUS catheter (CVIS Inc., Sunnyvale, CA) was used to precisely measure the diameter of the vessels before deployment of the endografts. Further IVUS images were then obtained immediately after implantation of the grafts to assess the adequacy of expansion and the geometry of the grafts, with particular reference to evidence of folding, twisting, or kinking of the graft wall. Three-dimensional reconstructions of the two-dimensional IVUS images obtained during timed catheter pullbacks allowed further delineation of the morphology of the expanded endografts and coated stents.

Anticoagulation was achieved at the time of graft implantation by administering intravenous heparin, but no interval anticoagulants or

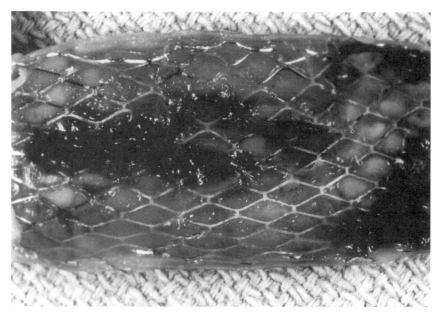

A

Fig. 7-7. A. Thrombus adherent to the metallic elements of a stent-graft device. B. Displacement of the PTFE graft segment from the stent occurred during implantation due to friction of the graft material against the sheath and vessel walls. The proximal edge of the stent, which should not be covered by graft, is indicated by the arrows.

antiplatelet agents were given. The grafts were restudied by angiogram, angioscopic inspection, and IVUS at the time of harvest at intervals of either one hour, one week, two weeks, four weeks, or eight weeks. The aorta and iliac arteries were then perfusion-fixed with 10% buffered formaldehyde at 100 mm Hg for 10 minutes and harvested en bloc.

Results

Two of six iliac arteries containing GAD-grafts were thrombosed at the time of harvest, whereas the other four iliac arteries and two aortas remained patent, for an overall patency rate of 75 percent. Nonoccluding thrombus was present in two further iliac arteries (Fig. 7-7A). Thrombus was associated with recognized folding of the PTFE graft wall in regions of inadequate expansion of the metallic

B

Fig. 7-7 *(continued)*

support ring. These folds of the graft wall were most accurately imaged by IVUS and not well visualized on angiograms obtained at the same time. At eight weeks, the GAD-graft was patent and free of thrombus and had a thin luminal covering of neointima.

In the group of six iliac Palmaz stent-grafts, there was one instance of displacement of the graft from the stent during deployment, due to friction of the graft against the introducer sheath (Fig. 7-7B). All devices remained patent, but nonobstructing thrombus was attached to the stents in three cases, harvested at one hour, one week, and two weeks. Good expansion of the grafts by even expansion of the stents was observed on the angiographic and IVUS images. In the longer-term specimens, a thin layer of neointima was detected overlying the stent struts. A definite but smooth transition region was demonstrated by both angioscopy and IVUS.

This study led to several important alterations in the construction of the GAD-grafts. In particular, we concluded that good support was required for any segments of graft implanted within the confines of relatively normal vessels to prevent serious folding or crimping of the graft wall. This has special relevance for the limbs of bifurcated grafts within human iliac arteries and for the segment of an aortic graft that would be attached within the proximal neck of an abdominal aortic aneurysm. It was clear that full expansion of the metallic support GADs was required if folds and kinks of the graft wall were to be avoided, and that IVUS would have a valuable role in confirming full graft expansion in subsequent clinical use of these techniques. Inadequate expansion of the GADs in these 6-mm diameter grafts was associated with vessel thrombosis and might have been corrected by further expansion by larger or less compliant balloons. On the other hand, small folds in the graft wall would most likely not be as significant in altering flow within a 20- to 26-mm diameter graft used for aortic aneurysm (Fig. 7-8).

We concluded that PTFE-coated stents or stent-graft combinations of the type described here would be suitable for endoluminal grafting of short segments of relatively straight vessel (since the stents are rigid) but that there were disadvantages caused by the possible displacement of the graft material from the stent during deployment. The GAD-graft design was more suitable for longer lengths of artery and for curved or angulated arteries or aortas because of the relative flexibility of graft between the metallic supports. There is also hope for individual customizing of grafts to cater to these regions of angulation. We also concluded that thin-walled Dacron prosthetics would be more suitable for human aortic grafting at present because of the difficulty in obtaining adequate compression of the currently available PTFE graft materials into an acceptable sheath size.

Clinical Program: Patients and Methods

The first clinical implantation of a GAD-graft device was in June 1993, for the successful transfemoral endoluminal management of a symptomatic abdominal aortic aneurysm in a 73-year-old patient with severe cardiac disease [9] (Fig. 7-9). As of April 1994, 21 Sydney endografts have been implanted.

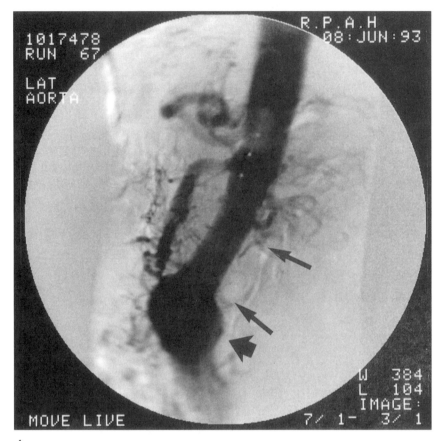

A

Fig. 7-8. Clinical use of endoluminal graft for abdominal aortic aneurysm repair. A. The preoperative angiogram (lateral view) in this patient demonstrates a long proximal neck (two thin arrows) and a well-localized abdominal aortic aneurysm sac (wide arrow). B. The postoperative angiogram (anteroposterior view) shows faintly the metallic markers in the graft wall and the lumen of the graft outlines with contrast. Small irregularities in the graft wall outline probably represent minor folds of the prosthetic material. The distal stent is indicated by the arrow.

In our clinical program, patients considered to be possible candidates for endoluminal grafting of aneurysms were studied by contrast-enhanced CT scan of the abdomen and pelvis (to include the entire length of the abdominal aorta and iliac arteries) and by

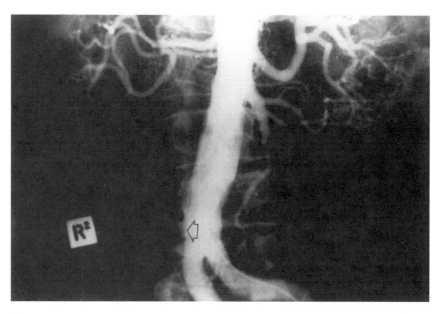

B

aortogram and runoff arteriography performed via a special angiographic catheter that has radiopaque calibration markings at 1-cm intervals. There were also trials of the value of three-dimensional reconstruction of the CT images. IVUS has been used selectively. Detailed measurements of the morphology of the aorta, aneurysm sac, and iliac arteries were calculated by reference to the calibration markers, with corrections made for vector angles. The most important measurements were the diameter of the neck of the aorta (immediately below the renal arteries), the length of this neck, the distance from the lowermost aspect of the renal arteries to the bifurcation of the aorta (i.e., the required length of endoluminal graft), the diameter of the aorta just above the bifurcation, and the diameter and angulation or tortuosity of the iliac artery chosen for access.

The maximal diameter of an aortic neck grafted to date has been 30 mm and the narrowest aorta 16 mm, whereas the narrowest diameter Sydney endograft used to date has been one of 12-mm diameter implanted into an aneurysm of the common iliac artery.

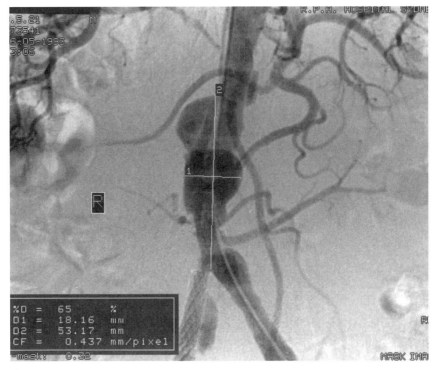

A

Fig. 7-9. Implantation of White-Yu GAD graft for endoluminal repair of a symptomatic abdominal aortic aneurysm in a high-risk patient with severe ischemic heart disease. A. Preoperative angiogram demonstrating a series of saccular aneurysms of the distal aorta. On-film dimensions have been calculated in this digital subtraction image. B. Completion angiogram showing exclusion of the aneurysmal segments of the aorta following transfemoral insertion of the endoluminal graft. This patient has remained well with no graft complications after a follow-up of nine months.

We have preferred to select patients who are able to undergo general anesthesia so that conversion to open operation can be an option in the event of failed endoluminal repair.

Graft Preparation

A conventional Dacron graft of diameter slightly wider than the measured aortic lumen was prepared by incorporating the metallic

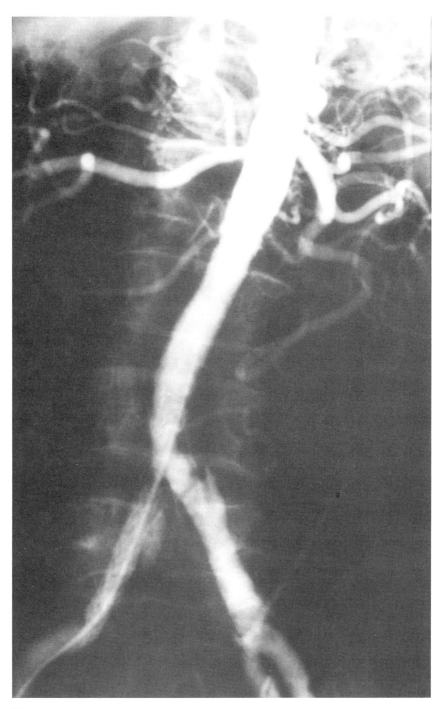

B

GADs. The endograft was then compressed over a balloon catheter and preloaded into a sheath system. In most cases the sheath system used was 24 French in diameter. A hemostatic valve device was used to minimize blood loss.

The approach used for access was either by direct exposure of the common femoral artery or by retroperitoneal exposure of the iliac artery. An 8 French sheath was initially inserted over a guidewire, and the guidewire was advanced up to the suprarenal aorta. On-table aortography was then performed, particularly to accurately locate the site of the renal arteries and the aortic bifurcation. The image intensifier was then locked into place to avoid problems associated with parallax error. Guidewire exchange was performed via the angiographic catheter, with an Amplatz super-stiff wire now positioned, so that the sheath system could be subsequently introduced without the risk of unwanted deviation over a more flexible wire.

Insertion of the 24 French sheath was achieved after a transverse arteriotomy had been made into the femoral or iliac artery. This arteriotomy incision incorporated the hole left by removal of the original access sheath. Passage of the relatively large sheath up into the aorta required great care and some element of twisting and rotation to follow the tortuous iliac course, especially at the point of maximal angulation of the iliac artery where it crosses the pelvic brim. Once the end of the sheath system had been advanced just beyond the renal arteries, its internal mandril was removed, and the preloaded graft and balloon were now advanced via the guidewire. When these components were satisfactorily positioned, the external sheath was usually retracted to the level of the orifice of the common iliac artery. This positioning served as an exact reminder of the location of the iliac artery and provided protection of the arterial wall at that level if part of the balloon inadvertantly inflated within the iliac.

The patient's blood pressure was controlled to a systolic measurement of approximately 80 to 105 mm Hg in preparation for inflation of the balloon and expansion of the endograft into position.

Clinical Series

As of April 1994, this graft has been tried in 21 patients. All patients in the clinical series were investigated by duplex scan, calibrated

Table 7-3. Results obtained with the Sydney endovascular graft in 21 patients

	Number	Success	% Success	Comment
Group I	10	10	100	All tube grafts
Group II	8	6	75	1 tube graft, 7 aortoiliac
Group III	3	3	100	Iliac aneurysms

angiogram, and angio-CT scan and then allocated to groups that we defined according to the following criteria:

1. Group I: Considered suitable for transfemoral implantation of a straight tube graft. Presence of a proximal neck of 2-cm length or longer between the renal arteries and the aneurysm, distal neck of 1.5 cm or longer, and iliac artery diameter more than 8 mm for access to the aorta.

2. Group II: Short neck of aneurysm, or requiring bifurcated or tapered aortoiliac grafts or access via iliac approach. Abdominal aortic aneurysm that did not fit the above criteria, usually due to associated aneurysms of the iliac arteries, lack of a distal neck, or a narrow iliac artery.

3. Group III: Peripheral aneurysms (Table 7-3).

All patients have been followed up by clinical examination, duplex scan, CT scan, and selective angiography.

Results

Intraluminal deployment of the graft was achieved in all 21 patients; however, two patients from group II subsequently required conversion to open procedures because of the following complications: (1) partial graft thrombosis resulting from inadvertent omission of systemic anticoagulation during deployment, and (2) both limbs of a bifurcated graft lodged into one iliac artery. One other patient in group II required surgical repair of access sheath trauma to a calcified, previously irradiated iliac artery.

Successful endoluminal repair was achieved in 10 of 10 (100 percent) patients in group I; the mean operative times and hospital stay were 1.75 hours and 6 days, respectively, in this group (Fig. 7-10). The success rate in group II was 6 of 8 cases (75 percent), and in group III 100 percent (see Table 7-3). Of the 11 patients whose abdominal aortic aneurysms were suitable for repair using a tubular Sydney endograft (including one recurrent, anastomotic aortic aneurysm), none has had a failure requiring conversion to an open operation. In two patients there were small leaks from the lumen into the aneurysmal sac at the upper end of the graft that sealed spontaneously in the first 72 hours. A third patient has had a persistent leak (at two months) from the graft lumen into the distal aspect of the aneurysmal sac, around the inferior end of the graft. This was caused by the graft being slightly too short for the length of the aneurysm. If this does not seal, a second endograft deployment is planned, overlapping within and distal to the existing one.

Of the seven patients whose aneurysms were unsuitable for endoluminal tube-graft repair, six were treated by tapered aortoiliac grafts and one by a bifurcated graft. The procedure failed in one patient with a tapered aortoiliac graft and required conversion to an open operation due to thrombosis in the graft. A dose of 150 units of heparin in diluted form had mistakenly been given instead of the full heparinizing dose that had been requested. The attempted endoluminal repair using a bifurcated graft had to be converted to an open operation when both limbs were deployed unilaterally in the common iliac artery.

These preliminary results (in a series of high-risk patients) have demonstrated that endoluminal abdominal aortic aneurysm repair with this graft can be achieved reliably and with low morbidity in patients whose aortic aneurysms fulfill the selection criteria for an endoluminal tube graft (group I) and in peripheral aneurysms (group III), but the results were less satisfactory in patients whose aneurysms did not have a good proximal or distal neck (group II). Further use of the bifurcated version of this graft design, along with improvements in access techniques and graft materials, are required for successful endoluminal grafting in a wider range of patients.

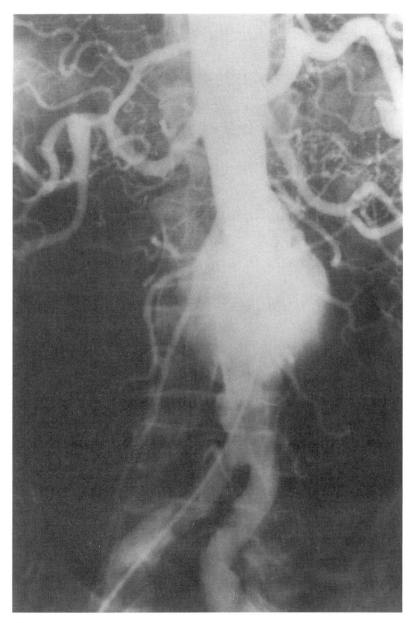

A

Fig. 7-10. Implantation of White-Yu GAD graft for endoluminal repair of infrarenal abdominal aortic aneurysm. A. Preoperative angiogram (anteroposterior view) demonstrating type I abdominal aortic aneurysm with approximately 2.5 cm of length of proximal aortic neck and a good

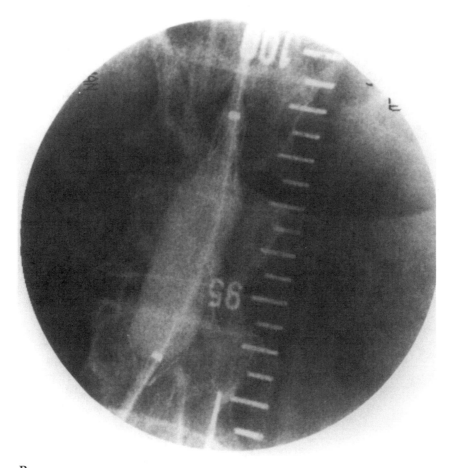

B

Fig. 7-10 *(continued)*

length of distal neck. This morphology of abdominal aortic aneurysm is ideal for endoluminal tube graft. B. Intraoperative image-intensifier film demonstrating the balloon being inflated with contrast solution to expand and fix the endoluminal graft. C. Intraoperative completion aortogram after graft implantation. The arrows indicate the faint outline of contrast within the graft. This film has been obtained by hand injection of contrast solution. The poor quality of such images illustrates some of the problems associated with radiologic imaging in the operative suite due to the use of radiopaque operating room tables, mobile image intensifiers, and hand-controlled injection (in comparison to power injectors).

142

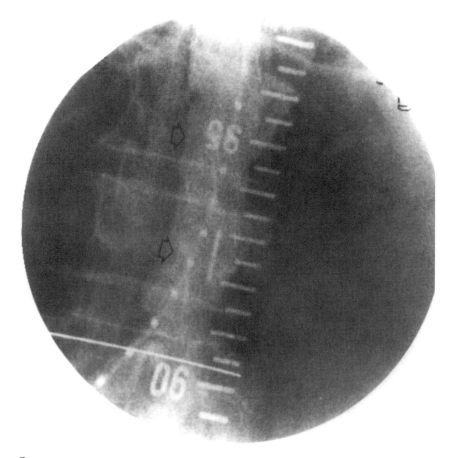

C

Endoluminal Grafting of Iliac Aneurysms

In the subgroup of three patients with iliac aneurysms, there were no failures requiring conversion to an open operation (Fig. 7-11). Each aneurysm involved the common iliac artery, and transluminal access for graft implantation was achieved by cutdown approach to the ipsilateral femoral artery. A smaller-diameter sheath can be used for these peripheral aneurysms since a narrower, less bulky graft is used.

The only complication in this small subgroup occurred in one patient who unfortunately developed a right-sided stroke 24 hours postoperatively, from which he has made a good recovery with minimal residual neurologic deficit.

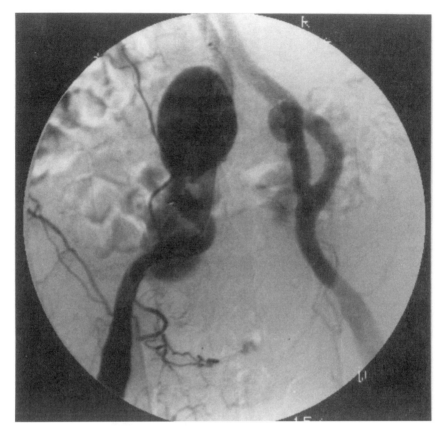

A

Fig. 7-11. Endoluminal repair of iliac aneurysm. This patient had previously undergone open repair of a large abdominal aortic aneurysm and had recently developed right-sided lower abdominal pains associated with expanding aneurysms of the common and internal iliac arteries. A. Preoperative angiogram (anteroposterior view) demonstrating large aneurysms of the right common and internal iliac arteries. B. Preoperative CT scan (contrast enhanced) demonstrating these two aneurysms. C. Intraoperative angiogram (anteroposterior view) obtained prior to graft implantation. A radiopaque ruler has been placed under the patient to aid in the accurate positioning of the endoluminal graft. D. Intraoperative image-intensifier film (anteroposterior view) showing the unexpanded endoluminal graft in the common iliac artery prior to graft implantation. E. Intraoperative angiogram (anteroposterior view) obtained after graft

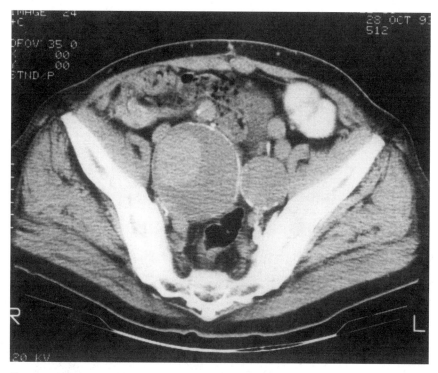

B

implantation. The expanded endoluminal graft has excluded blood flow into the aneurysms and retained normal flow to the leg. The patient was discharged from the hospital two days after this procedure with no complications and with resolution of symptoms.

Endoluminal Grafting of Aortic Dissections

Special application of transluminal endovascular grafting has been made in two patients with aortic dissection [12, 13]. In recent years there has been considerable interest in the use of various endovascular techniques in the management of aortic dissections [14–16]. These techniques have included use of IVUS to evaluate the pathologic changes in the arterial anatomy and to guide interventions such as percutaneous fenestration, balloon dilatation, and stent placement to restore and maintain flow in major aortic branches. We have investigated the use of endoluminal grafting in selected patients with complex aortic dissections.

145

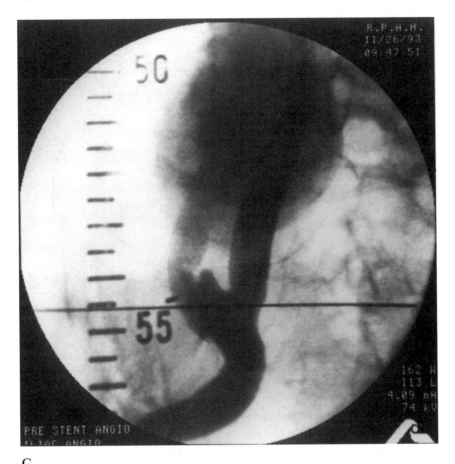

C

Fig. 7-11 *(continued)*

In one of these cases, a 46-year-old man presented with back pain and claudication of the left leg, which was found to be associated with an unusual spontaneous dissection of the infrarenal aorta [13]. The inferior mesenteric artery and left iliac artery were being perfused from the false lumen of the dissection. Initial management consisted of fenestration (by guidewire) of the dissection plane in the distal aorta under IVUS control, with subsequent balloon dilatation of the newly opened channel from the true lumen into the left iliac system followed by stent placement. Attempts were then made to close the proximal entry site of the dissection immediately below the

146

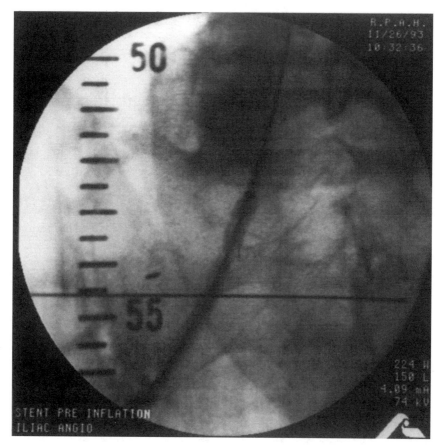

D

renal arteries, again by transluminal balloon angioplasty and stent placement (Fig. 7-12). This procedure was initially successful in obliterating the false lumen, but this channel reformed several months later through the interstices of the proximal stent.

An endoluminal graft was subsequently positioned within the aortic lumen, with its proximal aspect overlapping and lining the previously placed stent just below the renal arteries. The graft was sized to end 1.5 cm above the aortic bifurcation. This procedure was successful in effectively dilating and diverting blood flow via the true aortic lumen (Fig. 7-13).

147

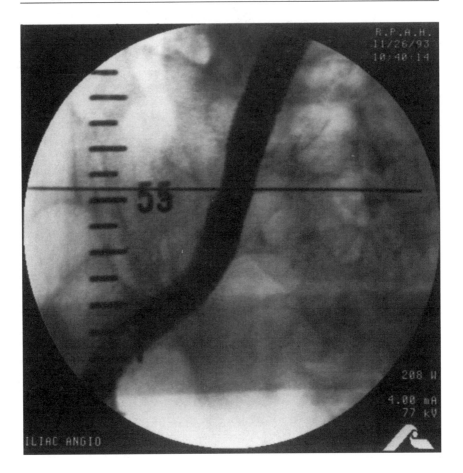

E

Fig. 7-11 *(continued)*

In another case, a 62-year-old man presented acutely with dissection of the descending thoracic aorta in addition to an infrarenal abdominal aortic aneurysm [14]. Investigation revealed that the thoracic dissection had arisen retrogradely from within the posterior wall of the abdominal aortic aneurysm and extended superiorly to the level of the left subclavian artery. Endoluminal placement of an endoluminal graft device below the renal arteries enabled simultaneous exclusion of the abdominal aortic aneurysm and the thoracic aortic dissection. The patient made an uncomplicated recovery. Postoperative aortography and CT scan demon-

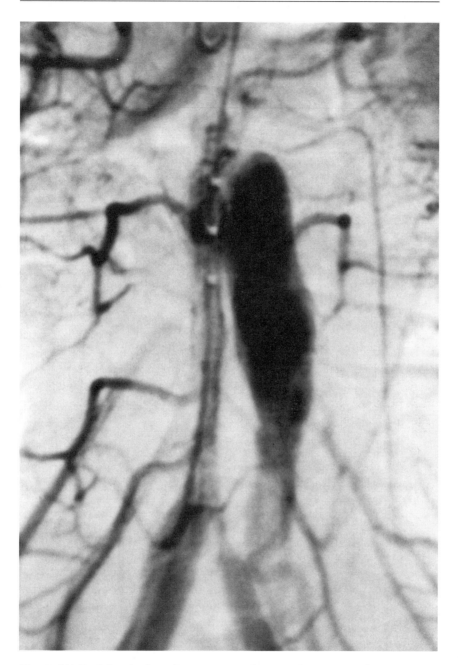

Fig. 7-12. Endoluminal graft treatment of aortic dissection. This angiogram shows flow into a false lumen immediately below the renal arteries and severe narrowing of the true aortic lumen.

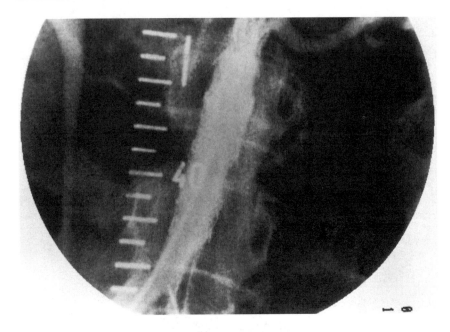

Fig. 7-13. Endoluminal graft treatment of aortic dissection. After implantation of an arterial stent and an endoluminal graft, the false lumen was obliterated and normal diameter of the true lumen reestablished. Stenosis of the proximal left common iliac artery was subsequently corrected by balloon dilatation.

strated normal flow through the aorta and endograft without leak of contrast into the abdominal aortic aneurysm sac or the false lumen of the dissection.

Summary of GAD-Graft Series Results

The Sydney endograft has been implanted in 21 patients to date, including three patients with iliac aneurysms, two with dissecting aortic aneurysms, and 16 with aortic or aortoiliac aneurysms. Two cases (9.5 percent) have required conversion to open repair, both because of technical errors during the implantation process. The success rate for abdominal aortic aneurysm of group I classification (selection criteria similar to that of the EVT device) is 100 percent, and for peripheral aneurysms is 100 percent.

150

Planned improvements in the near future include reducing the diameter of the compressed device during implantation by using ultra–thin-walled prosthetic graft material as well as narrower balloon catheters and access sheaths. Further refinements in techniques for insertion of bifurcated GAD-grafts are also ready for clinical trials.

References

1. May J et al. Transluminal placement of a prosthetic graft-stent device for treatment of subclavian artery aneurysm. *J Vasc Surg* 1993;18:1056–1059.

2. White GH, Yu W, May J. Experimental endoluminal grafts and coated stents [abstract]. *Angiology* 1993;4:26.

3. May J et al. Advantages and limitations of intraluminal grafts for thoracic and abdominal aortic aneurysm [abstract]. *Angiology* 1993;4:21.

4. May J et al. Transluminal Placement of Aorto-iliac Grafts for Treatment of Large Abdominal Aortic Aneurysms. In S Weimann (ed), *Thoracic and Thoracoabdominal Aortic Aneurysm*. Bologna: Monduzzi Editore, 1993.

5. May J et al. Endoluminal Stent-Grafts for Intrathoracic and Abdominal Aortic Aneurysm. In DD Liermann (ed), *Proceedings of International Stent Symposium* 3. Frankfurt, 1993.

6. May J et al. Treatment of complex abdominal aortic aneurysms by a combination of endoluminal and extraluminal aorto-femoral grafts. *J Vasc Surg* 1994;19:924–933.

7. May J et al. Intraluminal stents for thoracic and abdominal aortic aneurysm. *J Cardiovasc Intervent Radiol* (in press).

8. Chuter TAM et al. Transfemoral repair of canine aortic aneurysm: Straight and bifurcated grafts [abstract]. *J Vasc Surg* 1993;17:223.

9. White GH et al. Transfemoral implantation of a new non-stented endoluminal graft in a high-risk patient with symptomatic abdominal aortic aneurysm: Initial result and 9 month follow-up. (Submitted for publication, 1994.)

10. Parodi JC, Palmaz JC, Barone HD. Transfemoral intraluminal graft implantation for abdominal aortic aneurysms. *Ann Vasc Surg* 1991;5:491–499.

11. May J et al. Endoluminal repair of large and small abdominal aortic aneurysm [abstract]. *J Intervent Cardiol* 1994;7:109.

12. White GH et al. Management of spontaneous dissection of the infrarenal aorta by vascular stents and endoluminal aortic graft. (Submitted for publication, 1994.)

13. May J et al. Simultaneous endoluminal repair of dissection of descending thoracic aorta and fusiform aneurysm of the abdominal aorta. (Submitted for publication, 1994.)

14. William DM, Brothers TE, Messina LM. Relief of mesenteric ischaemia in Type III aortic dissection with percutaneous fenestration of the aortic septum. *Radiology* 1990;174:450–452.

15. Shimshak TM, Giorgi LV, Hartzler GO. Successful percutaneous transluminal angioplasty of an obstructed abdominal aorta secondary to a chronic dissection. *Am J Cardiol* 1988;61:486–487.

16. Walker PJ et al. The use of endovascular techniques for the treatment of complications of aortic dissection. *J Vasc Surg* 1993;17:1–10.

Endoluminal Stent-Grafting in the Thoracic Aorta

8

Charles P. Semba
Michael D. Dake

Thoracic aortic aneurysm is a life-threatening condition that develops at sites of acquired or congenital weakness within the media of the vessel. The descending aorta is the most common site of thoracic aneurysm. The vast majority are caused by atherosclerosis [1]. Thoracic aneurysms tend to remain clinically silent and rarely produce symptoms unless they progressively enlarge and cause compression of adjacent structures or rupture.

Rupture of a thoracic aortic aneurysm is a catastrophic event and uniformly fatal. Joyce's review of untreated thoracic aneurysms suggests a 50 percent 5-year and 70 percent 10-year mortality rate [2]. Rupture of the aneurysm occurs in 33 to 50 percent of the fatal cases; the remaining fatalities usually are related to comorbidity factors from generalized cardiovascular disease [3, 4].

Conventional therapy for thoracic aneurysms is surgical repair and constitutes the only proven method for treatment [5]. Surgery is urgently indicated if the aneurysm is 6 cm in diameter or greater, especially when serial examinations show progressive enlargement of the aneurysm, sudden onset of aortic regurgitation, or acute chest pain. Standard surgical technique requires resection of the aneurysmal segment and replacement with a Dacron graft. For aneurysms distal to the left subclavian artery and above the celiac trunk, resection can be performed by clamping the aorta above and below the aneurysm without the need for extracorporeal circulation [6].

Despite the technical challenges, the surgical mortality rate is relatively low (15 percent) when the surgery is performed by experienced cardiothoracic surgeons in patients who have good cardiac reserve and who are excellent surgical candidates [5]. However, the operative mortality rate approaches 50 percent in patients requiring emergent treatment or those with significant comorbidity including advancing age, chronic obstructive pulmonary disease, and coronary artery disease [3, 7].

Transluminal endovascular stent-grafting offers an alternative method of treatment that is potentially less invasive, less expensive, and less risky than standard operative repair. Based on techniques and principles of percutaneous interventions, we have been placing endovascular stent-grafts for the repair of descending thoracic aortic aneurysms. This chapter focuses on our experimental protocol for endoluminal stent-grafting in the thoracic aorta at Stanford University Medical Center.

Technical Considerations

The technical principles of stent-grafting can be simplified into three main components: stents, graft material, and delivery systems. The overall goal has been to devise a strategy that will allow placement of standard surgical graft material into the aorta to effectively exclude blood flow to the aneurysm, resulting in thrombosis of the aneurysmal sac using basic interventional radiologic principles.

Stents

Stents provide a sutureless method of securing graft material into the normal proximal and distal aortic neck. There are two general designs for stents: balloon-expandable, such as the Palmaz stent (Johnson & Johnson Interventional Systems, Warren, NJ) and self-expanding stents such as the Wallstent (Schneider, Inc., Plymouth,

154

MN) and modified Z-stent (Cook Inc., Bloomington, IN). After extensive testing in experimental models, we have found self-expandable stents to be better suited for the thoracic aorta. The stents we use are custom-built for each patient based on dimensions obtained from spiral computed tomographic (CT) data. The stents are composed of 0.016-inch surgical-grade stainless steel wire formed into Z-shaped elements. Individual stent bodies are 25 mm in length with variable diameters ranging from 25 to 40 mm. Depending on the length between the proximal and distal necks, several stent bodies are then sewn together using 5-0 polypropylene suture. Thus, an aneurysm that would require 7 cm length of graft material would require three stents to ensure adequate coverage of the aneurysm. The entire Z-stent endoskeleton is used as a frame to support the graft material (Fig. 8-1). Multiple stents are used to support the Dacron sleeve to avoid kinking, buckling, torsion, or collapse of the graft. We have found that the Z-stent design can provide the appropriate hoop strength and high expansion ratio that are required to anchor the graft material into position. The current design of the Z-stent relies on a small amount of excess radial expansion force to seat itself in the neck of the aneurysm to prevent graft migration. The stent also provides a hemostatic seal at the proximal and distal ends of the graft material, preventing seepage of blood around the ends of the graft into the aneurysm. No hooks or anchoring wires are used to prevent migration.

Stent-graft placement in the thoracic aorta presents unique technical challenges compared to placement in the abdominal aorta. First, the normal thoracic aortic diameters tend to be significantly larger than the abdominal aorta. While the balloon-expandable designs originally described by Parodi for treating abdominal aortic aneurysms have the advantage of precise placement at the infrarenal proximal neck, the "normal" thoracic aorta is typically 30 to 40 mm in diameter [8]. There are no commercially manufactured, standard angioplasty balloons to accommodate these large diameters (the largest valvuloplasty balloons are 28 mm). The second problem facing a balloon-expandable design is temporarily occluding blood flow in the proximal descending thoracic aorta. The proximity of the thoracic aneurysm to the tremendous pulsatile forces of the left ventricle makes temporary balloon occlusion nearly impossible

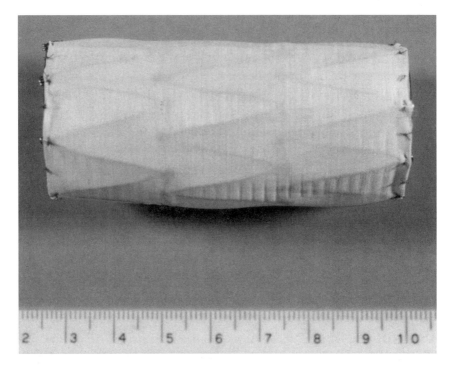

A

Fig. 8-1. Self-expanding endovascular stent-graft. A single woven Dacron jacket is used to cover the **Z**-stent endoskeleton (A). The **Z**-shaped stainless steel elements are secured to the inner surface of the graft (B).

using existing techniques. The vigorous hemodynamic forces tend to push the balloon downstream and the proximal stent may migrate with the graft material into the aneurysm, or worse yet, out of the thorax and into the abdominal aorta. Because of these considerations, we have abandoned the balloon-expandable approach in favor of the self-expanding stent.

The Wallstent design uses braided metallic filaments to create a self-expanding, longitudinally flexible stent. It is currently available only in small diameters (8 to 12 mm) [9]. Though the flexibility of the stent is desirable especially when working in the arch, because of its small size this stent is not suitable for aortic aneurysm repair at this time. The hoop strength is significantly less when compared to the rigid Palmaz stent or the **Z**-stent, and we have reserved this

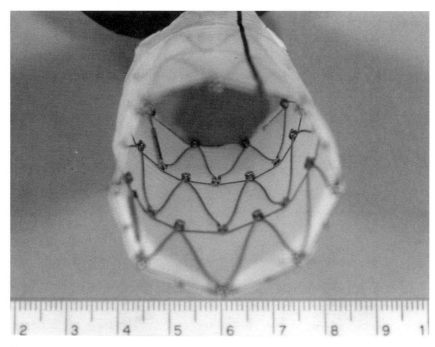

B

device for stent-grafting smaller vessels (e.g., iliac and subclavian arteries) using a polytetrafluoroethylene covering.

We have experimented using alternative stent shapes and materials. Nitinol is a nickel-titanium alloy with a super-elastic character. The Z-stent can be made using nitinol wire instead of stainless steel. The advantage is its high expansion ratio (expanded stent diameter to unexpanded stent diameter) and lower profile; however, its longitudinal stiffness and hoop strength are less compared to stainless steel Z-stents. The result is a stent-graft that is difficult to push through the delivery sheath and anchor the graft material into the neck of the aneurysm.

Stent-grafting within the arch presents special problems since the Z-stent prosthesis is best suited for deployment along the straight portion of the thoracic aorta. Many of the patients have long-standing hypertension and atherosclerosis that ultimately leads to elongation of the aortic arch. Most of the thoracic aneurysms distal to the left subclavian suitable for stent-grafting involve this curved, elon-

157

gated, and ectatic segment of aorta. We have used asymmetric Z-stents that, when attached together, form a gentle curve. This preformed curved shape requires precise orientation within the delivery sheath to ensure proper positioning within the arch. The use of radiopaque markers to identify the greater curve or the lesser curve is helpful in appropriately orienting the device.

Graft Material

Graft material for our prosthesis was woven polyethylene terephthate (Cooley Veri-Soft Dacron, Meadox Medicals, Inc., Oakland, NJ) with the crimps removed to reduce bulk by using a standard laundry iron. The main advantages of woven Dacron are its resistance to radial stretch, low porosity, and nominal thickness (less than 0.25 mm). A single piece of graft material is cut to the appropriate length and fitted over the Z-stent endoskeleton and secured with multiple interrupted sutures of 5-0 polypropylene. The freshly cut edges of the graft material are sealed using a cautery probe to prevent fraying during handling and deployment. After the stent-graft is assembled, the entire device is gas-sterilized prior to insertion. Other commonly used graft materials such as knitted Dacron or Gore-tex are typically too bulky for the delivery system we currently use.

Delivery System

The delivery system allows the stent-graft to be placed into the thoracic aorta from a remote entry site, typically the common femoral artery (Fig. 8-2). Our system consists of four components: (1) a single 24 French (8-mm diameter by 80-cm length) Teflon sheath fitted with a hemostatic valve apparatus at the hub; (2) a tapered dilator that allows the sheath to be advanced over a 0.035-inch diameter stiff guidewire; (3) a 24 French Teflon loading cartridge in which the stent-graft is placed; and (4) a 22 French Teflon rod that is used to push the stent-graft through the delivery sheath.

Teflon has the combined properties of excellent tensile strength relative to wall thickness (less than 0.080 inches), stiffness, and lubricity, and it resists softening when placed in the warm, blood-filled

158

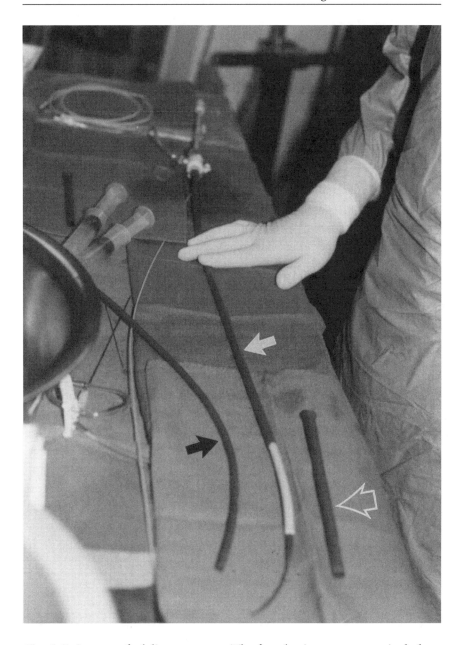

Fig. 8-2. Stent-graft delivery system. The four basic components include a 24 French Teflon delivery sheath with a smooth tapered dilator (white arrow). The stent-graft is placed into the loading cartridge (black arrow) and pushed through the delivery sheath with the solid Teflon pushing rod (open arrow).

159

aorta. Teflon has better overall qualities when compared to other polymers including polyethylene, Silastic, and polyurethane. A curved Teflon sheath is used to prevent kinking of the delivery system when attempting to place a thoracic stent-graft in the arch of the aorta.

Patient Preparation

Indications for endoluminal stent-grafting are (1) thoracic aortic aneurysms limited to the descending aorta distal to the left subclavian artery and proximal to the celiac artery; and (2) penetrating aortic ulcers with intramural hematoma. The proximal and distal necks must be at least 15 mm in length. Patients must be considered surgical candidates in case the device fails to deploy properly and an open procedure is necessary. Typically, the patients who undergo stent-grafting are high surgical risks with otherwise poor medical options. The patients are evaluated by both the cardiothoracic surgery and interventional radiology teams, and full informed consent is obtained for both the conventional surgical and stent-graft procedures.

All patients undergo extensive preoperative imaging with conventional chest radiography, three-dimensional spiral CT scanning, and angiography. Chest radiography is used to establish a baseline and screen for any underlying pulmonary disease. Spiral CT angiography is performed to measure the dimensions of the proximal and distal aortic neck and is the gold standard for the measurements used to build the prosthesis [10, 11]. Conventional angiography is used to evaluate the relationship of the aneurysm to the left subclavian and celiac arteries, the relative degree of curvature of the arch, and the size and tortuosity of the iliac and femoral arteries.

Endovascular Procedure

All stent-graft procedures are performed in the operating suites with the patient under general anesthesia with endobronchial intubation and mechanical ventilatory support. Pulmonary artery, radial artery, and transesophageal echocardiography (TEE) monitoring probes are inserted by the cardiac anesthesia team. Cardiopulmonary bypass standby is made available. The patients are placed on a dedicated radiolucent surgical table in a shallow right lateral decubitus position. If the proximal aneurysm neck is in close proximity to the left subclavian artery, a 5.0 French sheath is placed in the left brachial artery and a pigtail catheter is advanced into the ascending aorta. The catheter serves as a radiopaque marker to delineate the position of the subclavian artery. The left arm is moved into an abducted "swimmer's" position to prevent the humerus from superimposing over the descending thoracic aorta during fluoroscopy. The patient's thorax is then prepped and draped in routine fashion for a conventional left lateral thoracotomy in case a surgical bailout is required. The lower abdomen, pelvis, and groin regions are also sterilely prepped for a femoral arteriotomy or, in cases where the iliac arteries are severely diseased, a left retroperitoneal approach is required to gain access directly into the abdominal aorta.

High-quality fluoroscopic imaging is essential for accurate deployment of the stent-graft prosthesis. Following the sterile preparation of the patient, a portable C-arm fluoroscopy unit (OEC Diasonics, Salt Lake City, UT) is moved into position and the image intensifier is centered over the chest. The entire fluoroscopic portion of the procedure is recorded on 3/4-inch VHS video and radiographic film using a 512×512 imaging matrix.

Based on the preoperative angiogram, a cutdown is performed and the common femoral artery is exposed. The cutdown should be performed on the side with the least amount of atherosclerosis and tortuosity involving the common femoral and iliac arteries. The arteries must be at least 8 mm in diameter from the arteriotomy site to the aorta to accommodate the delivery sheath. After the femoral artery is isolated, an 18-gauge needle is used to make a single wall entry into the artery and a 0.035-inch diameter, 145-cm length soft-tip Bentson guidewire (Cook, Inc., Bloomington, IN) is advanced into the thoracic aorta. The needle is removed and a 5 French sidearm hemostatic vascular sheath is placed over the wire and advanced into the artery. After removal of the sheath dilator, a 5 French pigtail angiographic catheter (Mallinckrodt Medical, St. Louis, MO) is advanced into the ascending thoracic aorta over the guidewire. Following removal of the guidewire, a digital subtraction thoracic aortogram is performed in a steep 45- to 60-degree left anterior oblique projection at three to six frames per second using a bolus power injection of iodinated nonionic contrast material (300 mg/ml; Omnipaque; Winthrop-Sanofi, New York, NY). The aneurysm is evaluated with the video playback feature of the fluoroscopy unit, and the proximal and distal necks of the aneurysm are confirmed both angiographically and with TEE.

After the preliminary angiogram, the pigtail catheter is removed over an exchange length (260 cm) 0.035-inch diameter J-tipped stiff wire and a transverse arteriotomy is performed. The patient is then fully anticoagulated with intravenous heparin (300 IU/kg). The stent-graft dilator and delivery sheath assembly are advanced over the guidewire under fluoroscopic guidance until the tip of the delivery sheath is proximal to the aneurysm. With the sheath placed across the aneurysm, the dilator and stiff guidewire are removed, and the stent-graft is introduced into the delivery catheter from its loading cartridge by using the Teflon pushing rod. The stent-graft is then pushed through the delivery sheath with the Teflon rod until the leading edge of the stent-graft is flush with the tip of the delivery sheath.

Prior to deployment of the stent-graft device, the mean arterial pressure is decreased to the range of 50 to 60 mm Hg using intravenous nitroprusside solution. We have found this to be extremely useful to prevent downstream migration of the partially deployed stent-graft caused by the rapidly flowing blood. The stent-graft is deployed by holding the pushing rod firmly in position and smartly withdrawing the sheath. This allows for very rapid deployment of the prosthesis and minimizes migration. Following deployment, the nitroprusside solution is stopped.

A postdeployment angiogram is performed immediately following placement of the prosthesis. It is not uncommon to detect a slight amount of leak through the graft material in the first few minutes following implantation since the patients are still fully heparinized and the graft material is not preclotted. The delivery sheath is then removed and the arteriotomy site is repaired. For aneurysms in the proximal descending aorta, care must be taken to avoid inadvertent coverage of the left subclavian artery. Reimplantation of the left subclavian artery into the left carotid artery or a carotid subclavian bypass graft may need to be inserted if the left subclavian becomes occluded by the device.

Postprocedure Monitoring

Patients spend the first postoperative day in the intensive care unit, where they are closely monitored for signs of the potential complications of bleeding, infection, and downstream emboli. In the majority of cases, the patients can be transferred to a regular nursing unit within two days and discharged. The patients are not anticoagulated. Postprocedure monitoring includes a follow-up chest x-ray, conventional angiogram, and contrast-enhanced spiral CT examination prior to discharge. Spiral CT studies are obtained at two weeks, six months, and 12 months and yearly thereafter. An angiogram is obtained at 12 months and then annually. Spiral CT angiography has been a valuable monitoring tool since it obviates the need for an invasive angiogram and has much higher contrast sensitivity than conventional angiography to better detect subtle graft leaks.

Complications

The potential for spinal cord injury due to obstruction of the anterior spinal artery is a known risk in standard surgical repair of thoracic aortic aneurysms [12]. We do not routinely search preoperatively for the spinal artery. Whenever possible we try to spare any patent intercostal arteries. The risk of paraplegia with endoluminal thoracic repair is not known.

Pleuritic chest pain has been experienced by patients following stent-graft placement. The etiology is unclear and appears to be self-limited, and the associated "sympathetic" pleural effusions resolve spontaneously in seven to 10 days.

Downstream emboli are possible since the inner surface of the stent-graft contains the stainless steel struts of the stent. These struts could potentially provide a thrombogenic surface for small platelet aggregates. However, in our animal models there is no significant thrombus deposition on the stent surface because of the high velocity of blood flow along the stent-graft surface [13]. The potential for significant mechanical hemolysis across the stent-graft interface is not known. Embolic material may shear off the diseased vessel wall during placement of the large delivery sheath or during deployment of the stent-graft. This has not been reported in the few early reports on stent-grafting in the abdominal aorta or peripheral vasculature [8, 14–16].

It is theoretically possible that graft dilatation or further expansion of the aneurysm wall could occur despite thrombosis of the excluded aneurysm. This has not been reported thus far in the endoluminal grafting data from abdominal aortic aneurysms [8].

Conclusion

From our preliminary experience, stent-grafting is technically feasible for repairing selected aneurysms in the descending thoracic aorta. Thus far, we have placed these devices in highly selected patients for thoracic aneurysms with small necks and penetrating aortic ulcers with intramural hematomas (Fig. 8-3). The use of this technique in the setting of acute trauma or in patients with complex aortic dissections is unknown and will require a much larger body of experience.

It is clear from these early studies that endoluminal stent-grafting holds tremendous potential in terms of reduced morbidity, mortality, and expense. But the ultimate question will not be answered for several more years: Will these new devices confer protection against aortic rupture, and how will the durability of these procedures compare with standard surgical repairs?

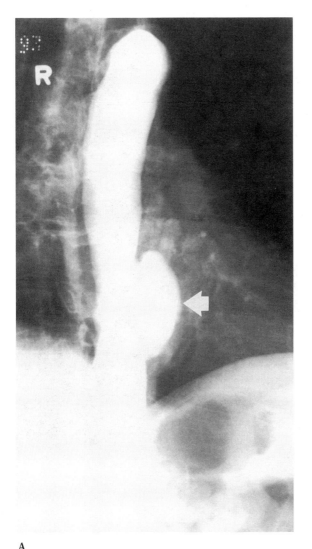

A

Fig. 8-3. A 72-year-old man with acute onset thoracic back pain. Preintervention imaging studies demonstrate a large focal aortic ulcer (arrow) on the anteroposterior thoracic angiogram (A) and the contrast-enhanced axial spiral CT scan (B). The stent-graft is deployed in the distal thoracic aorta to exclude flow into the aneurysmal sac (C). Follow-up imaging studies show exclusion of the aortic ulcer using spiral CT angiography shaded-surface display reconstructions (D) and axial projections (E). The follow-up scan was performed two weeks postdeployment and shows complete resolution of the aortic ulcer.

165

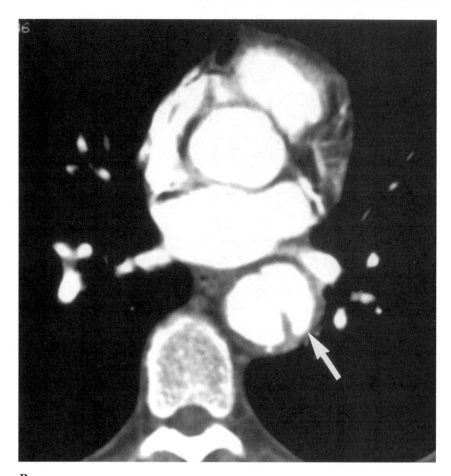

B

Fig. 8-3 *(continued)*

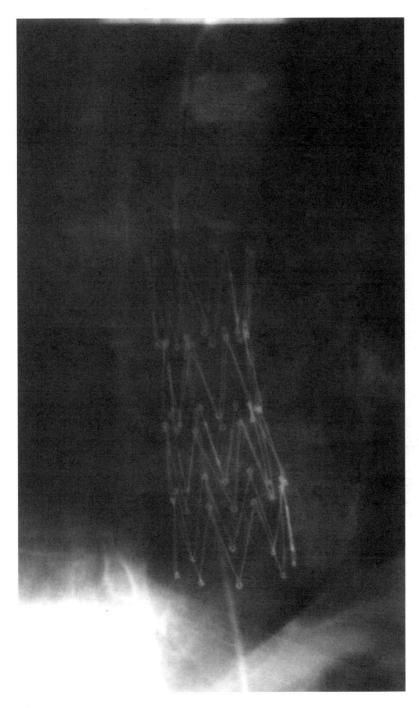

C

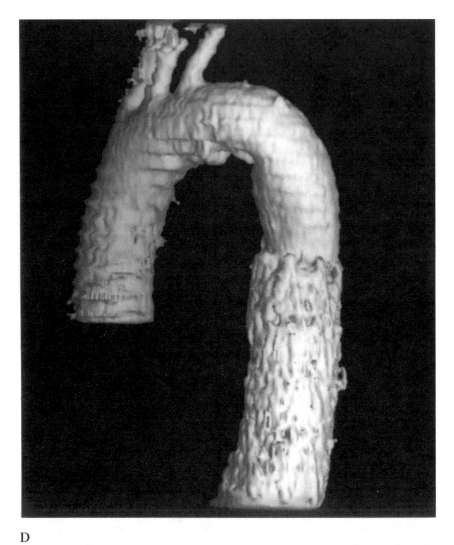

D

Fig. 8-3 *(continued)*

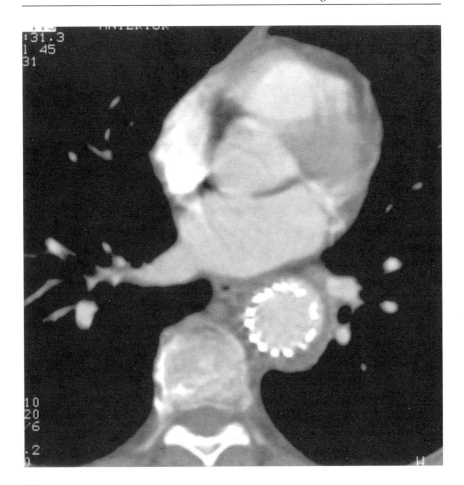

E

References

1. Lindsay J, DeBakey ME, Beall AC. Diagnosis and Treatment of Diseases of the Aorta. In RC Schlant, RW Alexander (eds), *The Heart* (8th ed.). New York: McGraw-Hill, 1994.

2. Joyce JW et al. Aneurysms of the thoracic aorta. A clinical study with special reference to prognosis. *Circulation* 1964;29:176–181.

3. Pressler V, McNamara JJ. Thoracic aortic aneurysm. Natural history and treatment. *J Thorac Cardiovasc Surg* 1980;79:489–498.

4. Bickerstaff LK et al. Thoracic aortic aneurysms: A population-based study. *Surgery* 1982;92:1103–1108.

5. DeBakey ME, McCollum CH, Graham JM. Surgical treatment of aneurysms of the descending thoracic aorta: Long-term results in 500 patients. *J Cardiovasc Surg* 1978;19:571–576.

6. Crawford ES, Rubio PA. Reappraisal of adjuncts to avoid ischemia in the treatment of aneurysms in the descending thoracic aorta. *J Thorac Cardiovasc Surg* 1973;66:693–704.

7. Moreno-Cabral CE et al. Degenerative and atherosclerotic aneurysms of the thoracic aorta. *J Thorac Cardiovasc Surg* 1984;88:1020–1032.

8. Parodi JC, Barone HD. Transfemoral intraluminal graft implantation for abdominal aortic aneurysms. *Ann Vasc Surg* 1991;5:491–499.

9. Rousseau H et al. Use of a new self-expanding endovascular prosthesis: An experimental study. *Radiology* 1987;164:709–714.

10. Semba CP, Rubin GD, Dake MD. Three-dimensional spiral CT angiography of the abdomen. *Semin Ultra CT* 1994;15:133–138.

11. Rubin GD et al. Three-dimensional spiral CT angiography of the abdomen: Initial clinical experience. *Radiology* 1993;186:147–152.

12. Marini CP, Cunningham JN. Issues surrounding spinal cord protection. *Adv Cardiac Surg* 1993;4:89–107.

13. Moon MR et al. Intravascular stenting of acute experimental Type B dissections. *J Surg Res* 1993;54:381–388.

14. May J et al. Transluminal placement of a prosthetic graft-stent device for treatment of subclavian artery aneurysm. *J Vasc Surg* 1993;18:1056–1059.

15. Marin ML et al. Percutaneous transfemoral stented graft repair of a traumatic femoral arteriovenous fistula. *J Vasc Surg* 1993;18:298–301.

16. Becker GJ et al. Percutaneous placement of a balloon-expandable intraluminal graft for life-threatening subclavian artery hemorrhage. *J Vasc Intervent Radiol* 1991;2:225–229.

Applications to Traumatic Lesions and Arterial Occlusions

III

Editorial Perspective: Role of Aortic Stent Therapy in the Evolution of Intravascular Prosthesis Development

The treatment of aortoiliac occlusive disease using a combination of thrombolysis, balloon dilation, and vascular stents represents landmark work addressing several issues critical to the development of intravascular prostheses.

The use of intraluminal grafts to treat aneurysms and other arterial lesions is not a novel concept. Many attempts to develop these devices have been considered over the last 20 years, but none has been successful due to the lack of an adequate intraluminal fixation mechanism. The development of intravascular stents provides a reliable fixation mechanism and has enabled the rapid evolution occurring in this field.

The following chapter by Dr. Diethrich addresses some of the fundamental issues involved in successfully choosing patients for intra-aortic stent placement and outlines the considerations required for safe application of this technology. The expansion of the concepts required for aortic stent deployment can easily be extended to the broader concept of using intraluminal stent-graft prostheses for the treatment of aneurysmal, traumatic, and occlusive lesions. The aortic stent data have been included in the text to emphasize their importance in the overall discussion of endoluminal prostheses and to highlight some of the unique aspects that are raised regarding the intravascular graft treatment of arterial occlusive lesions.

T.A.M.C.
C.E.D.
R.A.W.

174

Endoluminal Therapies for Aortic Occlusive Disease

9

Edward B. Diethrich

Not since the development of prosthetic graft materials has there been such a dramatic impact on the treatment of peripheral arterial occlusive disease as that created by percutaneous interventions. As new efficacious intraluminal procedures and tools are combined with conventional vascular surgical techniques, the focus of therapy is moving inexorably toward maximal revascularization with minimal invasion and cost. Without a doubt, endovascular surgery will soon become the preferred therapeutic approach to peripheral vascular occlusive disease in almost every vascular bed.

A perfect example of the benefits to be derived from our ability to bring a therapeutic device to a diseased vascular segment without direct surgical exposure is found in the abdominal aorta. The triad of thrombolysis, balloon dilation, and stent implantation is a versatile and efficacious remedy for nearly all distal abdominal aortic pathologies, including ulcerative lesions, bifurcation disease, and occlusions and stenoses compromising both the native artery and anastomosed prosthetic grafts. When the potential for percutaneous aneurysmal exclusion with an intraluminal graft-stent prosthesis is also considered, we can easily foresee a day when conventional aortic surgery will be rarely needed.

This ability to avoid an extensive laparotomy and graft interposition in patients with abdominal aortic disease conveys numerous advantages in addition to the likelihood of reduced costs. General anesthesia is not usually required, shorter hospitalization is common, lower mortality can be anticipated, fewer complications will occur as the opportunity for infection is reduced, and reapplication of the technique in the event of recurrent disease is simpler. Moreover, for male patients, removing the risk of impotence after a catheter-based procedure is a significant benefit over the sexual dysfunction that sometimes results from aortoiliac surgery.

Although both thrombolysis and balloon dilation have been used successfully in the abdominal aorta for more than a decade, the application of endovascular stents is the single most important technique to affect the future of occlusive and aneurysmal disease treatment in large-bore arteries such as the aorta. The strategies for selecting these interventions and the techniques for their application must now be a part of every endovascular surgeon's armamentarium.

Patient Selection

Nearly all manifestations of atherosclerotic occlusive disease in the distal abdominal aorta or aortoiliac segment can be considered potentially suitable for endoluminal treatment. A history of previous surgical or percutaneous interventions does not preclude a subsequent intraluminal aortic therapy, nor does the coexistence of coronary artery disease or most other chronic systemic disorders, including renal dysfunction. In fact, the relative technical simplicity and low risk of abdominal aortic angioplasty make this approach particularly attractive for patients who are ill, fragile, debilitated, acutely symptomatic, or opposed to conventional surgery.

Patients with aortic occlusive disease may present with variable signs and symptoms demanding precise diagnostic acumen. For example, a patient with a blue toe and early gangrene may have a strong femoral pulse, indicating the possibility of embolization from an aortic source. Another patient may have femoral pulses at rest that disappear with exercise testing, suggesting severe proximal occlusive disease. Compounding these diagnostic challenges is the likelihood of multiple lesion sites in the pelvic and limb arteries, where symptoms may be masked by the proximal disease. Because of these variables, comprehensive examination for peripheral arterial disease must include resting and exercise Doppler testing, duplex scanning, arteriography, and magnetic resonance blood flow evaluation when appropriate.

Arteriographically documented occlusions of the abdominal aorta are nearly always due to atheromatous formations complicated by local thrombosis. This situation is most likely to occur in conjunction with significant occlusive disease in the iliac arteries, although there are many exceptions. Thrombotic occlusion may also develop in patients with narrowing above or at the site of proximal anastomoses of aortoiliac or aortofemoral grafts. Such patients are appropriate for thrombolytic therapy followed by dilation and/or stenting of the native aorta or the anastomotic junction (Fig. 9-1).

Because thrombolysis is so effective in these situations, the contraindications must be appreciated. The patient should not have active internal bleeding, known intracranial pathology, or a cerebrovascular accident within three months of therapy. Other relative contraindications that may weigh in the decision to use thrombolytic therapy are recent major surgery, minor gastrointestinal bleeding, coagulation disorders, uncontrolled hypertension, and severe liver disease.

Patients with flow-impeding stenoses of the infrarenal aorta are good candidates for a percutaneous intervention. Equally important, disease in this location may threaten the viability of existing distal reconstructions. In the same fashion, a stenosis can occur proximal to an aortoiliac graft and hinder inflow, although anastomotic involvement is more common.

The rarer suprarenal aortic stenoses that can affect renal perfusion may also be managed with angioplasty, though care must be exercised to avoid compromising the renal ostium during balloon inflation (Fig. 9-2). Even renal artery lesions can be approached during the same percutaneous intervention (Fig. 9-3).

Patients with Leriche's syndrome or hypoplastic distal abdominal aortas may present with isolated aortic stenoses that are ideally suited to percutaneous dilation. Similarly, ulcerative abdominal aortic

177

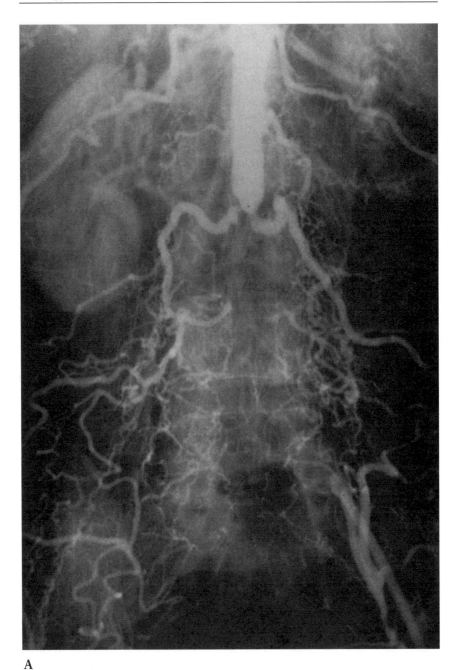

A

Fig. 9-1. A 76-year-old woman presented with severe symptomatology related to the complete occlusion of her abdominal aorta (A). After 24 hours of urokinase therapy (B), the aorta was sufficiently cleared to allow

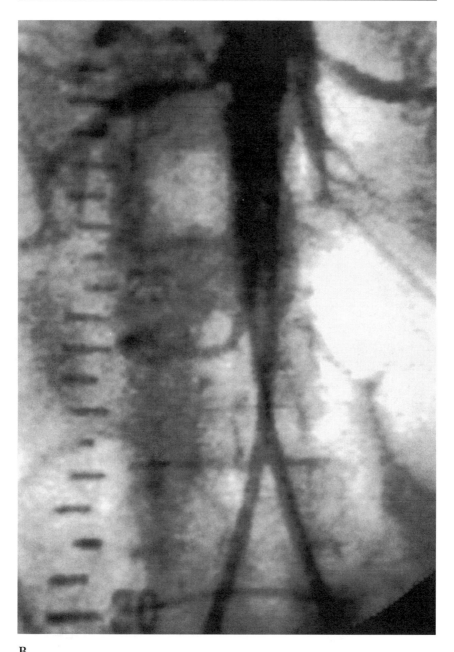

B

balloon dilation and subsequent implantation of two Palmaz P294 stents above the bifurcation with an additional two P308 stents deployed in the left common iliac artery (C).

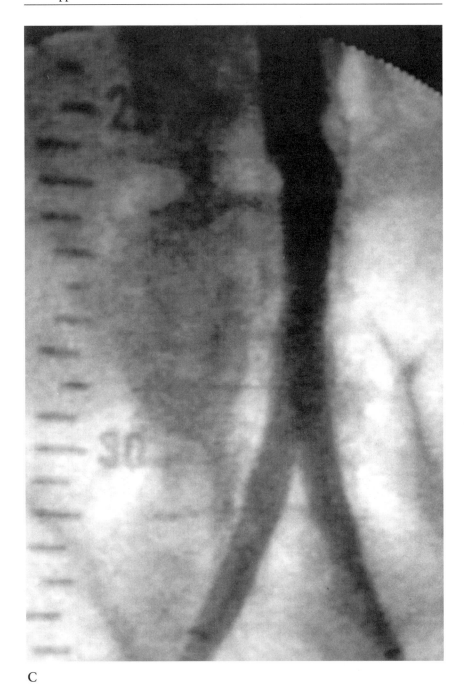

C

Fig. 9-1 *(continued)*

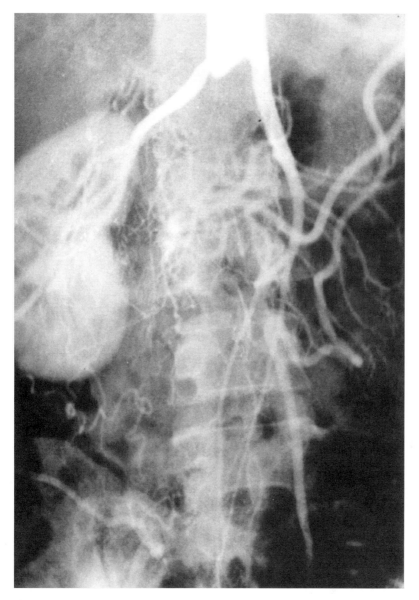

A

Fig. 9-2. A 36-year-old woman with complaints of chronic back pain and intermittent lower extremity numbness that worsened with exertion exhibited weak femoral pulses and no distal pulses on physical examination. An aortogram (A) demonstrated complete aortic occlusion beginning below the origin of the right renal artery and encompassing the origin of the left

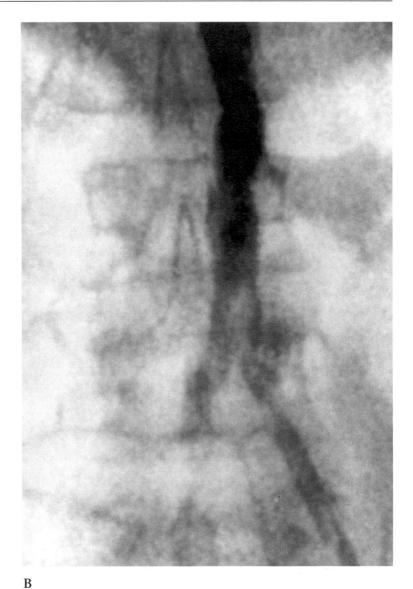

B

Fig. 9-2 *(continued)*

renal artery. The glomerular filtration rate in the left kidney was 26 percent. Antegrade urokinase infusion opened the aorta (B), but multiple filling defects were seen along its course, with occlusion of the right common
iliac artery and diminished flow in the left iliac system. Another overnight
course of urokinase was administered antegrade to the common iliac arter-

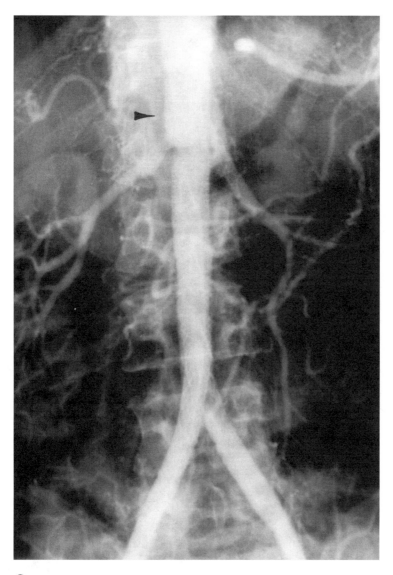

C

ies. The next day, balloon dilation of the supra- and infrarenal aorta and both common iliac arteries was followed by stent implantation: Two Palmaz P394 stents were placed in the distal aorta and another P308 was deployed in the suprarenal aortic position (C, arrowhead). One Palmaz P308 was placed at the origin of each common iliac artery; two additional P394 stents were deployed in the right common iliac artery.

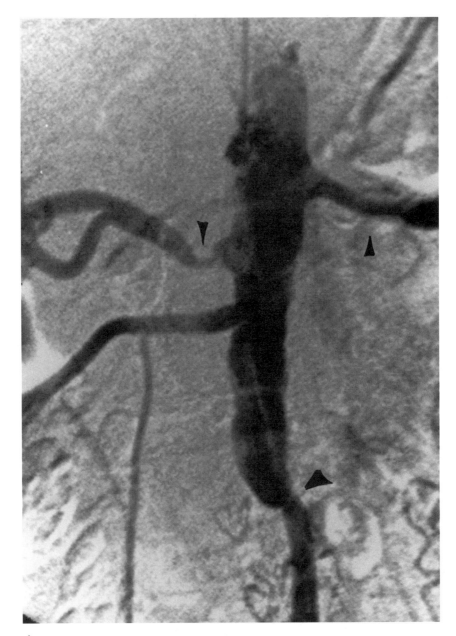

A

Fig. 9-3. A 55-year-old man with complete occlusion of the aortoiliac segment at the inferior mesenteric artery (A, large arrowhead) and high-grade stenoses (small arrowheads) of both renal arteries. Access was gained through the left brachial artery and the right common iliac artery

184

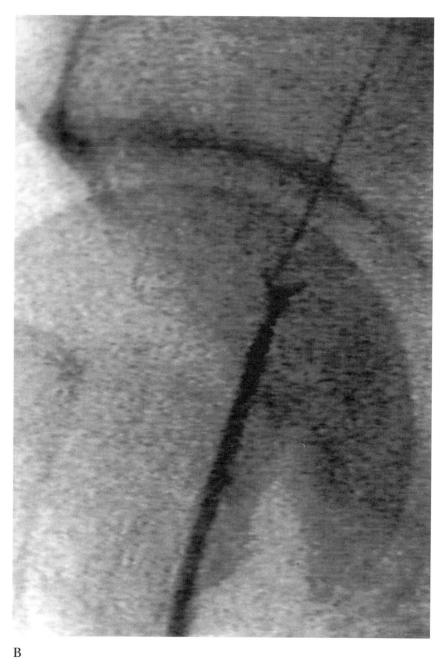

B

(CIA) initially, but when the retrograde wire could not pass the CIA lesion, the antegrade aortic wire was passed down the right CIA to the level of the sheath. A biopsy forceps (B) inserted through the sheath was

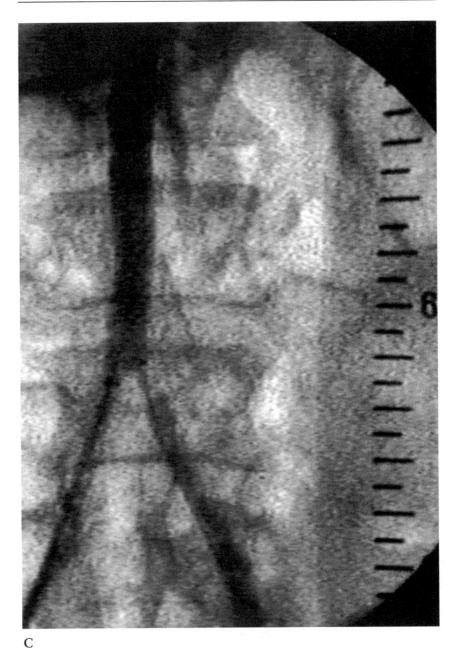

C

Fig. 9-3 *(continued)*

used to grasp the antegrade wire and pull it through the sheath. A left CIA approach was also necessary when the antegrade wire would not traverse the left CIA lesion. Both CIAs and the distal aorta were dilated, and

186

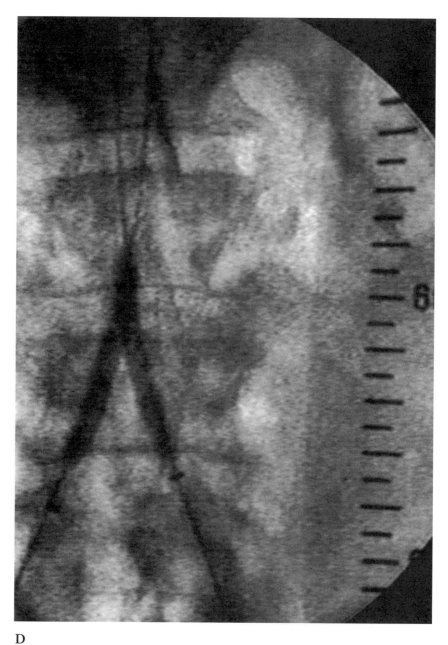

D

two Palmaz P308 stents were deployed in the distal aorta (C). Subsequently, both CIAs were stented with P294s, and one Wallstent was deployed in each external iliac artery as well. Persistent iliac gradients were eventually obliterated by kissing-balloon dilation of the aortic and

187

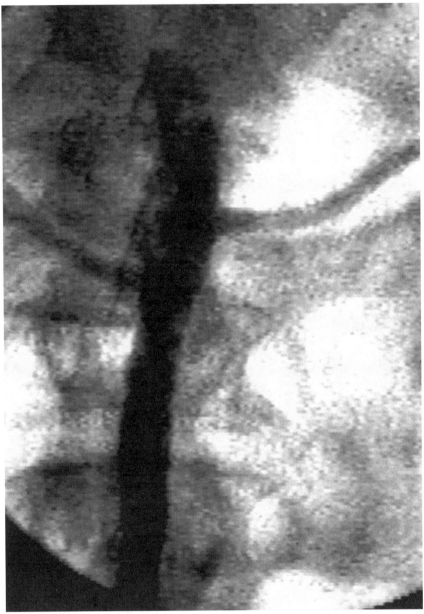

E

Fig. 9-3 *(continued)*

common iliac artery stents (D). Both renal artery stenoses were then addressed with balloon dilation and P204 stenting of the respective lesions with an excellent result (E).

lesions that produce atheroembolic microembolism ("blue toe syndrome") can be controlled by stent implantation that captures the atherosclerotic debris and traps it against the vessel wall (Fig. 9-4).

Stents were introduced to not only combat restenosis but also to treat abnormal dilation characteristics (e.g., resistance, recoil) and dilation failure (e.g., persistent filling defect, dissection, intimal flaps). So well has the Palmaz model performed this function that it is now used routinely for distal aortic stenoses and after recanalization of all occluded iliac arteries (Fig. 9-5). Moreover, multiple stents are not infrequently used in cases of extensive aortoiliac disease to ensure an adequate, continuous lumen over the entire course of the involved segment (see Figs. 9-1 and 9-5).

Assessment

The endovascular treatment suite must be suitably equipped for multidimensional intraprocedural assessment if complex percutaneous interventions are to be performed. High-resolution fluoroscopic imaging is essential and, in our opinion, is best provided by a ceiling-mounted surgical C-arm roentgenographic unit with image enhancer (ISS-2000 Plus Intraoperative Imaging System, International Surgical Systems, Phoenix, AZ) integrated with a 3/4-inch videotape recorder and monitors for contrast injection visualization and road mapping with an Eigen disk (Fig. 9-6).

To optimize the usefulness of this radiographic equipment, a nonmetallic, carbon fiber surgical table (International Surgical Systems) is available especially for interventional techniques. This thin but highly stable table is supported at only one end to provide complete clearance beneath for a panning x-ray system. Its telescoping pedestal allows vertical travel from 28 to 48 inches, 20-degree side-to-side roll, and 20-degree Trendelenburg tilt (standard and reverse). The table itself can be removed from the pedestal for exchange with other types of tabletops.

The importance of total arterial assessment without fluoroscopic compromise from the radial arteries, down the thoracic aorta to the infrapopliteal area, cannot be overemphasized. The treatment of

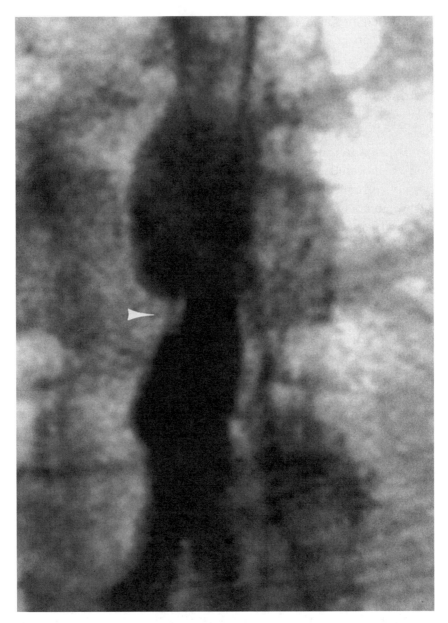

A

Fig. 9-4. This ulcerative plaque (A, arrowhead) associated with a high-grade stenosis was found in the distal abdominal aorta in a 71-year-old man. A single Palmaz P308 stent (B) was deployed primarily at the lesion site, creating a debris-free blood path.

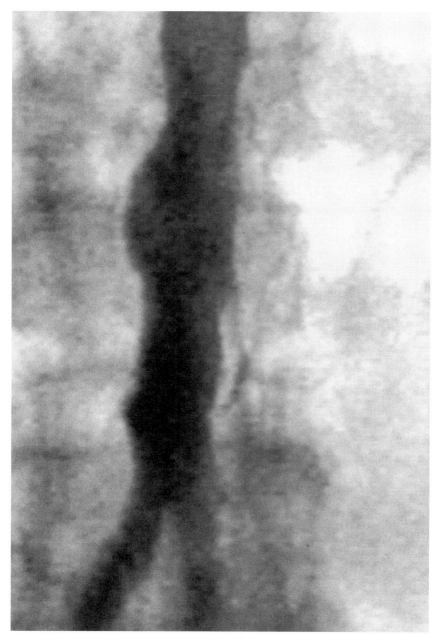

B

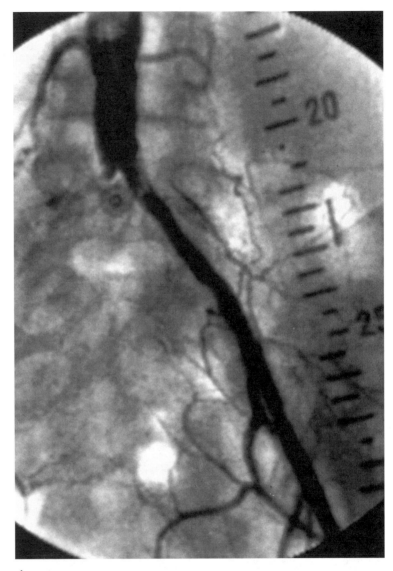

A

Fig. 9-5. A 56-year-old woman with claudication demonstrated total right common iliac occlusion with a 50 percent narrowing of the left common iliac artery and disease involvement at the bifurcation (A). Access through both common femoral arteries and the left brachial was achieved, but a wire could not pass the right common iliac artery lesion either retrograde or antegrade. A holmium laser catheter was successful in recanalizing the right common iliac artery. Balloon dilation was performed throughout both com-

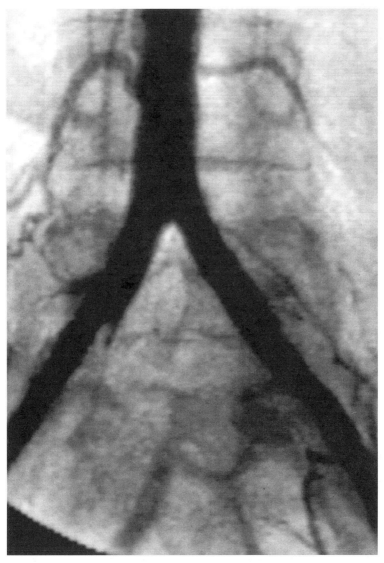

B

mon iliac arteries, and the bifurcation was stabilized by the kissing-balloon technique. IVUS interrogation revealed significant atherosclerotic disease remaining, confirmed by a residual pressure gradient, which dictated the deployment of stents. Palmaz P308 stents were deployed in the distal aorta (one) and along both common iliac arteries (two in each). A satisfactory result was confirmed by arteriography and absence of pressure gradients (B).

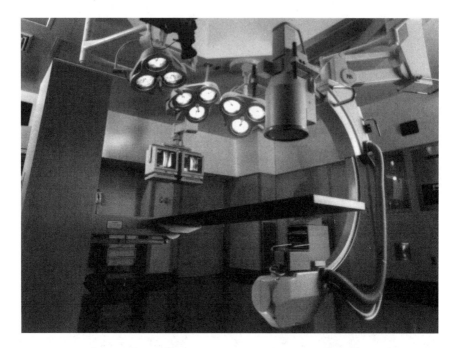

Fig. 9-6. Endovascular interventions require high-resolution imaging technology. This ceiling-mounted **C**-arm roentgenographic unit with image enhancer is integrated with a videotape recorder and monitors for contrast injection visualization and road-mapping with an Eigen disk. The carbon fiber surgical table features complete clearance beneath for unobstructed neck-to-toe imaging and rapid horizontal panning; multiple position adjustments regulate height, tilt, and roll.

complex aortic occlusions, renal stenoses, and, in the near future, both thoracic and abdominal aneurysm exclusion with endoluminal prostheses demands the ability to rapidly parallel-scan broad areas of the arterial tree for optimum results.

In addition to standard monitoring equipment for electrocardiography and measurement of pressure differentials across the aortic lesions, intravascular ultrasound imaging (IVUS) is a mandatory component of intraprocedural monitoring, particularly for interventional procedures involving the aorta. IVUS is invaluable for both preprocedural evaluation and postinterventional assessment. It provides baseline luminal dimensions pre- and postangioplasty (intraluminal cross sections and arterial circumferences) along with precise

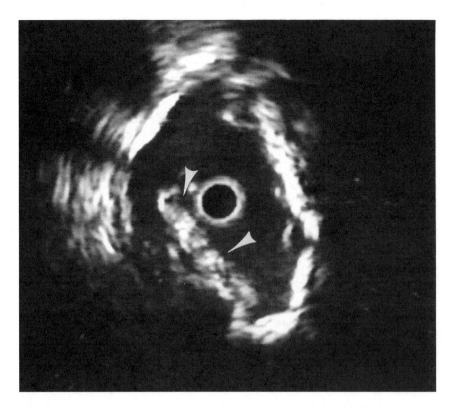

Fig. 9-7. IVUS interrogation assisted in the treatment of this linear dissection (arrowheads) in the infrarenal aorta of a 70-year-old man with bilateral iliac artery stents. The fluoroscopic image could not define the extent of the dissection, but with the assistance of IVUS imaging, three stents were positioned to completely cover the defect.

determination of arterial architecture and lesion pathology, data the fluoroscopic image cannot provide (Fig. 9-7).

In most cases, the IVUS examination following balloon dilation plays a significant role in both determining the need for stenting and assessing adequate deployment of these devices. Our experience indicates that improper stent deployment occurs more commonly than is indicated by the control arteriogram. Frequently, the postprocedural IVUS will show that the struts of the stent are not in perfect apposition with the arterial wall (Fig. 9-8). Additionally, while the angiogram may give the appearance of a perfect match between the stent and the arterial diameters, the precise cross-sectional measure-

195

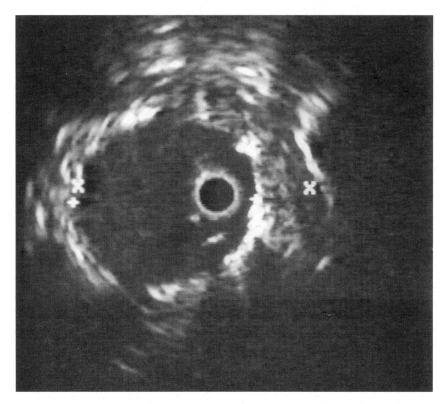

Fig. 9-8. IVUS examination of a Palmaz stent deployed in the abdominal aorta shows underexpansion of the stent (between plus signs) compared to the true luminal diameter (between Xs). Redilation was necessary to achieve an adequate apposition of the stent and vessel wall.

ments afforded by the IVUS study will indicate that the stent actually requires further dilation to attain a correct match with the vessel.

Anastomotic sites and inflow lesions are imaged two-dimensionally with the SONOS (Hewlett-Packard, Andover, MA) imaging system using either of several IVUS catheters: 20 MHz Sonicath (4.6 or 6.2 French) by Mansfield/Boston Scientific (Watertown, MA); 20 MHz (6 French) by Diasonics (Milpitas, CA); or 30 MHz by Cardiovascular Imaging Systems (8 French) (Sunnyvale, CA). Three-dimensional reconstruction is achieved with a real-time processing system (ImageComm Systems, Inc., Santa Clara, CA).

Although angioscopy offers a wealth of complementary information that only direct visualization can provide, it is not yet rou-

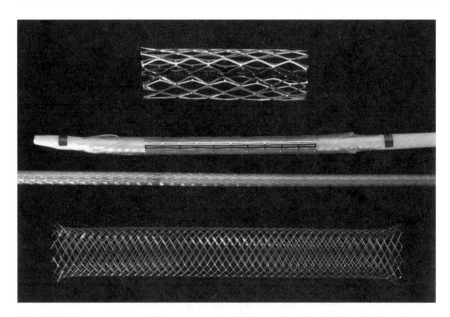

Fig. 9-9. Two stent models appropriate for use in the abdominal aorta are the stainless steel, slotted, balloon-expandable Palmaz design (top: expanded and loaded) and the self-expanding Wallstent, composed of braided stainless steel monofilaments (bottom: loaded and expanded).

tinely applicable in the high-flow arteries such as in the aortoiliac system. Special flow occlusion techniques using balloons above and below the site to be viewed are necessary in this region. Angioscopy can be very helpful in differentiating thrombus from intimal hyperplasia even in the large-bore artery.

There are several models of stents now being used in the abdominal aorta (Fig. 9-9). The Palmaz balloon-expandable peripheral stent (Johnson & Johnson Interventional Systems, Warren, NJ) is a stainless steel tube designed with multiple rows of staggered rectangular slots that assume a diamond shape when expanded, reducing to 10 percent the amount of metal in contact with the luminal surface. The Palmaz design is available in varying lengths from 10 to 39 mm with expansion ranges of 4 to 18 mm; newer models will permit expansion to even larger diameters, but these will not be available in the United States for some time. Its longitudinal rigidity and large diameter make it ideally suited for straight vessels like the distal aorta and the renal and iliac arteries.

Another promising stent design is the Wallstent (Schneider, Minneapolis, MN), a cylindrical device constructed by braiding multiple stainless steel monofilaments. It comes in a variety of lengths ranging from 50 to 150 mm and in diameters from 5 to 10 mm. Because of its springlike structure, the Wallstent is flexible, compliant, and self-expanding, making it useful for delivery through curved arteries, implantation overlying the graft-artery junction in end-to-side anastomoses, and in vessels subject to flexion from adjacent joints or structures, such as the common femoral and popliteal arteries. Although it is a self-expanding stent, we have found that after initial deployment with the self-expanding mechanism, the Wallstent must be further expanded with another balloon to ensure complete stent-vessel wall apposition.

Other models and variations of the existing devices will be forthcoming in the near future. In the long term, the potential for stent technology is excitingly varied—from bioabsorbable models to stents coated to time-release genetically engineered drugs; all these and more are currently under investigation.

Medication

Twenty-four hours before angioplasty, patients begin an antiplatelet regimen consisting of 325 mg per day of nongeneric aspirin and 75 mg dipyridamole three times daily (although the value of this medication has not been confirmed, and there is a relatively high incidence of patient intolerance).

After the procedure, the aspirin-dipyridamole therapy is restarted in the intensive care unit. Following discharge, the dipyridamole is discontinued after three months; the aspirin therapy continues indefinitely. No long-term anticoagulation therapy is needed for patients with stents in the aortoiliac segment because the likelihood of thrombosis is small in these larger arteries. Similarly, if a renal stent is deployed, no postoperative anticoagulation is required. However, when stents have been placed both above and below the inguinal ligament, warfarin therapy is initiated in the intensive care unit and continued indefinitely. The presence of a stent in the superficial femoral or popliteal arteries demands anticoagulation to achieve satisfactory results.

Thrombolysis

Catheter-directed thrombolysis is extremely valuable as a primary treatment tool in cases of aortic occlusion. Because thrombosis is usually a manifestation of an underlying pathology, clot lysis affords both diagnostic and therapeutic benefits. If the thrombus is relatively young (four to six weeks), lytic infusion is almost universally effective in opening a channel for treatment of the culprit plaque. However, even more chronic occlusions older than a year can respond well to lysis intervention.

If thrombus contributes to an obstruction, preangioplasty thrombolytic therapy can be initiated antegrade from percutaneous cannulation of the brachial artery with placement of the catheter at the lesion.

The selection of a thrombolytic agent depends on personal experience. Urokinase is the most widely used lytic agent for regional thrombolysis because of its specificity as a plasmin activator and its low complication rate, but recent observations suggest that higher potency t-PA may be more successful, with a shorter time to clot lysis than either streptokinase or urokinase. If the assumption is correct that major bleeding complications are related more to the length of the infusion than to the total dose of drug, then the more rapidly acting t-PA may become the preferred agent. However, recent studies using a loading dose of t-PA to reduce lytic infusion time have shown an increased incidence of intracerebral and local hemorrhage during even regional delivery. Hence, at present, the commonly suggested dosages for t-PA range from 0.05 to 0.10 mg/kg/hour with no loading dose.

If urokinase is the selected agent, the dosage schedule depends on the projected time to create a luminal channel. For a relatively young clot, a high-dose regimen (100,000 to 120,000 units/hour drip infusion) is used because lysis should occur quickly. Chronic occlusions will undoubtedly require longer lytic infusion times (up

199

to 48 hours), so the dosage is lowered to 40,000 to 60,000 units/hour. The low-dose protocol helps avoid the bleeding complications related to lytic therapy. In either case, an initial 250,000 IU bolus is delivered at the time of catheter placement.

Recently, more rapid delivery of urokinase has been observed using a pulsed infusion system (Pulse Spray, AndioDynamics, Glen Falls, NY). If a guidewire can be passed across the lesion, the pulse spray catheter (Fig. 9-10) is positioned so that the entire length of the occlusion is in contact with the delivery ports (the catheter comes with 5-, 10-, 20-, and 30-cm–long infusion patterns). The injecting system can be programmed to any desired infusion cycle. Typically, 500,000 units of urokinase are delivered in a 30-minute period, but longer cycles may be preferable when the thrombus is older. At the conclusion of the programmed infusion period, a repeat angiogram is performed to determine the need for a repeated cycle or longer, more classical infusions. The early results with this method have been favorable, especially when the thrombus appears to be less than 30 days old.

If the thrombotic occlusion extends to one or both common iliac arteries, the catheter can be advanced progressively after the proximal aortic occlusion is opened, thereby delivering a high dose of drug at the target lesion.

With either agent, the partial thromboplastin time is maintained in the 40- to 90-second range (1.5 to 2.0 times control) with a concomitant heparin drip (800 to 1,200 units/hour after a 1,000- to 3,000-unit bolus). Serial bedside arteriography is performed using either a portable C-arm or a standard chest x-ray unit to monitor lytic progress and gauge the advancement of the delivery catheter as described above.

Balloon Dilation

Following successful clot lysis, angioplasty of the aortic stenosis can be performed either through the antegrade access already established or a standard retrograde route. Selection of the approach depends somewhat on the size of the abdominal aorta and the ulti-

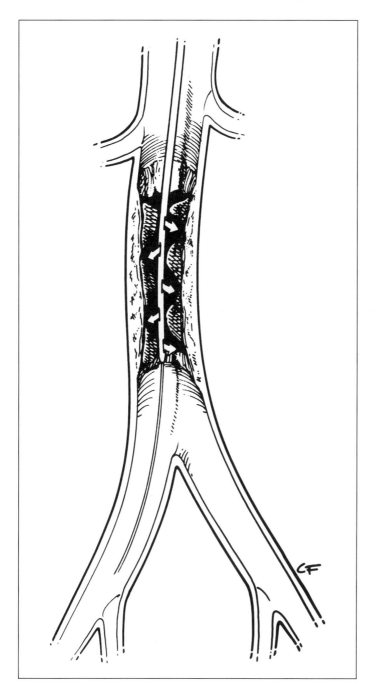

Fig. 9-10. This multiholed pulse spray catheter system is particularly useful in maximizing drug infusion in cases of long aortic thrombotic occlusions.

mate balloon shaft diameter that will be required for complete dilation and potential stent deployment. The only current limitation of the brachial artery approach is the small size of the artery, which may not accommodate a large sheath. However, the catheter manufacturers are responding to the need for lower-profile systems, and this hindrance may be less important in the near future. For example, long sheaths (8 French, 70 cm; Daige Corp., Minnetonka, MN) now allow the stent to be delivered at the precisely designated location while being protected during passage.

Likewise, the retrograde femoral approach is using progressively smaller delivery systems. The only limiting factor is the shaft size of the delivery balloon. In the presence of bifurcation disease or if lesion sites in the iliac arteries are being treated, access through both femoral arteries is necessary. A pressure line is attached to the side port of the sheath(s) for pressure differential monitoring. Once sheath placement is confirmed with a contrast injection, 2,500 to 5,000 units of heparin (depending on patient size) are given intravenously. Activated coagulation time is monitored throughout the procedure to maintain the level above 250 seconds.

A 0.035-inch (0.89-mm, 150- or 240-cm length) hydrophilic wire (Glidewire, Medi-tech, Watertown, MA) is then passed into the aorta from the common femoral artery. If retrograde crossing of the aortic or iliac lesion(s) is difficult, another Glidewire is passed through the antegrade lytic catheter across the aortic occlusion and grasped with a 5.4 French disposable biopsy forceps (Cordis Corp., Miami Lakes, FL) via the retrograde sheath. The wire is then pulled through the femoral sheath, thereby converting to a retrograde procedure.

In any case where it is impossible for either antegrade or retrograde wires to cross a residual iliac arterial occlusion, pulsed holmium-YAG laser energy (3.6 J per pulse at 10 Hz) delivered by a 2.5-mm Spectraprobe-Max (Trimedyne Inc., Tustin, CA) can be used to clear a retrograde channel through the obstruction, thus permitting wire passage from either above or below.

Once balloon dilation is complete, dilatation is assessed and the necessity for stenting is determined using several techniques, including pull-through pressure gradients and IVUS. Use of these multiple assessment modalities as complements to standard arteriography is mandatory in percutaneous interventions because the control arteriogram notoriously underestimates the postdilation condition of an artery and is of no real help in the three-dimensional monitoring of adequate stent deployment.

The measurement of pull-through pressure gradients is a particularly sensitive hemodynamic indicator of satisfactory luminal dimensions. By using special 4 French or 5 French wire-guided, radiopaque-tipped catheters (Medi-tech or Cook, Inc., Bloomington, IN) placed retrograde across the aortic lesion, the exact proximal origination point of the gradient can be determined by pulling the catheter back through the lesion and noting the level at which the radial artery and catheter pressure begin to differ. Complete abolition of this gradient is the only end point for a successful angioplasty in any situation, and failure to achieve this goal constitutes a major criterion for stent implantation.

Stent Deployment

The decision to deploy a stent in the abdominal aorta with or without initial balloon angioplasty depends on the nature of the lesion. For example, one procedure may involve primary stent implantation without preliminary dilatation for treating ulcerative plaques causing peripheral embolization. Primary dilation of these lesions can theoretically dislodge particles of atherosclerotic debris that embolize before the deployed stent can compress the material against the aortic wall.

A similar benefit of primary stent deployment occurs when there is residual thrombus on the aortic wall following lytic therapy. Quite often, however, balloon dilation precedes stent deployment under these conditions to widen the aortic lumen, fracture the plaque, and facilitate stent implantation.

Graft anastomoses are another circumstance in which stenting may be indicated primarily. Stricture at the graft-vessel junction in large arteries such as the aorta is often the result of fibrosis and scar tissue or progressive atherosclerotic disease in the artery itself. In smaller vessels, intimal hyperplasia is more often the culprit in anastomotic stenosis.

203

From a purely technical standpoint, most nonulcerated athero-sclerotic aortic lesions are dilated initially. This provides information about lesion recoil and proper aortic sizing. The decision to apply one or more stents will then be made intraprocedurally based on the IVUS interrogation and the presence of a residual pressure gradient.

The major determinant for stenting in the abdominal aorta is almost never the periprocedural arteriogram. Often, following large-balloon dilation of the aorta, the angiogram appears quite satisfactory and even the pressure gradient may be zero, but IVUS imaging will delineate an inadequate postdilation luminal diameter, residual plaque, anastomotic or lesion recoil, dissection, or atherosclerotic debris (ulcerated plaque or intimal flaps) judged to have embolic or flow-limiting potential.

If dilation is judged unsatisfactory for one of the above reasons, a wire exchange is performed to prepare for stent deployment. Over a 4 or 5 French angiographic catheter inserted through a groin sheath, a 0.035-inch (0.89-mm) Amplatz Super Stiff (150-cm length, Medi-tech) is substituted for the Glidewire. The Cordis sheath is then removed, and a 300-mm 9 French sheath equipped with a radiopaque band at the distal tip to monitor positioning (Check-Flo II, Cook, Inc.) is inserted and passed retrograde across the target aortic lesion.

Using the aortic cross-sectional measurements from the IVUS as a size guideline, a stent (usually the Palmaz P308 model) is manual-ly crimped onto an appropriately sized balloon that has a 6 French shaft that can be accommodated in the 9 French sheath. (To a great extent, balloon catheter selection is at the discretion of the practi-tioner, provided the size and expansion characteristics are appropri-ate for the deployment.) The stent is delivered to the target site, with its placement guided by road-mapping, bony landmarks, and cali-brations on the graduated ruler beneath the patient's pelvis.

When perfect stent position is obtained, the long sheath is retracted to expose the stent on the delivery balloon. As the bal-loon is inflated under fluoroscopic control, the characteristics of the stent expansion can be viewed as it deploys against the aortic wall. The balloon is then deflated, deflagged by clockwise shaft rotation, and withdrawn. Following successful stent deployment and full expansion, the stent-to-artery apposition is verified with IVUS. If further expansion is desired to obtain a larger lumen, or if the stent struts are not in perfect apposition with the aortic wall, a larger balloon is selected.

When multiple tandem stents are deployed, the most proximal device is implanted first. However, if the situation arises in which a second stent is required proximal to one already deployed, the safest technique for deployment of the second stent is to advance the delivery sheath with the obturator across the initial stent, thereby reducing the chance of the two stents coming into contact. It is important to slightly overlap sequentially applied stents to ensure no gaps exist, and it must be remembered that as the diameter of the stent increases with balloon expansion, the length shortens slightly. Concomitant iliac artery stenting, when necessary, follows the aortic implantation(s).

To complete a procedure, pressure gradients are again performed to ensure no gradient remains, IVUS imaging is repeated, and a control arteriogram documents the satisfactory arterial contours and blood flow. The patient is transferred to the intensive care unit with the sheaths in place; heparin is not reversed. The activated coagulation time is allowed to return to less than 150 seconds before the sheaths are removed. Ambulation is encouraged 12 hours after the procedure provided there are no contraindications, and the patient can usually be discharged within 24 hours. (Some patients have actually been treated on an outpatient basis, being discharged the same day of the procedure.)

Complications and Late Outcome

Our complications have been few—primarily access-related hematomas. We did encounter two instances of distal thromboembolism secondary to urokinase infusion and one pseudoaneurysm in an external iliac artery three weeks after stenting to repair an extravasation site (unrelated to the abdominal aortic stent deployment).

One of the few technical difficulties we have encountered in abdominal aortic stent placement came during our first case of transanastomotic stenting. The device was being expanded by a 10-mm balloon positioned with the stent's midpoint aligned with the anastomotic junction. Because the native aorta was considerably narrower than the graft, only half of the stent was impacted against the aortic wall, and the elastic recoil at the site pushed the stent into the proximal aorta during balloon inflation. The stent was retrieved by threading a low-profile balloon on a 5 French shaft through it and expanding the balloon slightly to engage the proximal end of the stent, then maneuvering it into position without incident. The distal portion of the stent still was not fully in contact with the graft wall; however, because there was firm proximal apposition to the aortic wall and no residual pressure gradient, further dilation was not pursued. In subsequent cases of this nature, we have used a short balloon positioned in the distal portion of the stent to "trumpet" the end of the device so it comes into better apposition with the graft wall.

Only one patient has experienced any long-term complication associated with the aortic stent. We were unaware that one female patient was an intravenous drug abuser who resumed her illicit drug consumption shortly after undergoing stent deployment for a 95 percent abdominal aortic stenosis. An abscess developed around the implant, and it had to be removed.

In no other patient have we witnessed any signs of aortic stent restenosis in the more than four years we have been performing this procedure (Fig. 9-11). One patient developed recurrent claudication 42 months after deployment of one stent each in the abdominal aorta and left iliac artery. Aortography (Fig. 9-12) revealed progressive atherosclerotic disease between the infrarenal abdominal aortic stent and the bifurcation. A single stent was placed across this location, returning the patient's ankle-brachial index to normal and relieving the claudication symptoms.

Routine arteriographic follow-up on more than 50 percent of our patients has shown no evidence of intimal hyperplasia or stent deformation, as determined by two-dimensional IVUS imaging at the time of follow-up arteriography.

Observations and Technical Notes

In the late 1980s, our center was one of the highest volume investigative sites for the Palmaz iliac stent, and we came to appreciate

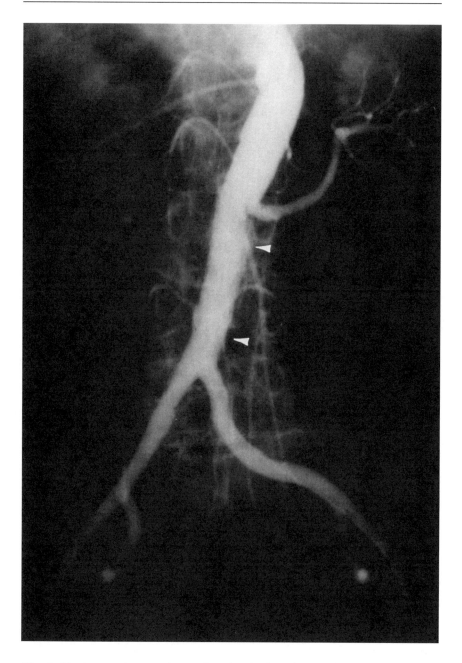

Fig. 9-11. An aortic stent (arrowheads) deployed to exclude an ulcerative plaque from the circulation in a 67-year-old woman with blue toe syndrome shows no appreciable changes three years after implantation.

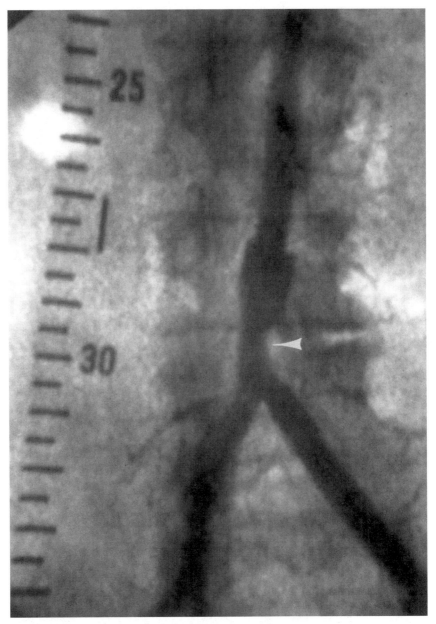

A

Fig. 9-12. A 70-year-old man had a Palmaz stent implanted at the site of an 80 percent stenosis in the infrarenal abdominal aorta in 1990. He recently reported recurrence of his claudication, and aortography (A) revealed progressive atherosclerotic involvement (arrowhead) between the

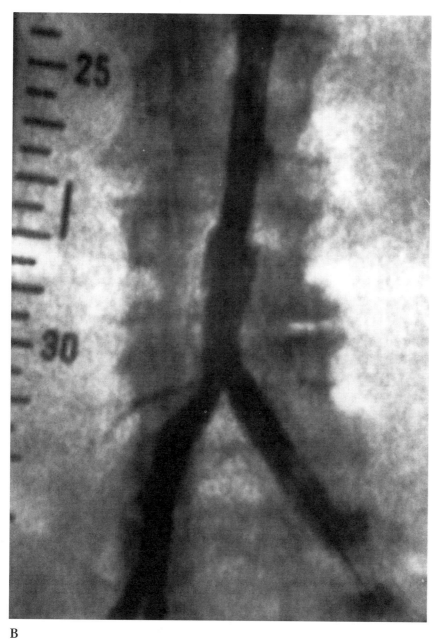

B

stent and the bifurcation. (Note the overdilation of the stent.) A second
stent (B) implanted distal to the original device restored adequate perfusion and eliminated the patient's symptoms.

the potential usefulness of this low-risk percutaneously applied device when our team was confronted with several cases in which the indications for iliac stenting were present in the abdominal aorta—namely, dissection, insufficient luminal diameter, and flow-restricting atheroembolic debris.

Now, some four years later, we have successfully implanted nearly 100 aortic stents for a variety of pathologies, including blue toe syndrome, anastomotic stenosis of aortofemoral grafts, and the ramifications of suboptimal or unsuccessful dilation.

The application of balloon dilation and stent deployment along the distal aorta also brings up the possibility of occluding the orifice of one or more of the smaller branch arteries. In our considerable experience with iliac artery stenting, we have not encountered a problem with placement of the Palmaz stent across the internal iliac artery orifice, and indeed, we have observed preservation of the lumbar arteries in cases of abdominal aortic stenting. Further, given the extensive disease that is often found in the aorta, the origin of small vessels like the inferior mesenteric artery is often already either occluded or severely compromised. It is doubtful that abdominal aortic stent placement will endanger small arterial branches.

Coincident with our progress in aortic stenting, we have also had considerable success with our antegrade infusion technique for abdominal aortic thrombolysis. Only occasionally does the lytic agent fail to achieve an open arterial channel, thereby necessitating retrograde lysing through an iliac artery.

Although the rationale for distal aortic thrombolysis is no different from that applicable to other vessels, there are a few technical considerations that must be recognized. First, fresh aortic thrombotic occlusions can extend retrograde to the orifices of the renal arteries. When lytic therapy commences, loosening of the thrombus under the pulsating aortic blood flow has caused fresh clot to propagate into the renal arteries (A. Montorjeme, personal communication, 1994). Whenever thrombolysis is used in an occlusion near the renal arteries, the potential for this complication should be kept in mind, since renal artery lysis may be required.

Second, retrograde thrombolysis in aortic occlusions is of little value unless the occlusion is recent enough to permit a guidewire to be passed from the groin across the aortic lesion. Otherwise, aortic thrombolysis must be initiated antegrade via a brachial artery approach. Our preference is access through the left upper limb to minimize the risk of cerebral embolization from pericatheter thrombus. Extension of thrombus from the aorta into the iliofemoral arteries is not a contraindication to local thrombolysis since lysis will occur as the more proximal thrombus is cleared.

The multiholed, coaxial infusion catheter must be positioned under fluoroscopic guidance at the proximal boundary of the thrombus, if possible, embedding the tip of the catheter into the thrombus to enhance lysis. If a wire can be passed across a long occluded segment, a pulse spray system will more efficiently lyse the thrombus. Angiography must also be executed periodically to assess fibrinolytic progress and guide repositioning of the catheter to maintain its position within the clot.

We have used urokinase in aortic occlusions without hematoma or bleeding, but the potential for both still remains, and careful monitoring of the coagulation profile is mandatory. There is less experience using t-PA for regional thrombolysis, but it appears that using a loading dose to accelerate the lysis time increases bleeding complications rather than lessens them.

Another complication of local thrombolysis—distal embolization—demands vigilance and prompt response. Residual thrombi may adhere to the wall of the aorta as the aortic flow washes away the urokinase at the end of treatment. These can then be dislodged spontaneously or by subsequent angioplasty procedures. More likely still is clot migration precipitated by the infusion procedure itself. Treatment of this complication may entail either open thrombectomy or "thrombolysis chasing" of the clot, in which the catheter is progressively advanced down the arterial tree to deliver the lytic agent onto the distal embolus until it is lysed. A third option is percutaneous aspiration of the thrombus using an antegrade femoral approach for access to the superficial femoral, popliteal, and trifurcation vessels. The choice is dictated by the clinical assessment.

The problem of embolization, however, is not unique to thrombolysis; it is one technical consideration common to all percutaneous interventions in the distal aorta. Surgeons familiar with the infrarenal abdominal aorta are mindful of the embolic potential from the loose atherosclerotic material so frequently found there. A few cases of distal embolization have been reported with balloon dilation, and although our two cases of distal embolization were more than likely the result of lytic therapy, the influence of balloon dilation and stent implantation cannot be ruled out. On the other hand, our use of stents to obliterate blue toe syndrome in several patients attests to the device's potential to prevent embolization.

Aortic Interventions: Present and Future

The opportunities for percutaneous interventions in the abdominal aorta are seemingly endless. The development of an endovascular graft-stent prosthesis to treat aneurysmal disease portends yet another application for intraluminal therapy in this arterial segment. This expanding array of endovascular techniques, combined with the low likelihood of restenosis in this large-bore artery, brings us closer to the day when efficacious transluminal procedures will make aortoiliac grafting nearly obsolete. Even now, lengthy surgical reconstructions can be abbreviated by applying endovascular techniques to the inflow lesions where success is greatest, followed by bypass grafting of the most distal disease for which intraluminal therapies are less effective.

This marriage of classical surgical techniques with catheter-based therapies for the treatment of peripheral vascular disease has given birth to the new subspecialty of endovascular surgery—an exciting opportunity for vascular surgeons to greatly expand their armamentarium. As the percutaneous techniques proliferate and improve in efficacy, endovascular surgeons will be increasingly more likely to offer their patients alternative therapies that feature lower morbidity and mortality, shorter hospitalizations, and reduced costs. The entire abdominal aorta, and soon the thoracic segment as well, will be added to the ever-expanding list of applications for percutaneous intervention.

212

References

Regional Thrombolysis

1. Ashida K et al. Complete recanalization of total occlusion in abdominal aorta by intraaortic infusion of a thrombolytic agent — a case report. *Angiology* 1993;45:574–579.

2. Bean WJ, Rodan BA, Thebaut AL. Leriche syndrome: Treatment with streptokinase and angioplasty. *AJR Am J Roentgenol* 1985;144:1285–1286.

3. Becker GI et al. Low dose fibrinolytic therapy. *Radiology* 1983;148:663-670.

4. Cunningham MW et al. Response of an abdominal aortic thrombotic occlusion to local low dose streptokinase therapy. *Surgery* 1983;93:541–544.

5. Gardiner GA. Thrombolysis of occluded arterial bypass grafts. *Cardiovasc Intervent Radiol* 1988;11:58–59.

6. Geoffette P, Kurdziel JC, Dondelinger RF. Local urokinase infusion for total occlusion of the lower abdominal aorta. *Eur J Radiol* 1989;9:121–124.

7. Graor RA. Thrombolysis with peripheral arterial percutaneous intervention. *Semin Vasc Surg* 1992;5:104–109.

8. Iyer SS, Hall P, Dorros G. Brachial approach to management of an abdominal aortic occlusion with prolonged lysis and subsequent angioplasty. *Cathet Cardiovasc Diagn* 1991;23:290–293.

9. Martin M, Fiebach BJO. Short-term ultrahigh streptokinase treatment of chronic arterial occlusions and acute deep vein thromboses. *Semin Thromb Hemost* 1991;17:21–38

10. Mathias K. Local thrombolysis for salvage of occluded bypass grafts. *Semin Thromb Hemost* 1991;17:14–20.

11. McNamara TO, Fisher JR. Thrombolysis of peripheral arterial and graft occlusions: Improved results using high dose urokinase. *AJR Am J Roentgenol* 1985;144:769–775.

12. Quiñones-Baldrich WJ. Regional Thrombolytic Therapy During Endovascular Surgery. In SS Ahn, WS Moore (eds), *Endovascular Surgery* (2nd ed). Philadelphia: Saunders, 1992.

13. Sullivan KL et al. Acceleration of thrombolysis with a high-dose transthrombus bolus technique. *Radiology* 1989;173:805–808.

14. Ward AS, Andaaz SK, Bygrave S. Thrombolysis with tissue-plasminogen activator: Results with a high-dose transthrombus technique. *J Vasc Surg* 1994;19:503–508.

Aortic Balloon Angioplasty

15. Belli AM et al. Percutaneous transluminal angioplasty of the distal abdominal aorta. *Eur J Vasc Surg* 1989;3:449–453.

16. Grollman JH, Del Vicario M, Mitlal AK. Percutaneous transluminal abdominal aortic angioplasty. *AJR Am J Roentgenol* 1980;134:1053–1054.

17. Heeney D et al. Transluminal angioplasty of the abdominal aorta. Report of 6 women. *Radiology* 1983;148:81–83.

18. Johnston KW. Factors that influence the outcome of aortoiliac and femoropopliteal percutaneous transluminal angioplasty. *Surg Clin North Am* 1992;72:843–850.

19. Johnston KW et al. 5-year results of a prospective study of percutaneous transluminal angioplasty. *Ann Surg* 1987;206:403–413.

20. Kumpe DK. Percutaneous dilatation of an abdominal aortic stenosis. Three-balloon-catheter technique. *Radiology* 1981;141:536–538.

21. Morag B et al. Percutaneous transluminal angioplasty of the distal abdominal aorta and its bifurcation. *Cardiovasc Intervent Radiol* 1987;10:129–133.

22. Ravimandalam K et al. Obstruction of the infrarenal portion of the abdominal aorta: Results of treatment with balloon angioplasty. *AJR Am J Roentgenol* 1991;156:1257–1260.

23. Shimshak TM, Giorgi LV, Hartzler GO. Successful percutaneous transluminal angioplasty of an obstructed abdominal aorta secondary to a chronic dissection. *Am J Cardiol* 1988;61:486–487.

24. Tadavarthy AK et al. Aorta balloon angioplasty: 9-year follow-up. *Radiology* 1989;170:1039–1041.

25. Tegtmeyer CJ, Nellous HA, Thompson RN. Balloon dilatation of the abdominal aorta. *JAMA* 1980;244:2636–2637.

26. Tegtmeyer CJ et al. Percutaneous transluminal angioplasty in the region of the aortic bifurcation. The two-balloon technique with results and long-term follow-up study. *Radiology* 1985;157:661–665.

27. Tegtmeyer CJ et al. Results and complications of angioplasty in aortoiliac disease. *Circulation* 1991;83(Suppl I):I-53–I-60.

28. Velasques C et al. Nonsurgical aortoplasty in Leriche syndrome. *Radiology* 1980;134:359–360.

29. Yakes WF et al. Percutaneous transluminal aortic angioplasty: Techniques and results. *Radiology* 1989;172:965–970.

Aortic Stent Implantation

30. Diethrich EB, Ravi R. Intraluminal stent implantation for the treatment of aortic graft stenosis. *J Invasive Cardiol* 1991;3:165–167.

31. Diethrich EB et al. Preliminary observations on the use of the Palmaz stent in the distal portion of the abdominal aorta. *Am Heart J* 1993;125:490–501.

32. Diethrich EB. Endovascular treatment of abdominal aortic occlusive disease: The impact of stents and intravascular ultrasound imaging. *Eur J Vasc Surg* 1993;7:228–236.

33. Diethrich EB. Endovascular techniques in abdominal aortic occlusions. *Int Angiol* 1993;12:270–280.

34. El Ashmaoui A et al. Angioplasty of the terminal aorta: Follow-up of 20 patients treated by PTA or PTA with stents. *Eur J Radiol* 1991;13:113–117.

35. Kueffer G, Spengel F, Steckmeier B. Percutaneous reconstruction of the aortic bifurcation with Palmaz stents: Case report. *Cardiovasc Intervent Radiol* 1991;14:170–172.

36. Palmaz JC et al. Aortic bifurcation stenosis: Treatment with intravascular stents. *J Vasc Intervent Radiol* 1991;2:319–323.

37. Vorwerk D et al. Stent placement for failed angioplasty of aortic stenosis: Report of two cases. *Cardiovasc Intervent Radiol* 1991;14:316–319.

38. Wolf YG et al. Initial experience with the Palmaz stent for aortoiliac stenoses. *Ann Vasc Surg* 1993;7:254–261.

Applications in Peripheral Vascular Surgery: Traumatic Arteriovenous Fistulas and Pseudoaneurysms

10

Carlos E. Donayre
Marco Scoccianti

The use of stents to anchor endoluminal-placed grafts in order to bypass and exclude abdominal aortic aneurysms has inspired the imagination of investigators around the world. The ability to deal with arterial lesions from a remote access site, along with the prediction of diminished morbidity, make endoluminal stented grafts particularly attractive as an alternative mode of therapy for various vascular disorders.

This chapter discusses the evolution and current applications of endoluminal grafts in peripheral vascular surgery. Their use in short or localized lesions (i.e., traumatic arteriovenous fistulas) is contrasted with the complex stenoses or occlusions encountered in femoropopliteal atherosclerotic disease.

Traumatic Arteriovenous Fistulas and Pseudoaneurysms

The incidence of arterial injury continues to increase because of both urban crime and violence and the widespread use of invasive interventional procedures [1, 2]. The close proximity of arteries and veins makes them vulnerable to the formation of arteriovenous fistulas and pseudoaneurysms when subjected to penetrating or iatrogenic trauma. Their operative management is often complex because of hemorrhage from an arterialized venous bed or difficult access that may require morbid surgical exposures. Since these traumatic injuries are more common in young, muscular men, even routine vessel exposure can be labor-intensive and complicated. Iatrogenic vascular injuries, on the other hand, tend to occur in elderly, debilitated patients with severe medical comorbidities. Not uncommonly, they follow attempts at myocardial revascularization by coronary balloon angioplasties, and the surgeon's task is compounded by having to intervene in a patient with a compromised heart. Operative morbidity and mortality are substantially increased in patients with vascular complications following diagnostic and therapeutic cardiac catheterizations [3].

Alternative, less invasive therapies include the use of intraluminal balloons and catheter-directed coil or particle embolization to achieve fistula closure [4, 5]. Duplex-directed external compression of the neck of traumatic pseudoaneurysms has also been used to thrombose and obliterate their lumens [6, 7].

The concept of minimally invasive endovascular techniques to exclude traumatic arteriovenous fistulas or bypass pseudoaneurysms, which could be associated with wider applicability, increased technical success, and a lower complication rate, was realized with the introduction of stented grafts. The first published report of the use of an intraluminal-lined stent to treat an arterial injury is that of Becker et al. [8]. A 43-year-old woman had a large-bore catheter mistakenly placed in her left subclavian artery during attempts at cannulating her subclavian vein. Due to the potential risk of hemorrhage or the need of a thoracotomy to obtain proximal control at the time of catheter removal, it was decided to deploy a covered stent to avoid such complications. A balloon-expandable, stainless steel, 30-mm Palmaz iliac stent was completely covered with a thin layer of silicone. It was then percutaneously deployed under flouroscopic guidance in the patient's left subclavian artery, as the large-bore catheter was removed. The covered stent was removed shortly afterward at the time of operative repair. The report focused on the use of lined stents to obtain vascular control, minimize blood loss, and decrease the operative exposure, not as a form of definitive arterial repair. Even though no follow-up was possible, they did demonstrate that a covered graft could be deployed safely and accurately through a remote site using a percutaneous approach.

The Parodi Device

Endoluminal treatment of arterial injuries by covered stents was a natural progression of Parodi's success with endovascular repair of abdominal aortic aneurysms (see Chapter 3). By modifying his initial concept, further clinical applications were investigated. A 62-year-old man was referred to him diagnosed as suffering from a "subclavian aneurysm" [9]. His history, however, was significant for having sustained a gunshot wound to the right chest two years earlier. The physical examination revealed all the classic signs of an arteriovenous fistula: pulsatile subclavian mass with a loud bruit, prominent subcutaneous venous pattern around the shoulder and chest, and hyperdynamic cardiomegaly. The angiogram demonstrated a large arteriovenous fistula with a subclavian and axillary artery of generous caliber and length at either end. The placement of a covered stent that could be delivered from a readily accessible artery and be used to obliterate the arteriovenous communication was entertained due to its technical simplicity. At the patient's request, endoluminal repair of his traumatic arteriovenous fistula was undertaken.

A Dacron graft was sutured to a Palmaz stent that could be fully expanded by a 10-mm balloon. In contrast to the aortic endoluminal grafts, the graft was totally supported by the stent (Fig. 10-1). The delivery sheath was introduced through the ipsilateral axillary artery,

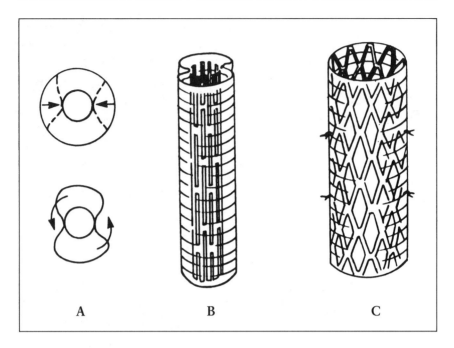

Fig. 10-1. Covered stent. A. Cross section of collapsed stent with graft attached, showing how graft is wrapped around the stent (arrows). B. Collapsed stent with Dacron graft attached, prior to folding. C. Fully expanded stent, with graft fully supported by the stent. (From JC Parodi. Endovascular repair of abdominal aortic aneurysms. *Adv Vasc Surg* 1993;1:96.)

and under fluoroscopic guidance the stented graft was properly deployed with balloon assistance. The clinical manifestations of the arteriovenous fistula immediately resolved, and a completion angiogram demonstrated closure of the fistula. Angiographic follow-up one month later (Fig. 10-2) displayed a patent subclavian artery without stenoses and absence of the arteriovenous fistula.

The technical and clinical success of this case led to its performance in six other patients (Table 10-1) [10]. One case merits further discussion. It involved a patient suffering from acquired immunodeficiency syndrome (AIDS) and a traumatic common carotid arteriovenous fistula secondary to a gunshot wound to the neck. To avoid a median sternotomy to gain proximal control and minimize blood exposure to the surgical team, endovascular repair

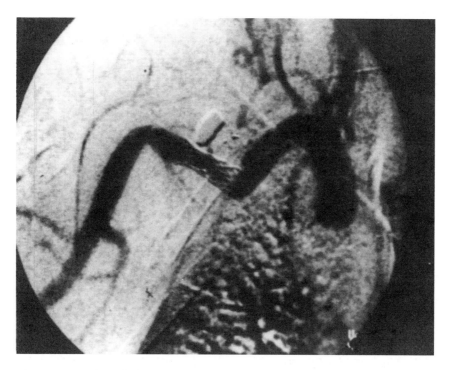

Fig. 10-2. Right subclavian angiogram one month after covered stent deployment demonstrates a patent subclavian artery without stenoses and absence of arteriovenous fistula. (From JC Parodi. Endovascular repair of abdominal aortic aneurysms. *Adv Vasc Surg* 1993;1:97.)

Table 10-1. Anatomic location of traumatic arteriovenous fistulas treated with a covered stent

Fistula location	Number (n = 7)
Subclavian artery and vein	3
Aorta and IVC	1
Right iliac artery and inferior vena cava	1
Superior femoral artery and vein	1
Common carotid and internal jugular vein*	1

*Treated with vein-covered stent.

of the injured artery was offered and chosen by the patient. There was concern over the use of Dacron or polytetrafluoroethylene (PTFE) material to cover a stent that was to be placed in both an immunocompromised patient and a freshly contaminated field. Thus, a properly selected Palmaz stent was wrapped with autologous, thin-walled vein and successfully deployed in a similar fashion as before. The greater saphenous vein remains the conduit of choice for operative arterial reconstructions in contaminated wounds, due to good long-term results and ease of access [11]. It seems likely that the same results will be achieved by stents covered with autologous vein, which decreases the potential for infection and subsequent thrombosis or vessel blow-out.

It can be readily surmised that the endovascular repair of peripheral arterial injuries requires the use of a smaller caliber carrier than that used in the treatment of aortic aneurysms. A single stent is required and can be covered by relatively thin material. Graft strength is not a major consideration, since the graft is supported by the stent in its entirety and does not have to heal inside thrombus. Thus, the next obvious step in the development of endovascular repair of arterial injuries was the percutaneous delivery of stented grafts, as initially demonstrated by Becker.

Marin and Parodi have reported the first percutaneous transfemoral insertion of a stented graft to repair a traumatic femoral arteriovenous fistula [12]. An 18-year-old man sustained a gunshot wound to the left thigh. On physical examination he was found to have marked leg swelling with a palpable thrill and diminished distal pulses. Femoral angiogram demonstrated a fistula between the superficial femoral artery and femoral vein and associated pseudoaneurysm (Fig. 10-3). Since distal vessels could not be visualized angiographically, duplex ultrasonography was used to define the size of the arterial defect and the diameter of the superficial femoral artery above and below the fistula (Fig. 10-4).

A 30-mm Palmaz balloon-expandable stent was covered by securing a 6- × 28-mm thin-walled PTFE graft to it. The stented graft was mounted on an 0.8- × 4-cm angioplasty balloon catheter and loaded into a 12 French introducer. Using local anesthesia, the ipsilateral common femoral artery was cannulated and a guidewire introduced, and the device was inserted percutaneously and, under

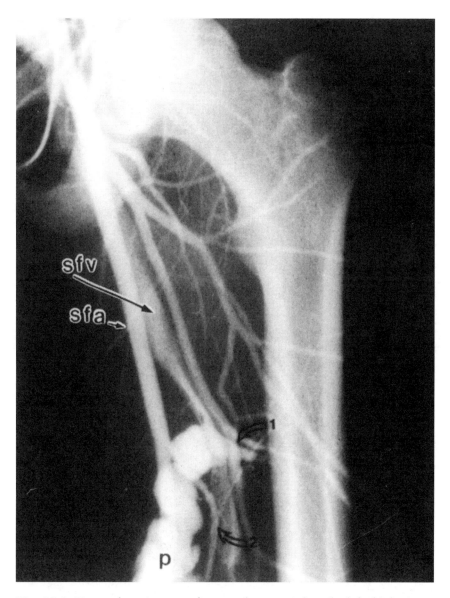

Fig. 10-3. Femoral angiogram after gunshot wound to the left thigh. An arteriovenous fistula is seen between left superficial femoral artery (sfa) and superficial femoral vein (sfv). Selective injection of deep femoral arterial branches (1) and SFA branch (2) showed these vessels were intact. (p = pseudoaneurysm.) (From ML Marin et al. Percutaneous transfemoral insertion of a stented graft to repair a traumatic femoral arteriovenous fistula. *J Vasc Surg* 1993;18:299.)

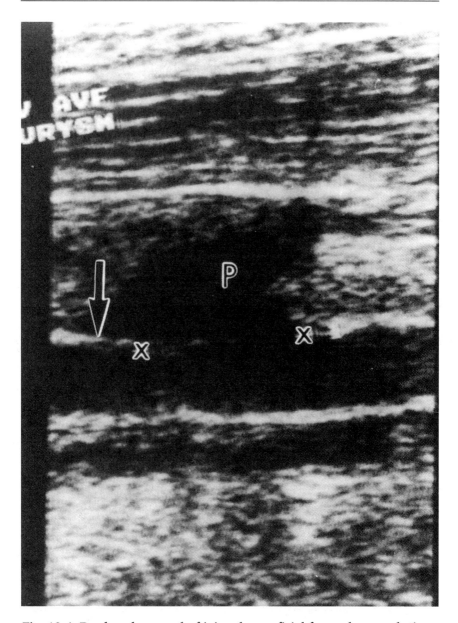

Fig. 10-4. Duplex ultrasound of injured superficial femoral artery depicted in Fig. 10-3. Loss of intimal stripe (arrow) and associated pseudoaneurysm (P) are seen. Arterial defect measures approximately 13 mm (distance between Xs). (From ML Marin et al. Percutaneous transfemoral insertion of a stented graft to repair a traumatic femoral arteriovenous fistula. *J Vasc Surg* 1993;18:300.)

fluoroscopic guidance, advanced over the guidewire. Once it was properly positioned, the delivery sheath was retracted, and the covered stent was balloon-expanded. Distal pulses returned immediately following graft deployment. Completion arteriography documented closure of the arteriovenous fistula and patency of the superficial femoral artery (Fig. 10-5).

Parodi et al. have reported their initial experience with the endovascular treatment of traumatic pseudoaneurysms and arteriovenous fistulas, with a follow-up of two to 20 months (average eight months) [13]. Their results have been impressive, with 100 percent patency of the treated vessels, persistent eradication of the fistulas or pseudoaneurysm, and no major complications.

Parodi's concept of endovascular repair has been successfully reproduced or modified by other investigators. May and White recently reported on the treatment of an iatrogenic subclavian artery pseudoaneurysm using a prosthetic graft-stent device [14]. A 78-year-old man with pyloric obstruction developed pulsatile swelling in his right supraclavicular fossa one week following attempts at catheterization of his subclavian vein for total parenteral nutrition. The patient was monitored for another week, but the swelling increased in size. A duplex scan showed a 5-cm pseudoaneurysm in the right subclavian artery. Innominate arteriography confirmed the duplex findings and demonstrated normal subclavian and axillary arteries proximal and distal to the pseudoaneurysm (Fig. 10-6).

The operation was performed under general anesthesia with the patient's arm outstretched 90 degrees to his body. A standard PTFE tube graft, 0.64 mm thickness, was not selected to minimize bulk. Instead, two PTFE patches (Gore-Tex, W. L. Gore & Associates, Flagstaff, AZ) 0.4 mm in thickness, were cut to appropriate length and sutured together to form a cylinder 1 cm in diameter. The completed graft was secured to an unexpanded 8-mm Palmaz steel stent and mounted on a balloon catheter (Johnson & Johnson Interventional Systems, Warren, NJ). The diameter of the subclavian measured 8.3 mm proximal to the aneurysm and 7.6 mm distally.

Access was obtained via an incision into the brachial artery in the upper arm. A 16 French peel-away sheath and dilator (William A. Cook, Queensland, Australia) were introduced into the brachial

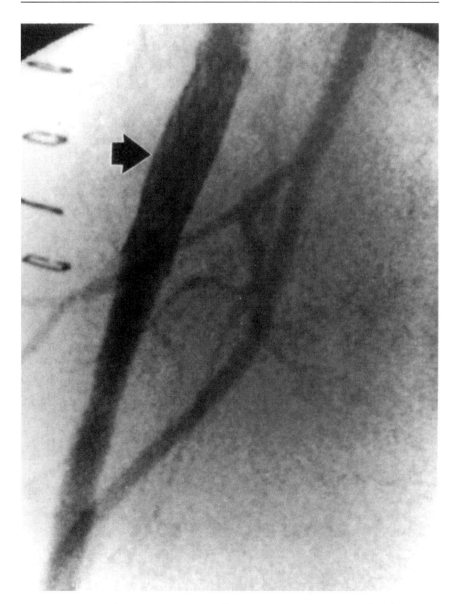

Fig. 10-5. Completion arteriogram demonstrates patent superficial femoral artery, proper positioning of stented graft (arrow), and no evidence of arteriovenous fistula or extravasation. Metal clips were applied to skin before procedure to facilitate fluoroscopic localization and proper placement of stented graft. (From ML Marin et al. Percutaneous transfemoral insertion of a stented graft to repair a traumatic femoral arteriovenous fistula. *J Vasc Surg* 1993;18:300.)

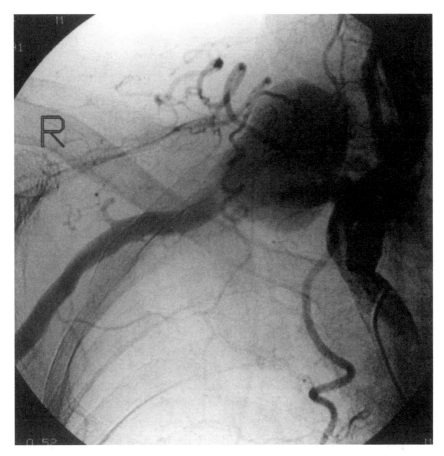

Fig. 10-6. Preoperative angiogram showing false aneurysm of the right subclavian artery. Subclavian and axillary arteries distal to aneurysm are of normal caliber. (From J May et al. Transluminal placement of a prosthetic graft-stent device for treatment of a subclavian artery aneurysm. *J Vasc Surg* 1993;18:1057.)

artery and advanced over the guidewire just distal to the pseudoaneurysm. The graft-stent device was delivered by advancing the balloon catheter over the guidewire and correctly positioned across the lesion. The stent was deployed, thereby anchoring the graft in place and excluding the aneurysm sac. The main difficulty encountered was that of balloon rupture within the stent. This was corrected by replacing the balloon with a high-pressure Blue Max (Meditech/Boston Scientific, Watertown, MA) 8-mm balloon to

227

achieve complete expansion of the covered stent. During the balloon exchange, displacement of the stent-graft was prevented by holding the introducing sheath against its distal aspect. Balloon rupture at the time of stent expansion may be caused by constriction of the prosthetic material around the stent, requiring excessive pressure for inflation, or by perforation of the thin-walled balloon by the metallic struts of the stent.

Completion arteriogram confirmed normal flow through the graft and no leak of contrast into the aneurysm sac (Fig. 10-7). The patient has had no complications and has normal circulation in the right arm 18 months after endovascular repair [15].

Corvita Endovascular Graft

Other experimental covered stents have also been developed to reduce the diameter of the device and permit percutaneous delivery and deployment. One such prosthesis that appears to be extremely suitable for percutaneous use is the Corvita endovascular graft, which was first conceived by Jean-Pierre Derume, head of the Department of Vascular Pathology at the Erasmus University Hospital in Brussels, Belgium. The stent component of this endovascular graft is comprised of a Didcott braided self-expanding stent (see Chapter 11) constructed of Elgiloy wire with a pitch angle of approximately 85 degrees and 40 percent length change when completely extended. Polycarbonate urethane fibers, with a fiber diameter of 10 to 20 μm, are then applied to the inner, outer, or both surfaces of the stent such that the pitch angle of the graft component matches the pitch angle of the fully expanded stent [16]. This endovascular graft can be produced in various lengths, with one or both ends of the stent exposed, and it can be easily cut to the appropriate length prior to insertion in the operating room. It is presently available in diameters ranging from 4 to 44 mm and in lengths from 3 to 30 cm (Fig. 10-8).

The advantages of the Corvita endovascular graft, a fully stented elastomeric prosthesis, are the following:

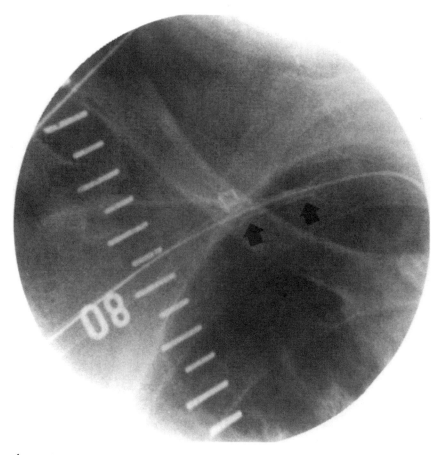

A

Fig. 10-7. A. Guidewire across pseudoaneurysm and covered stent in place prior to deployment. Arrows mark both ends of the stent. B. Completion arteriogram showing normal flow through the right subclavian artery without leakage of contrast into the aneurysm sac. Proximal and distal ends of the graft-stent device are indicated (arrows). Heavy metallic markings of radiopaque ruler are seen in both figures. (From J May et al. Transluminal placement of a prosthetic graft-stent device for the treatment of a subclavian artery aneurysm. *J Vasc Surg* 1993;18:1059.)

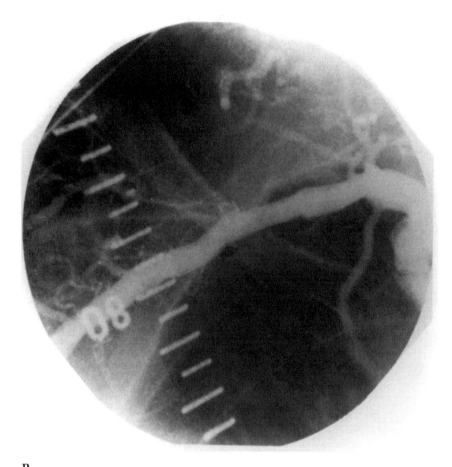

B

Fig. 10-7 *(continued)*

1. Ease of deployment and the fact that hooks are not needed to anchor the prosthesis and prevent its migration.
2. Percutaneous insertion is facilitated, since it can be compressed into a delivery sheath with a very small diameter (as small as 9 French). Furthermore, its small size and flexibility allow it to negotiate tortuous or stenotic access vessels.
3. After deployment it seems to adapt well to an arterial lumen of varying diameters

European implantation of an early version of the Corvita endovascular graft began in February 1993. Only high-risk

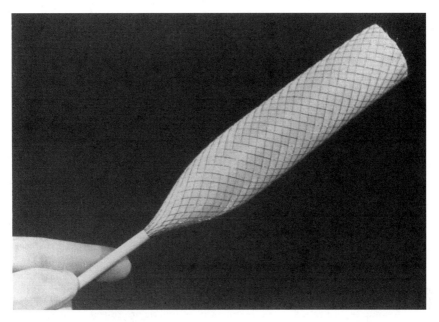

Fig. 10-8. Corvita endovascular graft (35 mm × 15 cm) being deployed from an 18 French sheath.

patients requiring urgent vascular intervention were eligible for enrollment in this study. Fourteen patients afflicted with a variety of vascular lesions were enrolled, and successful deployment was achieved in 11 of them. The advantages of this prosthesis make it particularly well-suited for the percutaneous endovascular repair of traumatic arteriovenous fistulas or pseudoaneurysms (Table 10-2). With the exception of one patient with an expanding aneurysm of the aortic arch who died two weeks postoperatively from a myocardial infarction, all patients are doing well with a follow-up of five weeks to 13 months [17].

Technical reasons accounted for failure of graft deployment in three patients with aneurysms. In one case, the endovascular graft was cut too short to cover the full length of an abdominal aortic aneurysm, and in the other two, iliac artery angulation did not permit the passage of the loaded introducer system. These three patients were successfully treated by standard surgical procedures.

231

Table 10-2. Clinical experience in Europe with Corvita endovascular graft[a]

Indication	Number (n = 11)
True aneurysms	3
Aortic arch	
Thoracic aorta	
Iliac artery	
Pseudoaneurysms	3
Subclavian artery	
Iliac artery (2)[b]	
Arteriovenous fistulas	4
Iliocaval (2)	
Axilo-axillary (2)	
Iliac artery stenosis	1

[a]Most common indication is the treatment of traumatic arteriovenous fistulas and pseudoaneurysms.
[b]One iliac artery pseudoaneurysm associated with a dissecting aneurysm.

Conclusion

The initial endovascular experience with the repair of traumatic arteriovenous fistulas and pseudoaneurysms using covered stents has met with high technical success and low morbidity. These injuries are usually localized to a small arterial segment, with normal vessel architecture at either end. Even if the vessel is totally transected, bleeding may be contained by muscle and fascial compartments to create a pulsatile hematoma. The major morbidity associated with their operative repair is related to the difficulty encountered in achieving adequate exposure and control of the injured vessel. Hemorrhage can be extensive since the procedure is performed in an area where the veins have become engorged from the direct connection to arterial flow. Muscles and tendons frequently need to be retracted or transected to allow access to the site of damage.

Endovascular access is achieved from a remote site, located distant from the area of injury, and on occasion can be gained by percutaneous techniques. Usually, only the affected vessel is manipulated, minimizing injury to the surrounding structures. If successful, the patient would benefit by having a shortened hospitalization and a quicker return to normal function. As experience is gained with this type of repair, it may be possible to treat even acutely bleeding patients by using advanced imaging modalities, such as intravascular ultrasound, to rapidly assess the site of injury and, in combination with intraoperative fluoroscopy, deploy a stented graft. Endovascular grafts with varying expansion ratios that can be cut to appropriate lengths and are ready for deployment, such as the Corvita graft, appear ideally suited for this type of approach.

The major concern is long-term function and patency of stented grafts because they are often placed in young patients. Autologous veins used as interposition grafts have performed well and have stood the test of time with documented patency of nearly 30 years in some cases [18]. Dacron and PTFE have also been used successfully as synthetic conduits in the operative management of arterial and venous injuries. They are used when autologous vein is not available or is of inadequate luminal size or quality, or if the patient requires expedient vascular reconstruction and vessel ligation is to be avoided. While the long-term patency rates appear to be less with these synthetic conduits, previous concerns about potential infection have not been realized in civilian reports [19, 20]. The patency of endovascular stented grafts used for the repair of traumatic arteriovenous fistulas and pseudoaneurysms may be affected by the fact that they tend to be short in length and are placed in vessels with relatively large diameter and high flow rates, such as iliac or subclavian arteries. Furthermore, the graft is entirely supported by a stent and usually bridges normal vessels.

If progressive stenosis is encountered with time, therapeutic options may be broadened by not having to intervene in an acutely injured patient. The stenotic areas may be dilated by a percutaneously performed balloon angioplasty or may require deployment of an additional stent. Until long-term follow-up is available, placing these patients on antiplatelet therapy seems prudent.

Another concern is the risk of stent compression when subjected to trauma, or when the stents are placed in locations where they may be scissored by osseous and muscular structures. This has been encountered with stents placed for subclavian vein stenoses. Salvage by balloon angioplasty may be feasible, but there should be careful attention to their anatomic placement at the time of deployment. Nonetheless, the endovascular repair of traumatic arteriovenous fistulas and pseudoaneurysms represents a major advance in the treatment of these lesions and may affect their current management if long-term patency is achieved.

References

1. Feliciano DV et al. Civilian trauma in the 1980s: A 1 year experience with 456 vascular and cardiac injuries. *Ann Surg* 1984;199:717.

2. Youkey JR et al. Vascular trauma secondary to diagnostic and therapeutic procedures: 1974 through 1982. *Am J Surg* 1983;146:788.

3. Messina LM et al. Clinical characteristics and surgical management of vascular complications in patients undergoing cardiac catheterizations: Interventional versus diagnostic procedures. *J Vasc Surg* 1991;13:593–600.

4. Keller FS et al. Iatrogenic internal mammary artery to inominate vein fistula. *Chest* 1982;81:255–257.

5. Nakamura T et al. Iatrogenic arteriovenous fistula of the internal mammary artery: Intravascular coil occlusion. *Arch Intern Med* 1985;145:140–141.

6. Schwend R et al. Obliteration of pseudoaneurysms by manual compression utilizing color duplex imaging. Presented at the San Diego Symposium on Vascular Diagnosis. February 1992, San Diego, CA.

7. Feld R, Patton GMN, Carabasi A. Treatment of iatrogenic femoral artery injuries with ultrasound-guided compression. *J Vasc Surg* 1992;16:832–840.

8. Becker GJ et al. Percutaneous placement of a balloon-expandable intraluminal graft for life-threatening subclavian arterial hemorrhage. *J Vasc Intervent Radiol* 1991;2:225–229.

9. Parodi JC, Barone HD. Transluminal treatment of abdominal aortic aneurysms and peripheral arteriovenous fistulas. Presented at the 19th Annual Montefiore Medical Center/Albert Einstein College of Medicine Symposium on Current Critical Problems and New Technologies in Vascular Surgery. November 1992, New York, NY.

10. Parodi JC. Endovascular treatment of abdominal aortic aneurysms. Presented at VII International Congress, Endovascular Interventions: On the Cutting Edge. February 1994, Scottsdale, AZ.

11. Rich NM, Baugh JH, Hughes CW. Acute arterial injuries in Vietnam: 1,000 cases. *J Trauma* 1970;10:359.

12. Marin ML et al. Percutaneous transfemoral insertion of a stented graft to repair a traumatic femoral arteriovenous fistula. *J Vasc Surg* 1993;18:299–302.

13. Parodi JC. Abdominal aortic aneurysms. Presented at the 1994 Research Initiatives in Vascular Disease, symposium on transluminally placed endovascular prostheses. March 1994, Bethesda, MD.

14. May J et al. Transluminal placement of a prosthetic graft-stent device for treatment of a subclavian artery aneurysm. *J Vasc Surg* 1993;18:1056–1059.

15. White G, May J. Transluminal placement of a prosthetic graft-stent device for the treatment of a subclavian artery aneurysm. Personal communication, 1994.

16. Wilson GJ et al. A compliant Corethane/Dacron composite vascular prosthesis: Comparison with 4-mm ePTFE grafts in a canine model. *ASAIO Trans* 1993;39:M526–531.

17. Derume J, et al. The Corvita endovascular graft: Device description and early clinical results. Personal communication, 1994.

18. Hierton T, Hemingsson A. The autogenous vein graft as popliteal arterial substitute: Long-term follow-up of cystic advential degeneration. *Acta Chir Scand* 1984;150:3770.

19. Feliciano DV et al. Five year experience with PTFE in vascular wounds. *J Trauma* 1985;25:75.

20. Feliciano DV et al. Management of vascular injuries in the lower extremities. *J Trauma* 1988;28:319.

Applications in Peripheral Vascular Surgery: Femoropopliteal Disease

11

Carlos E. Donayre
Marco Scoccianti

Balloon Angioplasty and Stenting of Iliac Vessels

The success of percutaneous balloon angioplasty in the treatment of atherosclerotic iliac disease is well established. In 1989 Becker et al. reviewed data from 2,697 iliac artery angioplasties reported in the literature and calculated a mean two-year patency rate of 81 percent and a five-year patency rate of 72 percent [1]. In the only randomized trial comparing iliac angioplasty against surgery, which involved 157 patients reported by Wilson et al. from the Veterans Administration in 1989, there were no significant differences between them at three years [2]. Transluminal angioplasty did encounter two primary limitations: intimal dissection and elastic recoil. To overcome this liability arterial stents were introduced. The stent performs as a scaffold, overcoming the recoil forces and compressing plaque in intimal dissections against the vessel wall.

A prospective, randomized trial of iliac stent placement versus angioplasty using the Palmaz stent was recently completed in Germany [3]. A five-year cumulative angiographic patency of 94 percent was obtained in the stent group, versus 65 percent in the angioplasty group ($p = .001$). In the United States, the only application of arterial stents approved by the Food and Drug Administration is for iliac angioplasty using the Palmaz balloon-expandable intravascular stent (Johnson & Johnson Interventional Systems, Warren, NJ). Indications for their use include suboptimal outcome of angioplasty based on hemodynamic measurements, total occlusions, restenosis, and extensive intimal dissections.

Balloon Angioplasty and Stenting of Femoropopliteal Vessels

Following the success of balloon angioplasty in treating iliac lesions, the short segmental stenoses or occlusions commonly encountered in the superficial femoral artery seemed ideal candidates for the same therapeutic modalities. Femoral angioplasty in the Nuremberg Cooperative Trial included 1,540 stenoses and 1,268 occlusions in patients afflicted mostly with claudication [4]. The overall one-year patency rate was 79 percent, and at three years the rate fell to 67 percent. The mortality was 0.17 percent, and no legs were lost acutely. When balloon angioplasty is compared to infrainguinal surgical bypass with untreated critical ischemia, the results are markedly different [5]. In this population the two-year patency rate after balloon angioplasty (18 percent) was significantly lower than after femoropopliteal (68 percent) or femorodistal (47 percent) bypasses. Furthermore, half of the 39 initially successful angioplasties reoccluded during the follow-up period.

Early treatment failures following angioplasty of femoral artery occlusions average 20 percent [6, 7] and have led to stent placement to improve these results. Current experience suggests that superficial femoral artery stenting should be limited to lesions shorter than 6 cm that have significant elastic recoil or flow-limiting dissection following balloon angioplasty. The segment of the superficial artery that appears to be most amenable to stenting extends from 5 cm below the inguinal ligament to the adductor canal.

Bergeron and associates recently presented their four-year results with Palmaz stent placement in the superficial artery [8]. They placed 54 stents in 41 arteries of patients with claudication (79 percent) and critical ischemia (21 percent). Early thrombosis before discharge occurred in only five percent. Mean follow-up of 24 months revealed a restenosis rate of 19 percent (34 percent for occlusions and 10 percent for stenoses) and a primary patency rate of 80 percent.

The use of self-expanding vascular stents in patients with failed femoropopliteal angioplasties was successfully performed by Triller et al. in 26 patients [9]. Five developed thrombosis in the first nine days, but four of them were salvaged by thrombolytic therapy. After nine months they report a patency rate of 87 percent. This group advocates the use of long-term anticoagulation to prevent thrombosis in patients undergoing stent placement in the femoral artery. Zollikofer et al. deployed self-expandable Wallstents across 15 lesions (stenoses in three, occlusions in 12) in the femoropopliteal region immediately following balloon angioplasty. Only two of the occlusions measured 3 cm or less, with occlusion length averaging 9 cm in length in the superficial artery and 18 cm in the femoropopliteal artery. Of the 11 patients available for follow-up, only six had patent stents at 20 months, with four of them requiring one to three secondary interventions. They concluded that stent placement for long femoral artery lesions should be performed with the utmost reserve, and the length of stent placement should be as short as possible to reduce the thrombogenic foreign-body surface [10].

Stented Grafts for Femoropopliteal Disease

Stents have been successful in lowering the immediate failure rate following balloon angioplasty of the femoropopliteal region, but their nemesis appears to be a high rate of restenosis. Stents undergo complete endothelial coverage by four months, with the thickness of the neointima being proportional to the time elapsed following insertion [8]. The greater proliferative response seen in the femoral region, lower flow rates, smaller vessel caliber, and compromised outflow are not improved with the placement of a stent. Current investigations are thus aimed at modulating the restenosis caused by vascular smooth-muscle cell proliferation elicited by angioplasty endothelial injury. In vitro and animal studies have shown that heparin inhibits smooth-cell proliferation by an action independent of anticoagulation. Jorgensen et al. treated six patients suffering from claudication secondary to superficial artery stenoses by balloon angioplasty and Palmaz stent deployment. This was immediately followed by 30 minutes of enclosed application of 2,000 anti-Xa units of Fragmin (low molecular weight heparin) at the stented site by means of a double-balloon catheter [11]. Regular examination by duplex scanning showed no signs of restenosis during an average of five months of observation. The results of this work suggest that short-term target of low molecular weight heparin may reduce the restenosis rate. Metal stents have also been coated with endothelial cells genetically engineered to produce tissue plasminogen activator in hope of retarding thrombosis [12].

Another concept involves placing a barrier between the stent and the site of the balloon-induced injury. This concept can be traced to Didcott, who developed a self-expanding dilator to treat and palliate benign and malignant esophageal strictures in the early 1970s. He manufactured his dilator by weaving together a series of stainless steel helices running in opposite curvature. This design was fashioned after the basic structure of fibrous layers seen running in some hollow organs of the body. The dilator was then covered by a thin layer of rubber to give it more elasticity and prevent tumor ingrowth (Fig. 11-1) [13]. Insertion and removal into the esophagus were performed by squeezing it into a streamlined thin-walled Teflon tube. The carrier tube and dilator were passed across the stricture, and the dilator extruded in situ by holding it steady with a rod while the Teflon tube was withdrawn. By placing a nylon purse string thread around the stent mouth, removal was made simple since pulling on the purse string caused elongation and collapse of the prosthesis (Fig. 11-2). The similarities of this covered stent with the currently available vascular endoprosthesis are remarkable. Upon submission of his manuscript in 1973, Didcott expanded on the potential uses of his dilator, including various vascular applications such as endo-

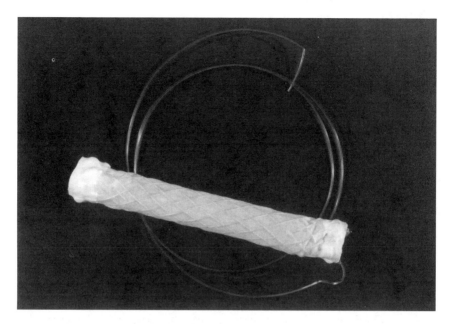

Fig. 11-1. Didcott dilator stainless steel stent covered with thin layer of rubber used to treat and palliate esophageal strictures.

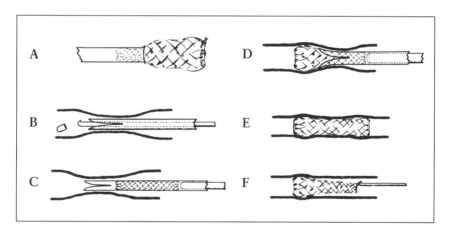

Fig. 11-2. Deployment of Didcott dilator. A. Dilator being loaded into introducer sheath. B. Removal of cap from introducer. C. Passage of dilator across stricture. D. Dilator being deployed across stricture site. E. Dilator in place. F. Removal of dilator.

luminal bypass of stenotic lesion, but this section was not published as the editors thought it should be the subject of further papers.

Cragg and Dake have the largest experience with the percutaneous revascularization of long-segment femoropopliteal occlusions [14]. Their rationale for this technique is to isolate the segment of diseased femoral artery by endoluminal bypass, thereby lessening the chance that intimal hyperplasia will intervene to produce restenosis (Fig. 11-3). The occlusions were traversed with wires and thrombolysis was carried out with urokinase to lyse clot whenever possible. A 6-mm thin-walled polytetrafluorethylene (PTFE) graft was attached with 7-0 polypropylene interrupted sutures to a self-expanding stent constructed of nitinol wire. The advantages of monofilament nitinol wire are its thermal memory, high hoop strength, longitudinal and radial flexibility, and little foreshortening following deployment [15]. The graft was delivered by compressing it in a tubular loading catheter and pushing it through a 12 French sheath. Deployment was then accomplished by withdrawing the sheath, followed by dilatation of the externally supported graft to 6 mm (Fig. 11-4).

Eight patients have been treated using a stented graft deployed with the aid of a variety of catheter-based techniques. In the patients enrolled in the study, there were no technical failures resulting from an inability to recanalize an occlusion or deploy the endoprosthesis. Six of the 8 of the patients are symptom-free and have a patent graft with a mean follow-up of five months. Only one patient has required further operative intervention for endograft thrombosis, one week following the procedure. He required an in situ saphenous vein bypass, but despite patency of his bypass a below-knee amputation had to be performed because of progressive ischemia. Another patient developed acute claudication in the treated leg after bending in his garden. Angiography revealed thrombosis of the graft due to partial collapse of the distal stent. Endovascular rescue with thrombolysis and balloon redilation of the stented graft was successful in restoring flow and relieving symptoms. The outcome for this patient illustrates the continuous concern about the effect of repeated bending on grafts placed across joints.

Currently the Endo Pro System 1 is undergoing clinical trials in France. It is a flexible, self-expanding endoprosthesis consisting of a

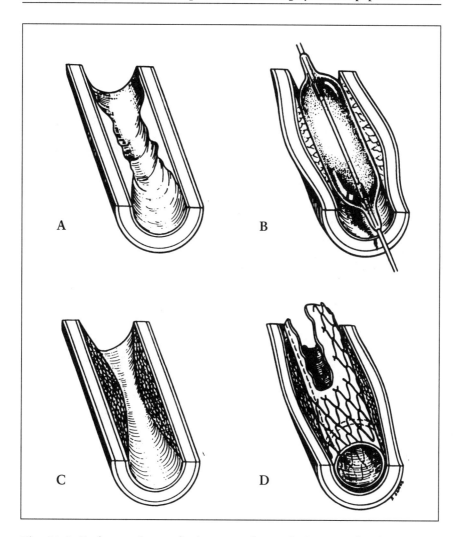

Fig. 11-3. Endovascular graft placement for occlusive vascular disease.
A. Vessel with stenosis. B. Balloon angioplasty. C. Late restenosis after
balloon angioplasty is usually due to fibrocellular intimal proliferation.
D. Endoluminal bypass with microporous graft should limit the develop-
ment of intimal hyperplasia in the anastomotic zones and improve long-
term patency of long-segment percutaneous revascularization. (From A
Cragg, M Dake. Percutaneous femoropopliteal graft placement. *J Vasc
Intern Radiol* 1993;4:461.)

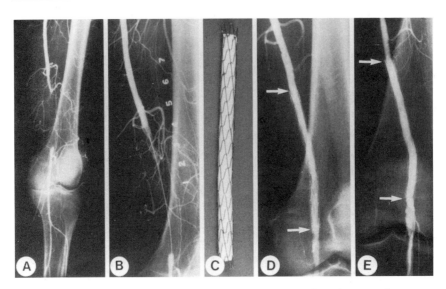

Fig. 11-4. Disabling left calf claudication. A. Femoral angiogram demonstrates a 10-cm long occlusion of the distal superior femoral artery and proximal popliteal arteries. B. Arteriogram after thrombolysis and angioplasty of the involved segment shows persistent occlusion. C. Self-expanding, externally supported PTFE endovascular graft; stent is largely outside the flow surface. D. Arteriogram after placement of stented graft shows widely patent arterial segment. E. Follow-up arteriogram 10 months after demonstrates widely patent graft. Arrows indicate the treated segment. Patient was asymptomatic, with normal ankle-brachial index after exercise. (From A Cragg, M Dake. Percutaneous femoropopliteal graft placement. *J Vasc Intern Radiol* 1993;4:456.)

Cragg stent covered with an ultrathin polyester woven fabric bonded with Fragmin R (fractioned low molecular weight heparin). The thickness of the stent is only 0.7 mm [16]. Its size and flexibility make it ideally suited for percutaneous deployment. The investigators further theorize that their fabric may heal better, may keep flaps and debris from going through the mesh of the stent, and may prevent migration of smooth-muscle cells; therefore it could inhibit fibrous proliferation.

In clinical use, nine symptomatic patients have been treated with the Endo Pro System 1. The lesions were located in the iliac (one), femoral (seven), and popliteal (one) arteries. The indications for use were four residual stenoses and delaminations after holmium laser and balloon angioplasty of long occlusions (6 to 10 cm), two long restenoses (8 to 10 cm) treated primarily with balloon angioplasty, and three suboptimal results after balloon angioplasty of a long stenosis. Seven patients received one stent measuring 10 cm in length and 6 mm in diameter, one patient required two stents with the above dimensions, and the remaining patient was treated with a stent measuring 6 cm in length and 8 mm in diameter. The deployment was simple, with the stents sufficiently expanded after balloon dilation to enlarge the arterial lumen. Technical success was 100 percent. Two thromboses occurred after two weeks and were successfully treated with thrombolysis.

In the United States the group at Montefiore Medical Center headed by Marin and Veith have inserted 27 endovascular stented grafts in 18 patients with limb-threatening aortoiliac or femoropopliteal occlusive diseases that coexisted with one or more major contraindications to standard revascularization procedures. In two patients with previously placed aortoiliac endoluminal grafts and in four additional patients with isolated limb-threatening femoropopliteal occlusions, a femoropopliteal endovascular stented graft was inserted via an open femoral arteriotomy. Total vessel occlusions were managed by traversing guidewires across them and performance of balloon angioplasty or laser recanalization. The grafts were constructed of 6-mm expandable PTFE material and attached distally to an appropriately sized Palmaz stent. A 14 French sheath measuring 30 to 40 cm was used to deliver the distally stented graft to its proper location. Distal fixation to the popliteal artery was achieved by balloon deployment of the Palmaz stent. The proximal end of each graft was sutured to the native artery using standard techniques. One patient died two weeks after implantation from unrelated causes but with a patent graft. Another patient's graft occluded after two weeks. The remaining four grafts remain patent three to eight months after implantation [17].

Marin and Veith also reported the successful exclusion of a popliteal artery aneurysm from the circulation using Parodi's concept of intraluminal bypass [18]. A 63-year-old man with an extensive cardiac history presented with an acutely thrombosed left popliteal aneurysm. On physical examination he lacked distal pulses on the left leg, but the motor and sensory examinations were normal. A large pulsatile popliteal mass was noted in the contralateral leg. Duplex scanning demonstrated a thrombosed left popliteal aneurysm and a right popliteal aneurysm measuring 2.6 × 15.0 cm. Findings were confirmed by angiography (Fig. 11-5). Due to his comorbid medical state and the viability of his left leg one month following presentation, operative intervention was not carried out.

Transfemoral grafting of the asymptomatic right popliteal aneurysm was undertaken because of its size, the presence of mural thrombus, and the patient's complex cardiac history. A proximal right femoral cutdown was performed under local anesthesia. The proximal end of a 6-mm stretch PTFE graft was sutured to a Palmaz balloon-expandable stent with two interrupted sutures, and the graft-stent device was mounted on a 3.0- × 0.8-cm angioplasty balloon. The completed device was loaded into a 14 French introducer catheter and passed over a wire under fluoroscopic control across the popliteal aneurysm. The proximal stent was deployed first to anchor the graft, and a second 15-mm Palmaz stent was deployed to fix the distal end to the below-knee popliteal artery. Postoperative angiogram documented exclusion of the aneurysm and normal flow to the tibial arteries (Fig. 11-6). His graft is patent, and he remains asymptomatic three months after endoluminal bypass.

General Considerations

The success of the endoluminal repair of aneurysms is predicated on the delivery of a stented graft inside a dilated, high-flow vessel with adequate vessel targets located proximal and distal to the aneurysm. The endovascular treatment of traumatic and arteriovenous fistulas relies on the delivery of a short graft, supported entirely by a stent, and again usually placed in areas of high flow and usually good outflow. Both appear to lower the morbidity and reduce the recovery time that is seen with standard operative repair and should deliver similar patency rates.

Femoropopliteal occlusive disease offers different challenges and obstacles for the successful performance of intraluminal bypasses. The vessels in question range in size from 4 to 7 mm, have diminished flow, and are hampered by a compromised outflow of either

246

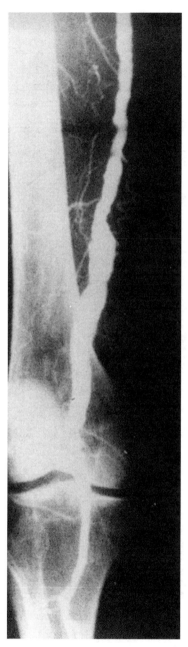

Fig. 11-5. Angiogram of right popliteal aneurysm. Popliteal artery is patent, tortuous, and aneurysmal. (From ML Marin et al. Transfemoral endoluminal stented graft repair of a popliteal aneurysm. *J Vasc Surg* 1994;19:755.)

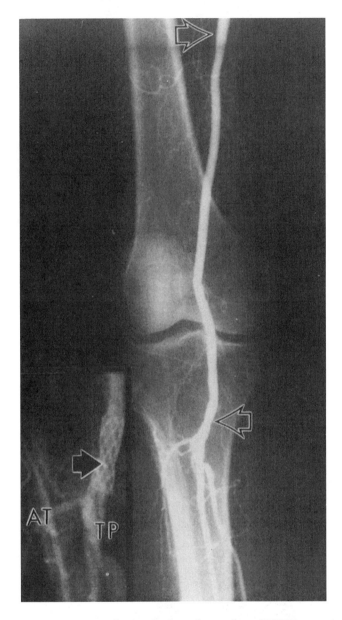

Fig. 11-6. Completion arteriogram obtained after placement of PTFE graft-stent device shows exclusion of the aneurysm (see Fig. 11-5) and graft patency. Arrows show area of stent deployment. Inset shows detail of stent in distal popliteal artery. (TP = tibioperoneal trunk; AT = anterior tibial artery.) (From ML Marin et al. Transfemoral endoluminal stented graft repair of a popliteal aneurysm. *J Vasc Surg* 1994;19:755.)

one or two patent calf vessels. The incidence of diabetes is higher in this patient population, and one has to be concerned with their thrombogenic potential. Added to these factors are the inherent limitations associated with the use of stents in the treatment of femoropopliteal occlusive disease. Grafts have been attached to stents with the hope of providing a barrier to the aggressive intimal proliferation that takes place following endovascular recanalization of these vessels. Grafts with balloon-expandable stents attached at either end to act as arterial anchors are simple to introduce and deploy. However, mismatch of artery and stent diameter by more than 20 percent, resulting in overexpansion of the arterial wall, may induce intimal proliferation. Compliance mismatch introduced by having a graft–arterial wall–stent interphase may cause flow disturbances and shear rates conducive to intimal hyperplasia and graft thrombosis. If the midgraft is not supported, folds may occur due to the tube-within-a-tube design and the associated elastic recoil and fibrosis that follow balloon dilatation of lengthy occlusions. If folds do form, further flow alterations will also be created. Morbidity is not reduced by a great extent; most patients will require surgical exposure of the common femoral vessels, and cost may adversely impact on the performance of these procedures.

Although the technical success and short-term patency of intraluminal bypasses for femoropopliteal disease have been adequate, several issues need to be addressed. Ultimately, the durability of these techniques must be proven and compared to traditional bypass surgery before they can be recommended on a wider scale.

References

1. Becker GJ, Katzen BT, Dake MD. Noncoronary angioplasty. *Radiology* 1989;170:403–412.

2. Wilson SE, Wolf GL, Cross AP. Percutaneous transluminal angioplasty versus operation for peripheral arteriosclerosis. *J Vasc Surg* 1989;9:1–9.

3. Richter GM et al. Further update of the randomized trial: Iliac stent placement versus PTA—Morphology, clinical success rates,

and failure analysis. *J Vasc Intervent Radiol* 1993;4:30.

4. Zeitler E et al. Results of percutaneous angioplasty. *Radiology* 1983;146:57.

5. Blair JM et al. Percutaneous transluminal angioplasty versus surgery for limb-threatening ischemia. *J Vasc Surg* 1989;9:698–703.

6. Martin EC et al. Angioplasty for femoral artery occlusion: Comparison with surgery. *AJR Am J Roentgenol* 1981;137:915–919.

7. Krepel VM et al. Percutaneous transluminal angioplasty to the femoropopliteal artery: Initial and long-term results. *Radiology* 1985;156:325–328.

8. Bergeron P, Pinot JJ, Benichou H. Four-year results of SFA Palmaz stenting. Presented at the VII International Congress on Endovascular Interventions. February 1994, Scottsdale, AZ.

9. Triller J et al. Vascular endoprosthesis for femoral-popliteal occlusive disease. *Rofo Fortschr Geb Rontgenstr Nuklearmed* 1989;150:328.

10. Zollikofer C et al. Arterial stent placement with use of the Wallstent: Midterm results of clinical experience. *Radiology* 1991;179:449–456.

11. Jorgensen B et al. Prevention of restenosis after superficial femoral artery stenting by target application of low-molecular weight heparin. Presented at VII International Congress on Endovascular Interventions. February 1994, Scottsdale, AZ.

12. Dichek DA et al. Seeding of intravascular stents with genetically engineered endothelial cells. *Circulation* 1989;80:1347–1353.

13. Didcott C. Esophageal stricture: Treatment by slow continuous dilatation. *Ann Royal Coll Surg* 1973;53:112.

14. Cragg A, Dake M. Percutaneous femoropopliteal graft placement. *J Vasc Intern Radiol* 1993;4:455–463.

15. Cragg AH, et al. Preclinical evaluation of the Cragg stent [abstract]. *Radiology* 1992;185(P):162.

16. Henry M, et al. Initial clinical experience with a Cragg stent in peripheral arteries. Presented at VII International Congress on Endovascular Interventions. February 1994, Scottsdale, AZ.

17. Veith F. Endovascular stented grafts in the treatment of aortoiliac and femoropopliteal occlusive disease. Presented at Symposium on Transluminally Placed Endovascular Prostheses. March 26, 1994, Bethesda, MD.

18. Marin ML, et al. Transfemoral endoluminal stented graft repair of a popliteal aneurysm. *J Vasc Surg* 1994;19:754–757.

Imaging Technology and Applications

IV

Patient Selection and Preoperative Assessment

Carlos E. Donayre
Krassi Ivancev
Rodney A. White

12

Endoluminal vascular grafting places greater than ever demands on imaging technology and techniques. The diseased vessel segments, as well as the associated vessels that need to be used for intraluminal access, must be characterized with precision, both dimensionally and geometrically. Explicit and accurate preoperative imaging modalities are required to select the proper device and are essential to the assembly of a customized prosthesis. These devices offer little opportunity for intraoperative adjustment, and the margins for error in graft sizing are often very small. Feasibility of stent-graft deployment and the ultimate success or failure of the procedure depend as much on precise imaging as the technical skills of the surgeon.

The ability to provide dimensional measurements to the millimeter level has never been a requirement of traditional imaging technologies such as conventional and digital subtraction angiography, computed tomography (CT), magnetic resonance imaging (MRI), and duplex ultrasound. Such measurements were also not particularly necessary for operative decision making. Apart from estimations of aneurysm sac diameters and determination of arterial stenoses, there has been no real need for a precise determination of vessel dimensions. Furthermore, when they are obtained they often carry a significant margin of error due to equipment and technical limitations and subjective interpretations by film readers.

The added challenge for the performance of endovascular repairs based on stent-graft deployment is that high-quality imaging must be transported to the operating room. Most surgical suites today are equipped with only conventional C-arm fluoroscopes. Sophisticated image-intensifying tubes, high-resolution intensifiers, immediate image replay, and television monitoring systems are unfortunately not available in most surgical centers due to cost and lack of space. The other alternative is to use the areas where these imaging modalities are located, such as the angiographic or cardiac catheterization suites. However, the patient must be prepared to quickly undergo conversion to a major operative intervention if any difficulties arise. Having to transport the patient, monitoring equipment, and the operating team rapidly from different areas in the hospital is a tremendous task.

Patient safety and an initial higher incidence of technical failures will force most endovascular teams to use the operating theater for the deployment of stented grafts. In this chapter we address the imaging modalities being used for patient selection and preoperative assessment, describe the imaging techniques available for the performance of endoluminal grafting, discuss new technologies such as intravascular ultrasound (IVUS), and appraise imaging systems designed specifically for the surgical environment.

Patient selection for the performance of endoluminal repairs is based on an understanding of arterial anatomy as displayed by preoperative imaging. In the past, angiographic measurements were made on cut films with the assumption that the approximate magnification was 20 to 25 percent. More accurate assessment of the magnification factor can be obtained using calibrated guidewires (or catheters) and modern digital-based angiographic equipment capable of incorporating this information directly into measurements.

The transaxial images, provided by conventional CT scanning, have been a standard source of information on the diameter and configuration of the infrarenal aorta. More recently, the limitations of transaxial imaging have been overcome by the development of three-dimensional processing of data obtained from conventional CT scans, spiral CT scans, MRI, and magnetic resonance angiography (MRA).

256

Several features of the distal arterial tree have important implications for the feasibility of endovascular grafting. These are the focus of the imaging work-up, which forms the basis for patient selection and graft sizing. The exact selection criteria vary according to the functional limitations of the particular system. However, all devices depend on the same anatomic features. These are discussed in detail in Chapter 2 and will be mentioned here only as they relate to imaging requirements.

All current systems require implantation of the device in the area of nondilated, fairly circular aorta between the renal arteries and the proximal end of the aneurysm—the aneurysm neck. The suitability for implantation depends on the length, diameter, shape, and angle of the neck, as well as the presence of thrombus.

Straight (tube) grafting systems also depend on the presence of a similar segment between the distal end of the aneurysm and the iliac arteries—the distal neck or cuff. The same features mentioned above also apply here. The presence of thrombus can distort the appearance of the neck at both ends of the aneurysm when only the lumen is examined, as in conventional angiography. Graft attachment to mural thrombus is associated with persistent leaks into the excluded aneurysm sac, progressive neck dilatation, and delayed rupture.

Mural thrombus is also important as a potential source of embolism and may depend on the consistency of the pannus. The characteristics of mural thrombus must be studied using modalities like CT scanning and MRA to identify those patients who are at high risk of distal embolization (Fig. 12-1).

Visceral arteries in the region of the graft must be identified and located. The presence of accessory renal arteries affects the level of proximal graft attachment and may preclude performance of the procedure (Fig. 12-2). Clinically significant renal artery stenosis must also be identified and, if possible, treated prior to the insertion of an endovascular graft. A large inferior mesenteric artery that may be indispensable for colonic perfusion and the presence of a meandering artery are considered contraindications for endovascular repair.

Iliac artery tortuosity and stenosis may both impede insertion of the delivery system, depending on its size and flexibility (Fig. 12-3). Iliac artery aneurysms must be identified and their relationship to the internal iliac artery origin determined, since this determines the feasibility of bifurcated graft repair in such cases.

257

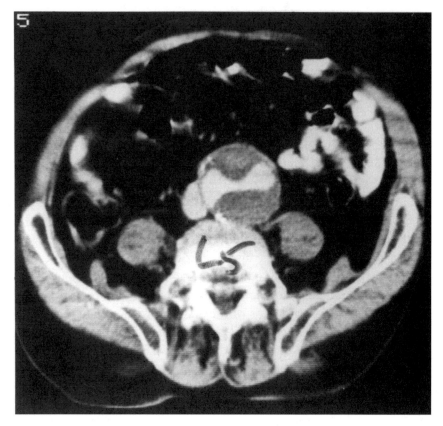

A

Fig. 12-1. A. Conventional CT scan: contrast study of aortic aneurysm.
Sagittal view at L-5 level shows "dumbbell" lumen with extensive thrombus in the aorta. B. Conventional CT scan: multiple lumens are seen
within the aneurysm sac (arrowhead) C. Angiogram of same patient.
Proximal portion of "common iliac aneurysms" (arrows) is a bifid lumen
created by thrombus in distal aortic aneurysm. Patient excluded as candidate for endovascular repair based on above findings.

Precise determination of the length of the infrarenal aorta is critical for successful aneurysm repair with a straight graft, because the
shortness of the distal implantation site allows little leeway for error.
In the bifurcated repair the length of the common iliac artery must
also be determined, although the distal implantation site available
for these cases is often longer, making sizing less critical.

258

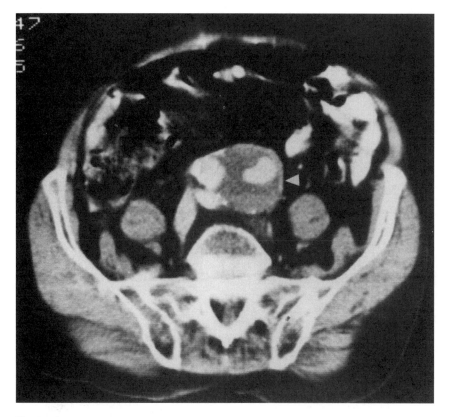

B

Conventional Computed Tomography

The most common imaging modality used today for the evaluation of abdominal aortic aneurysms prior to standard operative repair is the CT scan [1, 2]. The majority of vascular surgeons operate on aneurysms based on information derived only from such a study. These are usually patients with aortic aneurysms limited to the infrarenal aorta and without clinical evidence of associated renovascular disease, mesenteric ischemia, or iliac occlusive disease. The CT scan also provides information about complex anatomy, such as the presence of a horseshoe kidney, retroaortic left renal vein, and inferior vena cava duplication, and can unmask clinically silent pathology (i.e., malignancies). Due to its frequent use, relatively low cost, and noninvasive nature, the CT scan is usually the study on which feasi-

259

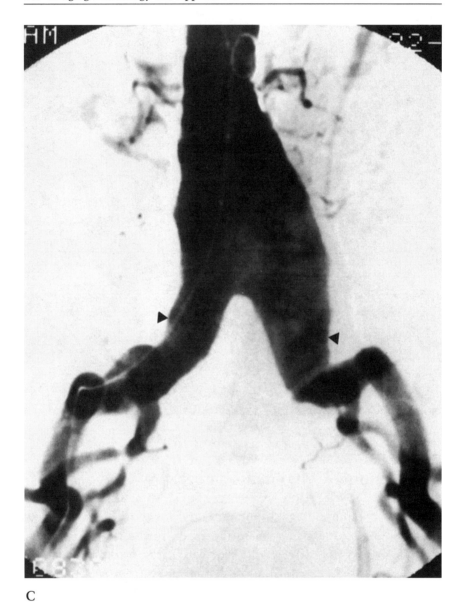

C

Fig. 12-1 *(continued)*

bility of endoluminal grafting is initially determined prior to submit-
ting the patient to further angiographic interrogation.

Generally, conventional CT studies are performed with oral contrast intake to opacify bowel loops, as well as with intravenously

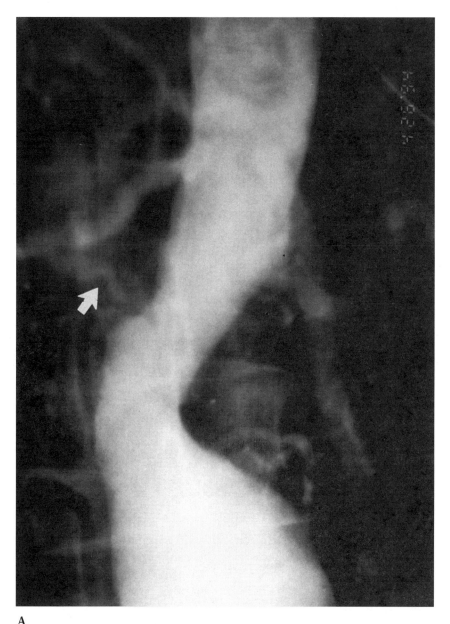

A

Fig. 12-2. Accessory right renal artery. A. Preoperative angiogram: long proximal neck in both renal arteries and accessory right renal artery (arrow) demonstrated. B. Intraoperative angiogram: stented graft (curved arrow) deployed just distal to right accessory renal artery (straight arrow).

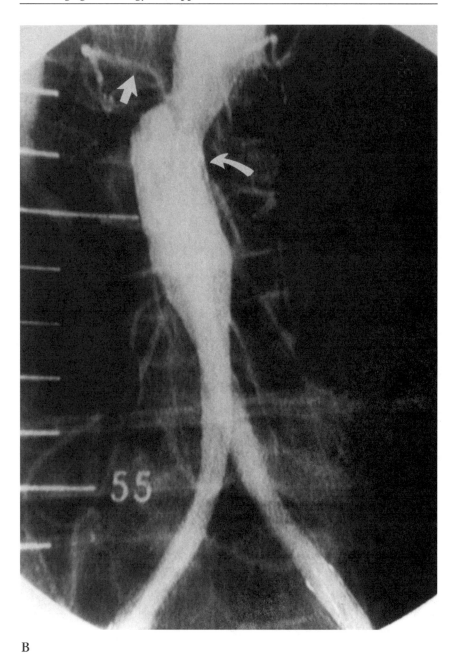

B

Fig. 12-2 *(continued)*

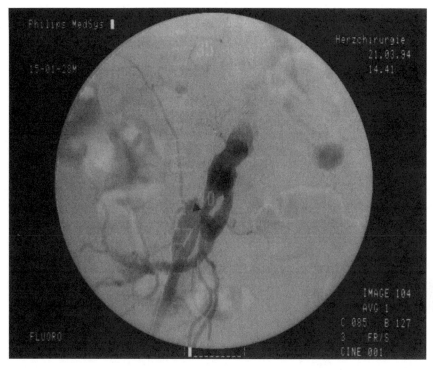

A

Fig. 12-3. Intraoperative angiogram. A. Stenosis (arrowhead) of right external iliac artery prevented delivery of endoprosthesis. B. External iliac artery (arrowhead) after balloon dilatation and placement of Wallstent. It tolerated an 18 French delivery sheath without difficulty.

administered iodinated contrast medium. Unfortunately, the coronal sections or slices obtained are 10 mm thick, which limits the anatomic information obtained. In the patient being screened as a potential candidate for endoluminal aortic repair, contiguous 5-mm thick slices should be used through the expected origins of the renal arteries (i.e., L1 to L3), followed by three contiguous 10-mm thick slices, and then 10 mm thick, 5-mm apart slices down to the level of the symphysis pubis to assess the distal aneurysm neck and iliac arterial system. Due to the prolonged imaging time with this technique, a second bolus of contrast is usually required to obtain high image definition.

While the CT scan can readily identify the origins of the main renal arteries, accessory renal arteries may be hard to demonstrate.

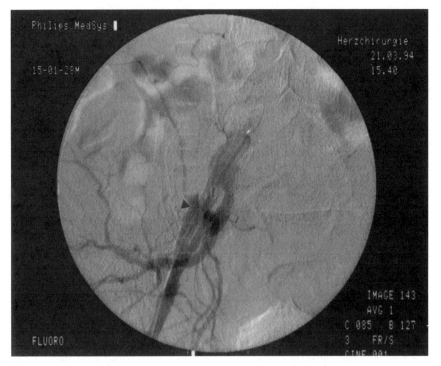

B

Fig. 12-3 *(continued)*

Papanicolau et al. prospectively compared the preoperative CT scan and angiographic findings of 50 electively repaired abdominal aortic aneurysms to those described at operation [1]. The CT demonstrated all 50 aneurysms and correctly identified the proximal neck in 94 percent. Angiography detected 48 of the aneurysms but correctly identified the proximal neck in all of them. The CT correctly identified 98 percent of the patients with two renal arteries (n = 41) but only two of the patients with multiple renal arteries (n = 9).

Measurements of the length and the diameter of the proximal neck can be reliably made when there is limited angulation or tortuosity, which, in turn, appears inversively related to the size of the aneurysm. CT has a tendency to exaggerate the diameter of the neck with increasing obliquity. In such cases the shorter, rather than the larger, diameter of the ellipsoid appearance of the neck is probably closer to the real dimension. The presence and extent of thrombus is easily appreciated if intravenous contrast is used.

Ectasia or aneurysmal involvement of the common iliac arteries can be at times difficult to differentiate from tortuosity. Common iliac artery involvement, or lack thereof, was accurately predicted by CT in only 84 percent of the patients studied by Papanicolau [1]. However, if a normal transverse diameter of these vessels is seen distally, this speaks in favor of tortuosity, as common iliac artery aneurysmal degeneration often involves the whole vessel.

Finally, transaxial images are not reliable for calculation of aneurysm length, especially with increasing tortuosity. Conventional CT evaluation of aortic aneurysms, although helpful in screening and selecting suitable candidates for endoluminal grafting, is not sufficient for obtaining the precise measurements required for the assembly of an endoprosthesis. In those patients in whom conventional CT suggests that endoluminal graft repair is feasible, further evaluation by conventional angiography is mandatory. If possible, the preoperative survey should be supplemented by newer imaging modalities* such as spiral CT angiography or MRA to be able to assess their strengths and limitations until a proper protocol is selected.

Spiral Computed Tomography Angiography

Spiral CT angiography is a new technology that provides three-dimensional images of the abdominal aorta and its main branches from any viewing angle [3–5]. This is achieved by a continuous 360-degree rotation of the x-ray gantry (one rotation per second) for up to 50 seconds with a simultaneous movement of the patient through the gantry. In this way a rapid acquisition of the imaging data is obtained from a cylinder covering 9 to 25 cm during each 30- to 50-second scan and requiring only a single breath-hold by the patient. As a result, contiguous patient data can be acquired with minimal movement and the elimination of respiratory misrepresentation. Proper timing of an intravenously administered contrast medium allows for depiction of only the aorta and its main branches during the peak arterial phase; this further enables reformation of the data to create angiographic

*Three-dimensional reconstruction is discussed in detail in Chapter 2 and is not covered in this section.

projections through any plane. The use of contrast for CT imaging, along with the capability of cross-section reconstruction without the superimposition of overlying structures, results in the ability of imaging vessel lumina, stenoses, atheromatous plaque, and calcification. Such information is important in the preoperative evaluation of aortic aneurysms considered suitable for endovascular repair.

Four different types of reconstruction displays are currently available [6]:

1. *Conventional transaxial images*, on which reliable measurements of aneurysm diameter can be obtained (Figs. 12-4 and 12-5).

2. *Shaded-surface display (SSD)*, a gray-scale three-dimensional rendering based on a selection of density threshold range (usually between 100 to 200 Housefield Units) [7]. Pixels with intensities below this threshold are not displayed. The aorta and its branches appear on SSD as a solid cast made of the column of contrast, which fills the aortic lumen, and any wall calcification. Although SSD provides an excellent overview of aneurysm morphology and very clearly is able to delineate the aorta and its main branches, it provides no information on the relative attenuation inside the created three-dimensional image. The extent of luminal thrombus or calcified plaques is therefore not displayed. In addition, osseous structures that have the same density as the contrast-enhanced aortic lumen appear equally bright. Again, no precise measurements can be made on SSD (Figs. 12-6 and 12-7).

3. *Multiplanar reformation (MPR)*, a tomographic view obtained at a single voxal thickness that depicts the relative density inside vessels in such a way that calcified plaques can be distinguished from the true vessel lumen and thrombus. The combination of axial images and MPR appears to be the most valuable with regard to image information acquisition, but it is time consuming, labor-intense, and difficult to demonstrate. Again, no reliable measurements can be made on MPR (Fig. 12-8).

4. *Maximum intensity projections (MIP)*, which are generated by casting imaginary rays through the volumetric data set [8]. Pixels at the highest Housefield Units (the brightest pixels) along the path of each generated ray form a given projection. It is a display that produces two-dimensional angiography-like images with the ability to discriminate between lumen and wall calcification, as well as

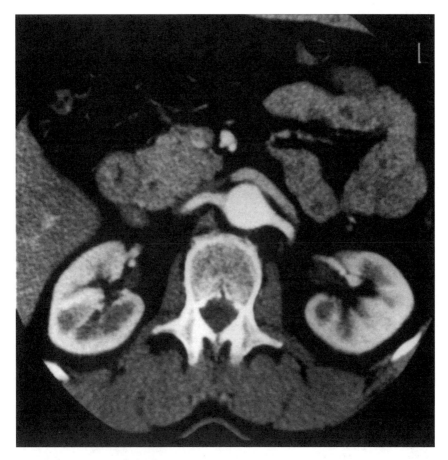

Fig. 12-4. Spiral CT angiography: transaxial view demonstrating normal renal arteries and beginning of the aneurysm neck.

thrombus. Editing out the skeleton and using a cine mode makes MIP reconstruction the display of choice for the imaging of abdominal aortic aneurysms. MIP, like SSD, can be rotated along the Z axis (head to foot), creating three-dimensional views from any angle. However, no reliable measurements can be made on MIP either (Figs. 12-9 and 12-10).

Spiral CT angiography is a minimally invasive, efficacious modality for evaluating aneurysm morphology to assess the feasibility of endoluminal stent-graft repair. It can be performed as an outpatient procedure and takes approximately 30 minutes to perform, with

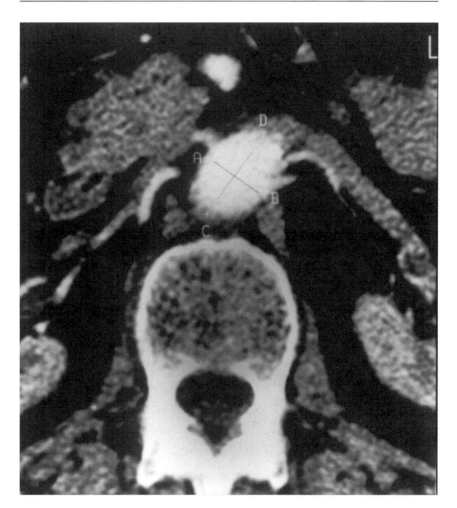

Fig. 12-5. Spiral CT angiography: transaxial view just below the origin of the renal arteries. The aneurysm neck appears ellipsoid because of its angulation. The shorter diameter reflects the true size (A to B cursor).

another hour for completing the different reconstructions. In addition, it is approximately only one-third the cost of conventional arteriography. Usually the combination of the different reformatting displays is required to obtain optimal imaging information. It reliably demonstrates aortic diameter, residual patent aortic lumen, and the location of mesenteric vessels and main and accessory renal arteries, and allows rotation of the reconstructed aneurysm in multiple viewing planes.

268

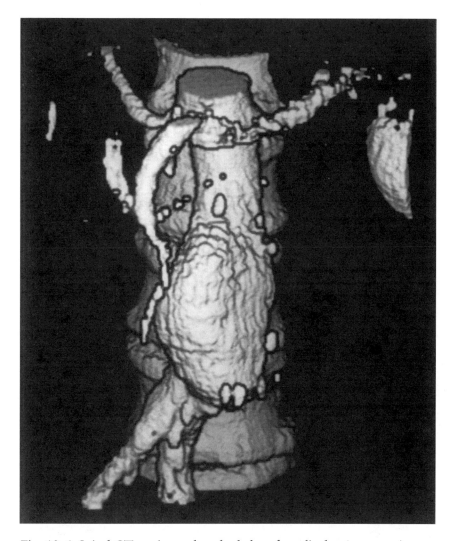

Fig. 12-6. Spiral CT angiography: shaded-surface display (same patient as in Fig. 12-7). Three-dimensional rendering clearly revealing the long aneurysmal neck, aortic aneurysm, and unaffected common iliac arteries.

Magnetic Resonance Angiography

MRA is increasingly being used as a noninvasive method in evaluating patients with suspected vascular disease. It does not require contrast. Two basic approaches are applied for the MRA of aortic blood flow.

269

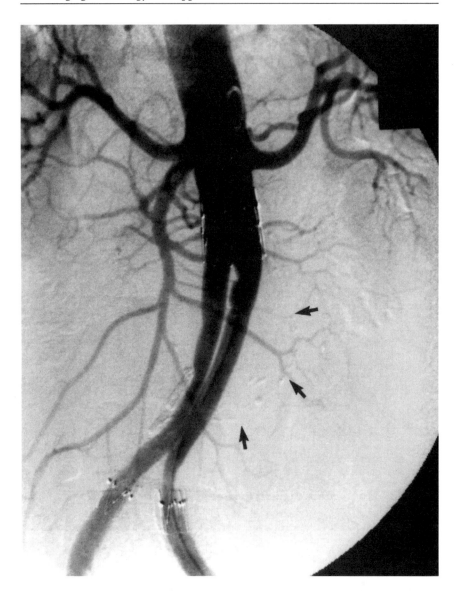

Fig. 12-7. Digital subtraction angiography: postoperative study one month after insertion of a bifurcated endovascular graft. Note the heavily calcified plaque in the lateral wall of the common iliac artery not revealed on spiral CT (shaded-surface display). Abdominal aortic aneurysm effectively excluded (arrows).

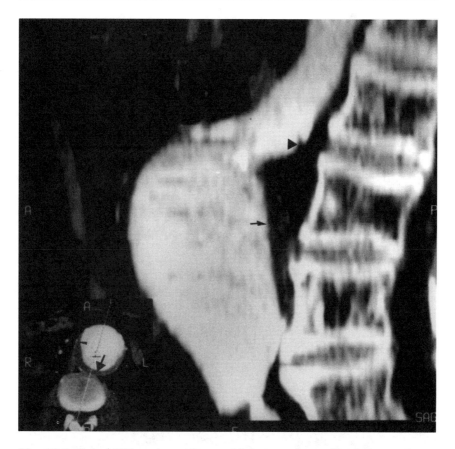

Fig. 12-8. Spiral CT angiography: multiplanar reformation (same patient as in Fig. 12-7). Sagittal view showing the angulated aneurysmal neck. The calcified plaque (arrowheads) is easily separated from the aortic lumen and thrombus (arrows).

Abdominal vessels are visualized by conventional spin-echo pulse sequences, in which normally flowing blood appears without signal—*black blood* MRA—and another that maximizes these signals—*bright blood* MRA [9]. The latter has been shown to be the most informative (Figs. 12-11 and 12-12). However, because of slow, turbulent flow often seen with aortic aneurysms, MRA can be deficient in providing quality images. Although a general road map of the aneurysm can be acquired by MRA, it does not always provide detailed information on the number and state of the renal arteries or the morphology of the iliac arteries.

271

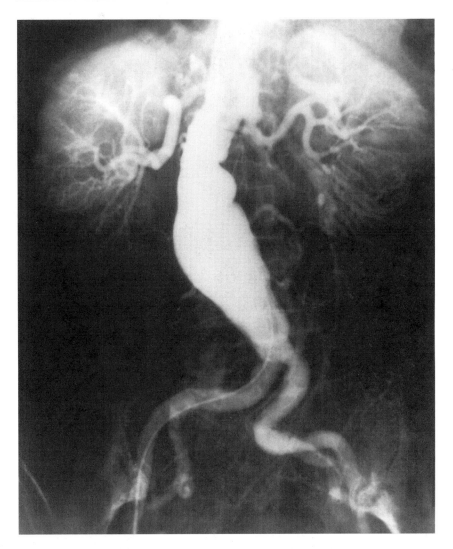

Fig. 12-9. Cut-film angiography: relationship between aortic aneurysm, renal arteries, and iliac arteries clearly demonstrated. Mild left renal artery stenosis is seen. (Courtesy of Dr. Charles P. Semba, Stanford University.)

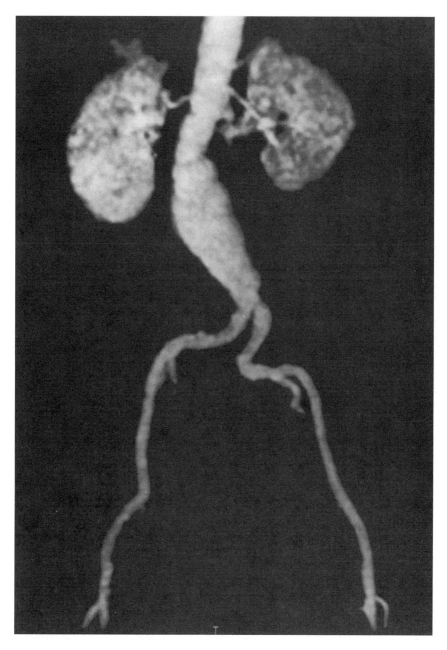

Fig. 12-10. Spiral CT angiography: maximum intensity projection, virtually identical to image seen in Fig. 12-9. (Courtesy of Dr. Charles P. Semba, Stanford University.)

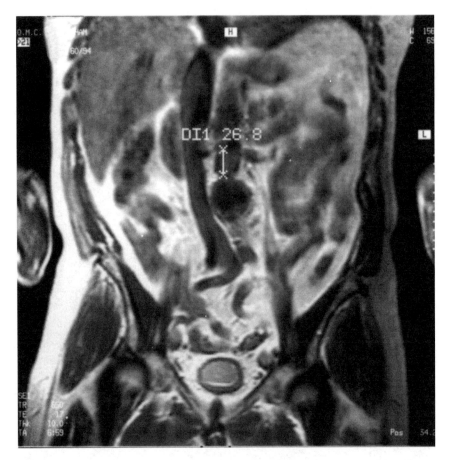

Fig. 12-11. Magnetic resonance angiography: coronal section in the plane of the aneurysm neck, showing the renal arteries proximally and the junction between the neck and the aneurysm, with cursor displaying the length of the neck.

Recently, gadolinium has been used to overcome these shortcomings [10]. Gadolinium is a paramagnetic contrast agent that is administered intravenously and makes the T1 image of blood shorter when compared with that of fat (T1 = 270 msec), muscle (T1 = 600 msec), and other background tissues. It is then possible to image the arteries directly and obtain excellent high resolution since this technique does not depend on blood inflow or blood motion. Three-dimensional imaging is possible by optimizing signal acquisition of the shortened T1 of blood. The obtained results and images are similar to those of spiral CT angiography.

274

Preoperative Measurements and Calculations

After selecting a patient for endovascular aneurysm repair, precise measurements of the aneurysm and access vessels need to be made to select the proper device, assemble the chosen endoprosthesis with the appropriate dimensions, and make an objective decision on the access route or approach. Dimensions of the following parameters are required:

1. Diameter and length of the infrarenal aortic neck
2. Length from the lowest renal arteries to the aortic bifurcation
3. Diameter and length of the distal aneurysm neck
4. Minimal internal diameters of the common and external iliac arteries

The angulation and tortuosity of the aneurysm, proximal and distal aortic necks, and iliac systems are also taken into account as they will affect the accuracy of the measurements obtained. The shape and diameter of the proximal and distal necks can easily be obtained from dynamic fine-cut (5-mm) CT scan sections using intravenous contrast and magnified views of the aorta. They also provide information on the presence of luminal thrombus, data that are not available when angiography is used. The remaining measurements are probably best acquired by using calibrated angiography and conventional puck films (anteroposterior and lateral views) of the abdominal aorta and iliac and femoral arteries, as well as selected vessel segments. A calibrated angiographic catheter with two or more metallic radiopaque markers interspaced at 10- or 20-mm intervals is used to perform the preoperative angiograms (Fig. 12-13). Off-line measurement of the diameters and lengths of the various segments of the vessel are taken from the films and the magnification factors are automatically corrected and stored. In this way the angiographic magnification produced is minimized, and vessel angulation is corrected for since the catheter theoretically should follow the same path that the endoprosthesis will take (Fig. 12-14).

White and May (Royal Prince Alfred Hospital, Sydney, Australia) have compared their results with precision imaging comprised of conventional angiography, digital subtraction angiography, and CT scan in a series of 21 patients who have successfully undergone

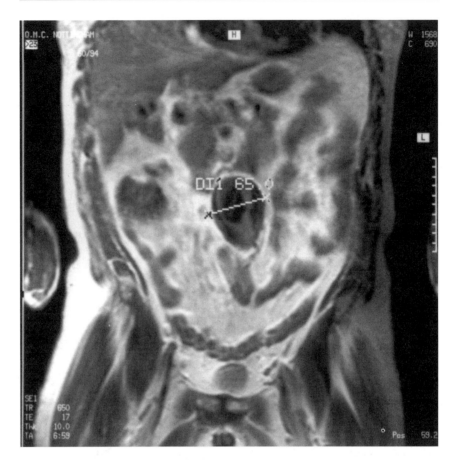

Fig. 12-12. Magnetic resonance angiography: coronal section through the aneurysm with the cursor showing its diameter.

endoluminal repair of their abdominal aortic aneurysms (Table 12-1) [11]. The mean on-film magnification factor for angiography was 1.33; it was 1.90 for digital subtraction angiography films of the iliac arteries and 0.49 for CT scans. As seen in Table 12-1, there was consistent overestimation of dimensions obtained from CT image measurements when compared with those obtained from calibrated angiography. One cause of this discrepancy is that the CT scan readings are usually taken from wall to wall of the aorta, whereas the angiographic study shows only the outline of contrast within the lumen. The differences obtained from these modalities are being studied in an ongoing comparative study.

276

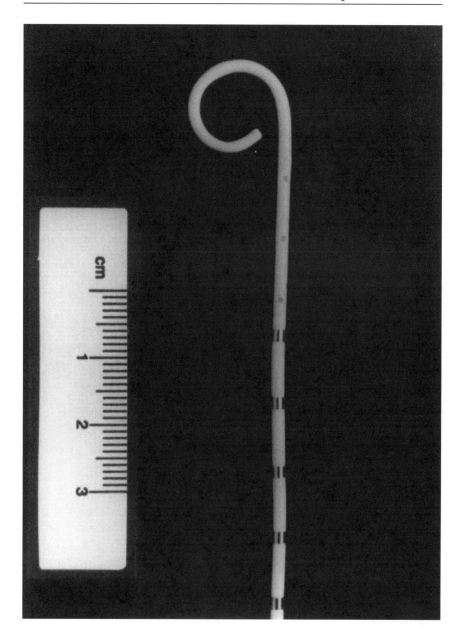

Fig. 12-13. Calibrated angiographic pigtail catheter. The metallic bands around the distal aspect of the catheter are spaced at 1-cm intervals and are used for calibration of radiologic magnification to allow accurate measurements of the aortic dimensions. Adjustments must also be allowed for angulation and curvature of the catheter or vessels.

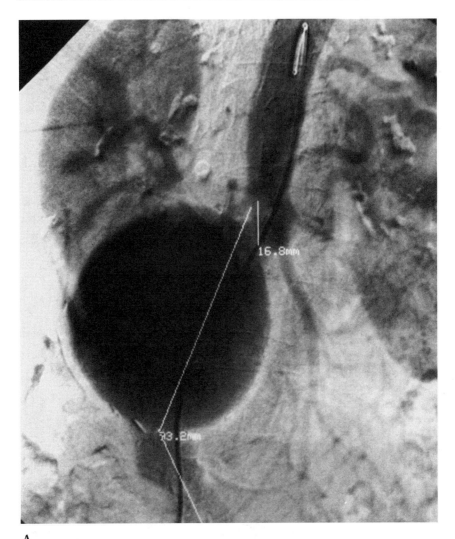

A

Fig. 12-14. Digital subtraction angiography: preoperative study of aortic aneurysm. Anteroposterior (A) and lateral (B) views show computer-generated measurements (white cursor) that do not correspond to those obtained from a calibrating wire (C) with 2-cm markings (arrows). Calibrating angiographic catheter should follow a similar path as the endoluminal graft.

278

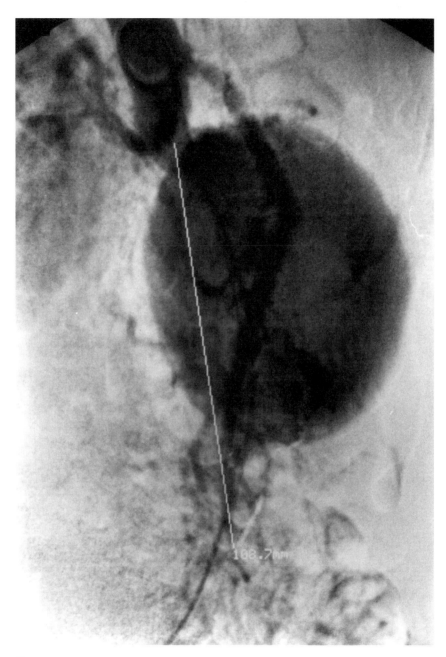

B

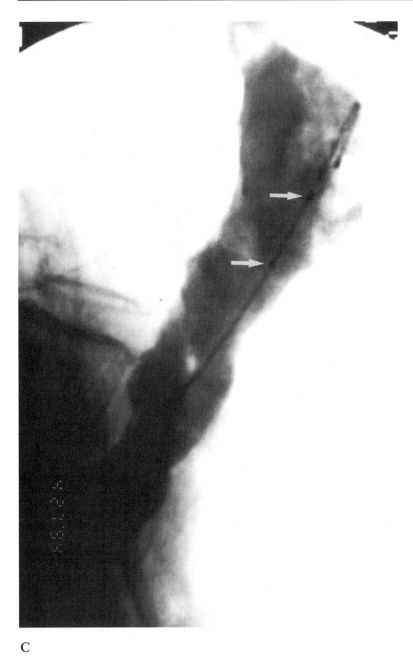

C

Fig. 12-14 *(continued)*

Table 12-1. Dimensions obtained from detailed calibrated radiology studies in 21 patients undergoing endoluminal abdominal aortic aneurysm graft procedures

	Angiogram: Mean (range) (mm)	Computed tomography: Mean (range) (mm)
Proximal neck diameter	20.0 (14.2–25.4)	22.8 (17.0–28.1)
Proximal neck length	26.7 (13.5–48.3)	28.3 (15.0–50.0)
Renal to bifurcated	108.3 (85.9–144.6)	110.3 (77.0–130.0)
Distal neck diameter	23.0 (11.9–47.5)	26.8 (14.6–51.9)
Distal neck length	9.8 (0.0–23.0)	9.2 (0.0–25.0)
CIA diameter	12.4 (6.9–22.4)	
EIA diameter	8.3 (5.0–10.7)	

CIA = common iliac artery; EIA = external iliac artery.

The mean distance from the renal arteries to the aortic bifurcation on angiogram was 10.8 cm and ranged from 8.5 cm to 14.5 cm, and the mean diameter of the aortic neck was 20.0 mm on angiogram and 22.8 mm on CT scan. The mean length of the neck was 2.67 cm, with six of 21 (28 percent) having a neck of less than 2 cm length, making implantation of an endoluminal graft more difficult. Seven patients (33 percent) had no distal neck of the aneurysm sac and therefore required a bifurcated or aortoiliac configuration of graft. To date, it has been the policy of the group in Sydney to rely primarily on the angiographic measurements for the selection of the endoluminal grafts and decision making, using the CT scan data to provide supplementary information, such as the extent of mural thrombus and the degree of mural calcification.

Another maneuver that can be used to measure lengths is the bent-wire technique. A guidewire is introduce into the aorta, and its end is located at the level of the left renal artery and bent as it exits the skin. The wire is then pulled back until the neck ends and a second bend is made. Next the wire is pulled back to the beginning of the distal neck and another bend is made. In this fashion a variety of length measurements are obtained by directly measuring the distance between each bend, since no magnification is introduced.

281

Again, the only assumption made is that the guidewire and endo-prosthesis will follow the same path.

Duplex ultrasound has also been of value for preoperative assessment of the iliac systems. It can be used to exclude any angiographically silent stenoses, as well as to confirm the diameters of these vessels.

References

1. Papanicolau N et al. Preoperative evaluation of abdominal aneurysms by computed tomography. *Am J Radiol* 1986;146:711–715.

2. Laroy LL et al. Imaging of abdominal aortic aneurysms. *Am J Radiol* 1989;152:785–792.

3. Zeman RK et al. Helical (spiral) CT of the abdomen. *Am J Radiol* 1993;160:719–725.

4. Costelo P, Gaa J. Spiral CT angiography of the abdominal aorta and its branches. *Eur Radiol* 1993;3:359–365.

5. Rubin GD et al. 3-dimensional spiral computed tomographic angiography: An alternative imaging modality for the abdominal aorta and its branches. *J Vasc Surg* 1993;18:656–665.

6. Rubin GD et al. Spiral CT of renal artery stenosis: Comparison of three-dimensional rendering techniques. *Radiology* 1994;190:181–189.

7. Magnusson M, Lenz R, Danielsson PE. Evaluation of methods for shaded surface display of CT volumes. *Comp Med Imag Graph* 1990;15:247–256.

8. Napel S et al. CT angiography with spiral CT and maximum intensity projection. *Radiology* 1992;185:607–610.

9. Arlart IP, Guhl L, Edelman RR. Magnetic resonance angiography of the abdominal aorta. *Cardiovasc Intervent Radiol* 1992;15:43–50.

282

10. Prince M. Gadolinium-enhanced MR aortography. *Radiology* 1994;191:155–164.

11. White G, May J, Yu W. Written communication, April 1994.

Intraoperative Imaging System Requirements

13

Carlos E. Donayre
Geoffrey H. White
Rodney A. White

Intraoperative Angiography and Fluoroscopy

Angiography is the oldest technique among the currently available methods of imaging the vascular lumen and remains the most widely accepted. Endovascular therapies have placed demands for unerring and exacting results on this technology. The major limitation of the use of intraoperative angiography and fluoroscopy is that when used as a single projection, they really represent only a two-dimensional view of the vessel lumen. Intraoperative oblique or lateral projections may be difficult or inadequate, due to constraints from a floor-mounted surgical table or inability to freely adjust the position of the patient. Precise and detailed preoperative imaging, which allows three-dimensional reconstruction of the aneurysm morphology, extent of luminal thrombus, and tortuosity or narrowing of the access vessels, must be readily available to complement and clarify the intraoperative images being obtained. All the available imaging studies must be used to conceptually reconstruct the target vessel prior to stent-graft assembly or deployment.

The major role of intraoperative angiography or fluoroscopy is multifold. It first must confirm and provide exact endoluminal landmarks for deployment of the selected or assembled stent-graft prosthesis. The ability of angiography to display large vascular territories in a short period of time is well proved. Second, it has to assess that proper device deployment has been achieved and that blood flow is restored by the endoluminal bypass. Finally, if complications arise, it must aid in the performance of a potential endovascular rescue.

The imaging systems required for the deployment of stented endovascular grafts range from the most basic composed of C-arm fluoroscopy and a lead-marked ruler placed under the patient to provide a constant reference point, to the most sophisticated system that uses a ceiling-suspended fluoroscopic system in combination with a wall-mounted carbon fiber surgical table to enable access over the entire length of the patient (see Chapter 8). Intra-arterial digital subtraction angiographic (DSA) capabilities are desirable to obtain high-quality predeployment and completion angiograms. This modality can produce exquisite images with newer systems capable of 1024 × 1024 matrix acquisition. The ability of DSA to store and replay images also allows the operative team to review the angiographic data obtained as many times as necessary without having to administer iodinated contrast agents repeatedly. The small field of view, determined by the size of the image intensifier, has been recently improved, and larger 21-inch screens may be available in the near future. The susceptibility of DSA to misregistration artifacts from any kind of patient motion is overcome by having the patient under general anesthesia and holding respirations when images are obtained.

It is always wise to obtain scout films after positioning the patient on the operating room table to ensure that the lead-marked ruler is properly situated along the lumbar spines and that no artifacts, such as a warming blanket, are obstructing the field of view. The C-arm movements must be unhampered by the operating table for unrestricted viewing from xiphoid to pubis.

The first task in the deployment of endovascular grafts is establishing a remote access and passing guidewires through an iliac system that is usually tortuous, across the thrombus-lined aneurysm sac, and into the suprarenal aorta. Digital innovations such as the road-mapping feature facilitate selective catherizations of tortuous vessels. The image intensifier is positioned over the area of interest, an angiogram is obtained, and the DSA density display is converted so that vessels appear white on a gray background. Real-time fluoroscopy can then be superimposed on this guide of the vascular anatomy as long as the image intensifier or operating table are not moved. Guidewires can be manipulated using the road map to gain access to the suprarenal aorta. The road map can also be used to recheck length measurements using the bent-wire technique described above.

Next, a predeployment angiogram of the proximal neck is obtained to mark the most distal renal orifice, and the target site is selected for graft anchoring (Fig. 13-1). Another useful feature of DSA is the maximum opacification function, which displays an angiogram that is a composite of multiple serial frames. In this way a single image can depict adequate vessel opacification even with slow rates of hand injection through small catheters. Having obtained a satisfactory angiogram, the left renal artery, the borders of the proximal aortic neck, and the markings of the ruler are marked directly on the fluoroscopy screen. The road-map feature can also be used at this time. The most important thing to remember is that the image intensifier or operating table cannot be moved while the endovascular prosthesis is being maneuvered into its target site. If movement occurs, another angiogram must be obtained and new markings made; if not, incorrect deployment and potential failure of the whole procedure may occur.

To ensure pinpoint proximal deployment accuracy of the stented graft, a small angiographic catheter can be placed from either the contralateral access vessel or from above via the brachial artery. Small contrast boluses at the time of stent-graft deployment allow real-time visualization of this important step (Fig. 13-2). The same imaging techniques can be used to deploy the distal balloon-expandable stent in a tube graft (see Chapter 3) or the distal self-expanding stents of a bifurcated graft (see Chapter 4).

After the endoluminal aortic prosthesis has been deployed, a high-quality angiogram must be obtained to evaluate the accuracy of deployment, exclusion of aneurysmal blood flow, and presence of proximal or distal leaks (Fig. 13-3). Technical mishaps such as graft torsion, inadequate graft length, or iliac limb stenoses must also be noted since they are amenable to endovascular rescue. Bifurcated grafts must traverse through iliac orifices that possess calcified, ath-

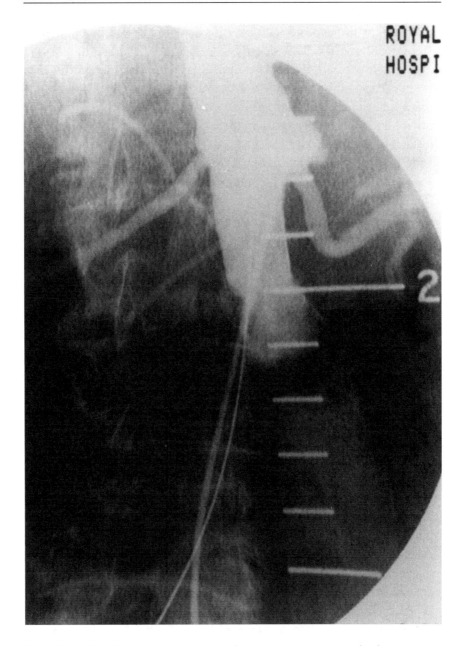

Fig. 13-1. Cinefluoroscopy-angiography: intraoperative study demonstrating renal arteries and proximal neck.

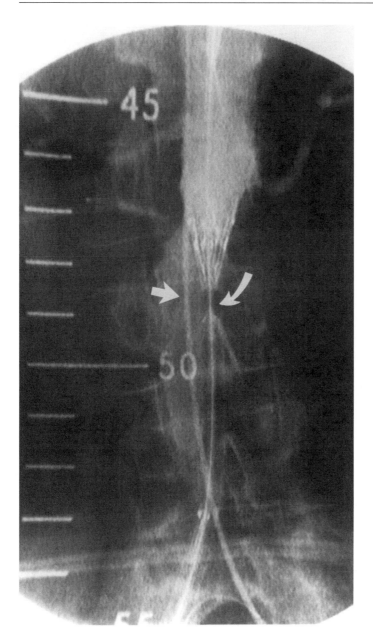

Fig. 13-2. Cinefluoroscopy-angiography: intraoperative study showing an endovascular graft with self-expanding stent (curved arrow) being positioned into proper location using a second angiographic catheter (arrow) to deliver contrast as the stent is being deployed.

289

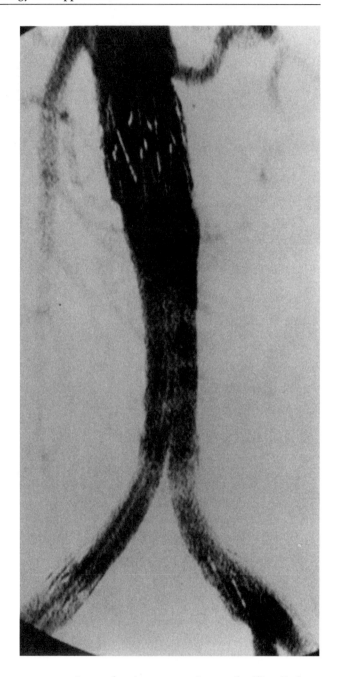

Fig. 13-3. Cinefluoroscopy-angiography: intraoperative study. Iliac limbs of stented bifurcated graft demonstrating good flow and no leaks or torsion.

erosclerotic plaque not seen on the preoperative studies. These lesions impinge on the unstented iliac graft portion and can lead to postoperative thrombosis. Deployment of a Wallstent restores normal graft contour and ensures graft patency (Fig. 13-4).

Intravascular Ultrasound Imaging

As mentioned above, vascular imaging modalities are developing very rapidly. Although arteriography remains the gold standard for determining the distribution and continuity of the vasculature, new imaging modalities, particularly intravascular ultrasound (IVUS), have demonstrated that conventional arteriograms are limited in their ability to accurately determine luminal dimensions, cross-sectional areas, and distribution of atherosclerotic plaques [1, 2]. IVUS has developed rapidly in recent years and provides a unique perspective for viewing vascular lesions and judging the effects of endovascular interventions. It combines advances in catheter technology, echographic data processing, and computerized image manipulation to produce accurate luminal and transmural images of blood vessels. A 360-degree cross-sectional image is obtained by scanning the ultrasound beam through a full circle and synchronizing the beam direction and deflection with the display. This is achieved by either mechanically rotating the imaging elements or by using electronically switched arrays mounted on catheters 4 to 8 French in diameter [3].

IVUS is a catheter-based imaging modality that provides precise and unique information regarding luminal and vessel wall cross-sectional dimensions [4, 5]. Diameters and cross-sectional surface areas are readily calculated (Fig. 13-5). It is also useful for detecting the presence of calcium and for inspecting the morphology of and distribution of intraluminal thrombus (Fig. 13-6) [6]. IVUS provides the only available intraoperative assessment of intraluminal thrombus in the proximal or distal neck prior to stented graft deployment. This information is critical to endovascular graft implantation, since, as mentioned, deployment in thrombus can result in leaks, distal neck expansion, and rupture.

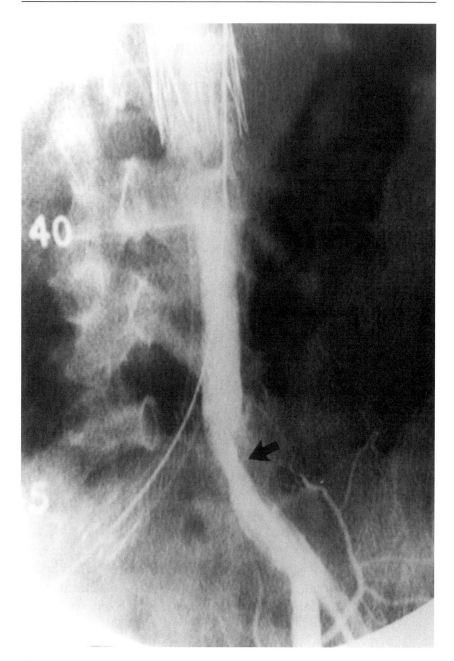

A

Fig. 13-4. Cinefluoroscopy-angiography: intraoperative study. A. Extrinsic distortion of iliac limb (arrow). B. After Wallstent deployment, left iliac

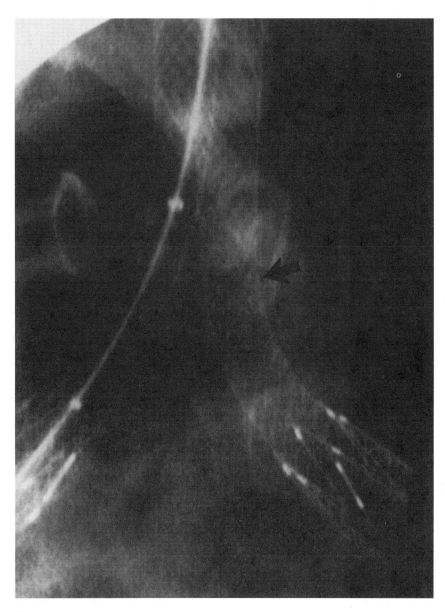

B

limb resumes normal contour (arrow). C. Completion intraoperative digital subtraction angiogram demonstrates normal flow in both iliac systems
with no further distortion of the left iliac limb (arrow).

293

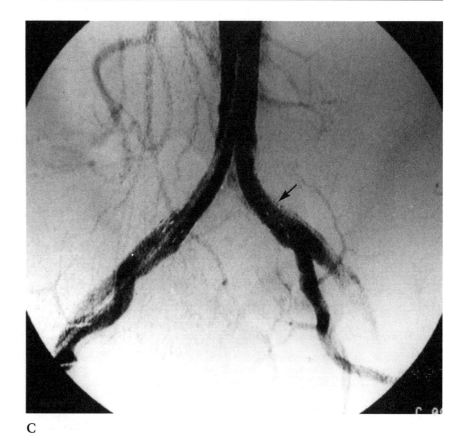

C

Fig. 13-4 *(continued)*

Another application of IVUS is the detailed luminal information it provides before, during, and after endovascular interventions. Furthermore, it provides a method for both guidance of endoluminal devices and immediate assessments of the results. These capabilities are applicable to therapeutic techniques such as balloon angioplasty, atherectomies, and, particularly, intravascular stent deployment [7]. Angiography, when compared to IVUS, has been shown to underestimate the degree of residual stenosis following atherectomy in up to 80 percent of patients and is unable to confirm complete deployment in up to 20 percent of cases where a stent was used [8].

Computerized three-dimensional image reconstruction of IVUS generates cross-sectional sections that allow the images to be viewed as a complete cylinder, adding to the applicability of IVUS in the clin-

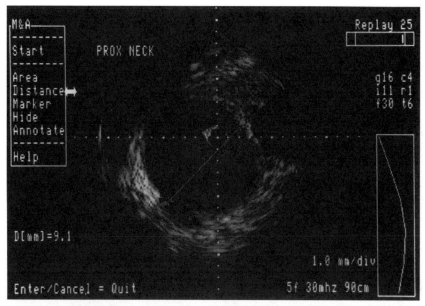

A

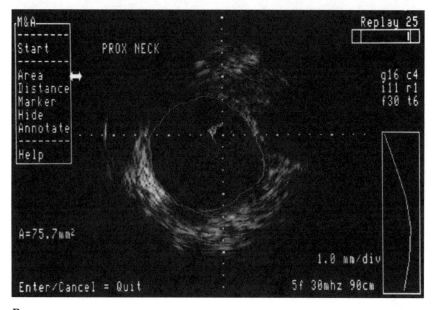

B

Fig. 13-5. IVUS: normal canine aorta. A. Measurement of diameter of infrarenal aorta. B. Cross-sectional area determination (arrowheads on cursors used to obtain measurements).

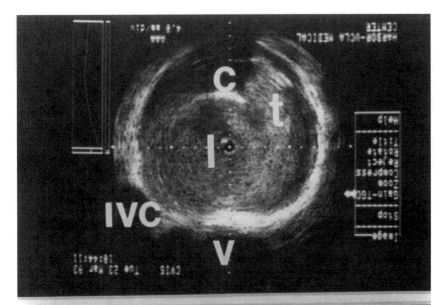

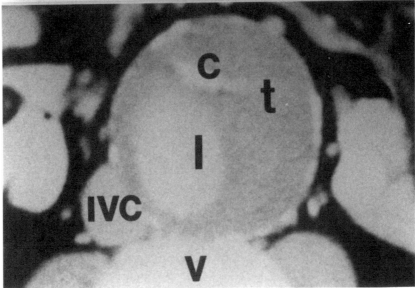

Fig. 13-6. Comparison of tomographic views by IVUS (top) and CT scan (bottom) of the aneurysm at the same location. (l = aortic lumen; t = thrombus in the aneurysm; c = calcification; IVC = inferior vena cava; v = vertebral body.) (From RA White et al. Innovations in vascular imaging: Angiography, 3-D CT, and 2-D and 3-D intravascular ultrasound of an abdominal aortic aneurysm. *Ann Vasc Surg* 1994;8:287.)

ical setting [9]. This imaging technique involves stacking a longitudinally aligned set of consecutive two-dimensional images that are acquired by slowly withdrawing the catheter through the selected vessel segment at a uniform rate. Longitudinal gray-scale and three-dimensional computer-generated images are produced, which can be manipulated and rotated on-screen (Figs. 13-7, 13-8, and 13-9). Image artifacts are introduced by the current catheter-based IVUS technology, since the cross-sectional images used for the three-dimensional reconstructions are acquired from variable positions within the vessel as the catheter is withdrawn from the lumen. When the three-dimensional images are reconstructed, the catheter is displayed as a straight line in the vessel lumen, even though the position of the catheter moves within the lumen during acquisition of the images. In addition, precise time sequencing of catheter passage through the lumen is required to provide accurate longitudinal three-dimensional data. Nonetheless, information about graft folds, torsion, and stent-vessel apposition can be readily seen with this technology (Fig. 13-10).

Recently, an IVUS transducer has been incorporated into an angioplasty balloon catheter (Balloon Ultrasound Imaging Catheter, Boston Scientific, Watertown, MA), allowing viewing the balloon dilatation process in real time. This technique provides quantitative and qualitative analyses of lumen and arterial wall alterations immediately preceding, during, and after transluminal balloon angioplasty [10].

Real-time IVUS imaging of endovascular graft deployments in a canine aortic aneurysm model has been performed at our institution and compared to cinefluoroscopy [11]. A 3.5 French Sonicath intravascular ultrasound catheter (0.035-inch, 20-MHz element) was passed through the central lumen of the balloon catheter to visualize real-time balloon expansion of a Palmaz stent-graft prosthesis (Fig. 13-11). IVUS interrogation of the aortic lumen before device deployment enabled accurate identification of the renal and branch arteries and selection of the appropriate site for proximal stent placement. It was also able to identify cases of incomplete stent expansion that were not apparent on angiography. Further enlargement of the stent to match the aortic diameter was carried out and confirmed by IVUS. The capability to document secure and full stent expansion is extremely important to avoid potential stent migration, aortic dilatation, or the development of late leaks.

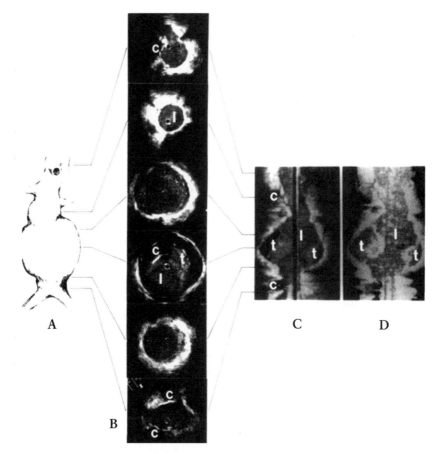

Fig. 13-7. IVUS. A. Schematic of abdominal aortic aneurysm. B. Selected cross-sectional IVUS images of the aorta and aneurysm at various levels. C. Longitudinal gray scale. D. Three-dimensional surface images of the aneurysm. Note the evidence of thrombus (t) and calcification (c) at several levels throughout the length of the vessel. (l = lumen.) (From RA White et al. Innovations in vascular imaging: Angiography, 3-D CT, and 2-D and 3-D intravascular ultrasound of an abdominal aortic aneurysm. *Ann Vasc Surg* 1994;8:286.)

The IVUS has developed into a powerful imaging modality, with clinical applications particularly relevant to the successful deployment of stent-graft endovascular prostheses. Its use is only hampered by cost and the need for invasive catheterization. In summary, it provides the following information:

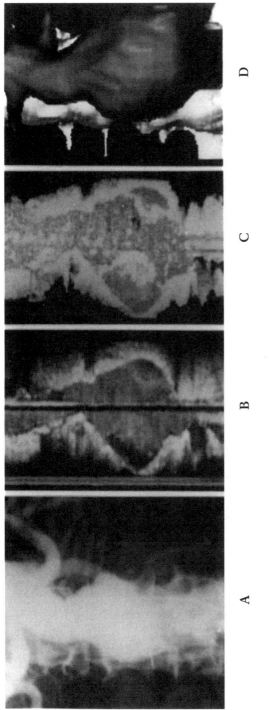

Fig. 13-8. Aortogram (A), longitudinal gray-scale IVUS (B), surface-rendered three-dimensional IVUS (C), and three-dimensional CT reconstruction (D) of the external surface of an aortic aneurysm. The views are of comparable lengths of the aorta with similar magnification to enable comparison of the imaging methodologies. (From RA White et al. Innovations in vascular imaging: Angiography, 3-D CT, and 2-D and 3-D intravascular ultrasound of an abdominal aortic aneurysm. *Ann Vasc Surg* 1994;8:287.)

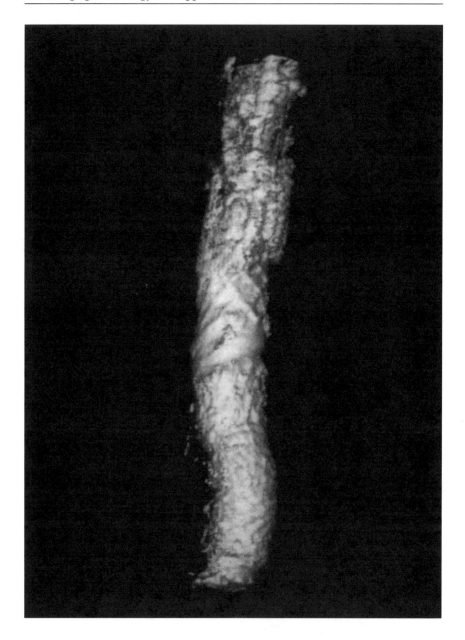

Fig. 13-9. IVUS–three-dimensional reconstruction: endovascular tube graft after deployment (Parodi device). No fold or torsion seen.

1. Diameters and cross-sectional areas (without magnification) of infrarenal aorta, distal aneurysm neck, and iliac vessels.
2. Using a pull-back technique, the length of the proximal neck, distance from the renal arteries to the aortic bifurcation, and length of the iliac vessels.
3. Presence of thrombus and extent of calcium at the selected site of implantation.
4. Real-time imaging of balloon-based stent deployment, with the ability to document full stent deployment and apposition of graft material to the aortic wall.
5. Evaluation of graft folds or torsion that are amenable to endovascular rescue.
6. Interrogation of bifurcated graft iliac limbs. IVUS can visualize extrinsic limb compression, or folds, and identify inadequate stent deployment or expansion.

One of the most important changes resulting from this increased requirement for detailed imaging has been a shift of the role of radiologic studies from one of pure diagnostic utility to that of a practical dimensional tool that requires direct input from the surgical team. It is critical that a surgeon with sound knowledge of the procedures and characteristics of the available endoluminal grafts be involved with the setup of related radiology protocols and the measurement process. This also applies to three-dimensional imaging. Advances and improvements in some of the newer modalities such as IVUS, spiral CT, and MRA may lead to their eventual replacement of angiography as the primary modality for assessing patients with vascular disease and may determine not only the feasibility of endovascular repair but also participate in the guidance and performance of the procedure.

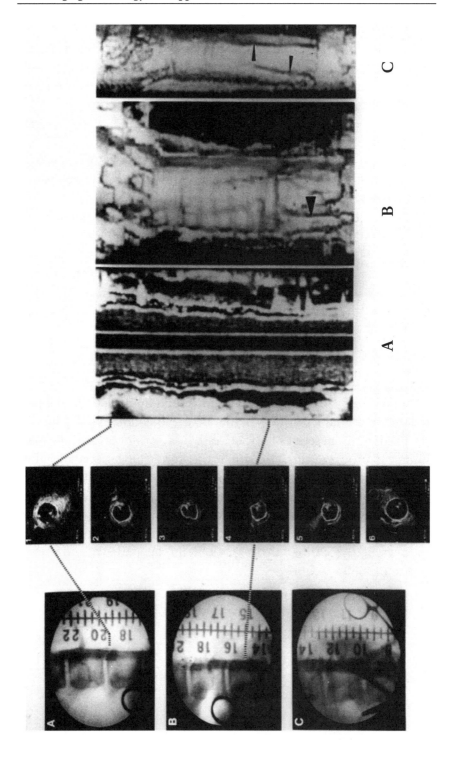

▲ Fig. 13-10. Endovascular tube graft after deployment in normal canine infrarenal aorta. No distal stent was used. *Left panel:* Cinefluoroscopy. Endovascular tube graft deployed in normal canine aorta. Normal flow and aortic contours shown. *Middle panel:* IVUS two-dimensional views of stented graft at different levels. Good stent apposition proximally (panel 1). Distal end of the graft was not stented; narrowing and separation from aortic wall clearly demonstrated (panels 3–5). Normal aorta (panel 6). These findings were not seen on cinefluoroscopy. *Right panel:* IVUS–three-dimensional reconstruction. A. Longitudinal gray scale shows separation of graft from the aortic wall. B. Luminal cast showing distal graft infolding and irregular lumen (arrowhead). C. Three-dimensional reconstruction showing proximal end with good apposition; distal graft folds clearly demonstrated (arrowheads).

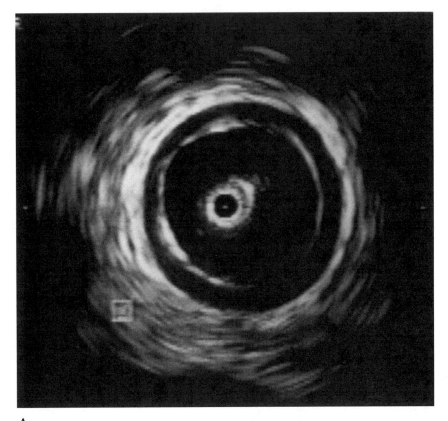

A

Fig. 13-11. IVUS–real-time study. A. Stent-graft prosthesis being deployed with real-time imaging. Stent partially deployed, vessel wall free of thrombus or calcifications. B. Stent-graft prosthesis in place, good vessel wall apposition, and full stent deployment.

References

1. Tobis JM et al. Intravascular ultrasound imaging of human coronary arteries in vivo. *Circulation* 1991;83:913–926.

2. Tabbara MR et al. In-vivo human comparison of intravascular ultrasound and angiography. *J Vasc Surg* 1991;14:496–504.

3. Cavaye D, White RA. The Principles of Diagnostic Ultrasound Imaging. In D Cavaye, RA White (eds), *Intravascular Ultrasound Imaging*. New York: Raven, 1993.

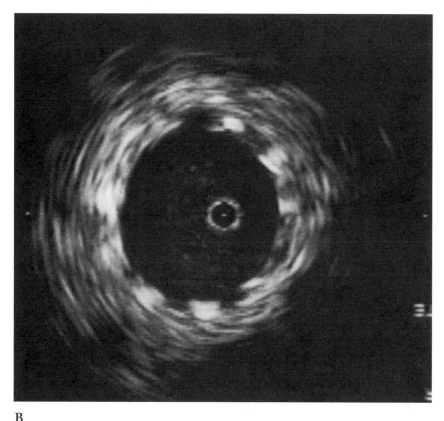

B

4. Cavaye DM et al. Intravascular ultrasound imaging: The new standard for guidance and assessment of endovascular interventions. *J Clin Laser Med Surg* 10:349–53, 1992.

5. Cavaye DM, White RA. Imaging technologies in cardiovascular interventions. *J Cardiovasc Surg* 1993;34:13–22.

6. Feltrin GP et al. Intravascular ultrasound evaluation for assessment and therapeutic decisions in aortic diseases. *Angiology* 1994;45:7–16.

7. Cavaye DM et al. Intraluminal ultrasound assessment of vascular stent deployment. *Ann Vasc Surg* 1991;5:241–246.

8. Katzen BT et al. Role of intravascular ultrasound in peripheral atherectomy and stent deployment [abstract]. *Circulation* 1991;94(Suppl II):2152.

9. White RA et al. Innovations in vascular imaging: Angiography, 3-D CT, and 2-D and 3-D intravascular ultrasound of an abdominal aortic aneurysm. *Ann Vasc Surg* 1994;8:285–289.

10. Isner JM et al. Combination balloon ultrasound imaging catheter for percutaneous transluminal angioplasty. *Circulation* 1991;84:739–754.

11. White RA et al. Intravascular ultrasound and the role in patient selection and device placement. Presented at the Society for Vascular Surgery, North American Chapter, International Society for Cardiovascular Surgery Research Initiatives in Vascular Disease Symposium. March 26, 1994, Bethesda, MD.

Future Perspectives and Development Issues

V

The Utility and Development of Endovascular Prostheses

14

Timothy A.M. Chuter
Rodney A. White

Utility

Substantial experience is accumulating to support the potential utility of endoluminal prostheses for treating a variety of vascular lesions. Although the technical ability to deploy stent-graft devices using low-profile endovascular delivery systems has been established, the long-term efficacy has yet to be proven for any particular indication.

Aneurysms

Using endovascular grafts to treat abdominal aortic aneurysms is appealing, especially when conventional surgical exposure is associated with significant morbidity and mortality. Initial results have been encouraging, although long-term follow-up is required to assess the patency and complications compared to standard operative repair. Early experience with endoluminal exclusion of aneurysms suggests that the residual aneurysm lumen fills with thrombus in the majority of patients, and continued enlargement by perigraft blood flow via lumbar and collateral vessels has not been observed [1]. Parodi has reported that color-flow duplex scanning following endoluminal aneurysm repair is a sensitive method to follow patients for continued flow within the aneurysm and to assess for aneurysm enlargement [2].

Traumatic Vascular Lesions

Endovascular prostheses have been used to treat traumatic lacerations, false aneurysms, and arteriovenous fistulas (see Chapter 10). The majority of patients who have been treated using these methods are young, active individuals who will require long-term follow-up to prove the value of the interventions.

Arterial Occlusive Disease

The use of endovascular grafts to treat arterial occlusive lesions as an adjunct to balloon angioplasty requires intense, careful investigation before conclusions regarding the theoretical advantages can be made. Since endovascular prostheses pass through the lumen of a recanalized artery, stenoses or occlusions will result if the lumen renarrows. Perhaps endoluminal grafts will retard proliferative responses that lead to reocclusion by excluding the injured vessel wall from blood elements [3]. The endoluminal graft may also serve as a barrier to luminal encroachment by preventing growth of myointima through the interstices of a stent. Alternatively, the graft may be used for topical drug delivery [4]. At present these hypotheses remain to be tested by appropriate animal experiments and clinical trials.

Developmental Issues

Endovascular technologies have evolved over the last 30 years with interventional radiologists, cardiologists, and vascular surgeons contributing to the field. The development, application, and training of physicians in the use of endovascular procedures has been addressed from several perspectives [5–9]. As endovascular methods have evolved to include the therapy of lesions usually treated by conventional surgical methods (i.e., abdominal and thoracic aneurysms), surgeons' interest and participation in development have increased [8, 10]. In addition, the risks of the procedures and the need for surgical exposures to obtain arterial access for introduction of larger-diameter (18 to 24 French) endovascular prosthesis delivery systems mandate that the procedures be performed in a facility that has the capabilities of an operating room, with a vascular surgeon participating in the procedure. Collaboration between vascular surgeons and interventional radiologists is required to foster optimal development of endoluminal graft devices, with each adding unique contributions to the field [10]. In most institutions neither subspeciality has the necessary influence, skills, or training to fully provide optimal care without a collaborative effort.

Experimental and Clinical Evaluations

One of the most controversial issues at present is the determination of appropriate methods to ensure safe and effective development of endoluminal prostheses while minimizing the investment of time and money. All researchers agree that preclinical bench and animal testing is required to determine healing in both normal and lesion models.

One approach to the testing of intraluminal prostheses is to rely on the extensive healing and performance data that have been compiled on contemporary prostheses. Although some would speculate that intraluminal grafts require unique characteristics, the delineation of new parameters has not occurred. There is significant experimental and early clinical data suggesting that contemporary prosthetic materials heal in a reliable and predictable manner when used as endovascular grafts similar to the healing encountered when the implants are used for "bypass" applications. On this basis it may be reasonable to suggest that preclinical evaluations be developed with guidelines similar to those established for current prostheses [11] and that new evaluation criteria be added as the need is identified. This position must be tempered by the fact that contemporary materials do not have the optimal mechanical properties, such as thin-wall compressibility and kink resistance, that are needed for

311

low-profile delivery systems. In addition, although contemporary materials heal in a predictable manner when apposed to viable tissue, healing in the thrombus-lined walls of an aneurysm remains to be confirmed.

For several applications (i.e., aortic aneurysms), comparison of early clinical study results with historical controls should be adequate to make efficacy and safety determinations, with controlled studies being reserved for final prototype devices, delivery systems, and procedures once the technology has matured. Safe application relies on the conduct of carefully designed preclinical in vitro and in vivo animal assessments with human introduction only after established requirements are met. As preclinical studies are limited in the ability to assess many factors that will arise in the clinical situation, flexibility is needed in early clinical protocols to accommodate changes in selection criteria, techniques, and device design. These variables should be addressed in Investigation Device Exemption (IDE) studies approved by the Food and Drug Administration that are appropriate for class III devices, if the evaluations are performed in the United States. Clinical studies must also have corresponding institutional human subjects and research committee approvals.

References

1. Shah DM et al. Treatment of abdominal aortic aneurysm by exclusion and bypass: An analysis of outcome. *J Vasc Surg* 1991;13:15–22.

2. Parodi J. Abdominal aortic aneurysms. Presented at 1994 Research Initiatives in Vascular Disease Symposium on Transluminally Placed Endovascular Prostheses. March 25, 1994, Bethesda, MD.

3. Libby P et al. A cascade model for restenosis: A special case of atherosclerosis progression. *Circulation* 1992;86(SIII):47–52.

4. Clowes AW, Reidy MA. Prevention of stenosis after vascular reconstruction: Pharmacologic control of intimal hyperplasia. A review. *J Vasc Surg* 1991;13:885–891.

5. String ST et al. Interventional procedures for the treatment of vascular disease: Recommendations regarding quality assurance, development, credentialing criteria, and education. *J Vasc Surg* 1989;9:736–739.

6. Spies JB et al. Guidelines for percutaneous transluminal angioplasty. *Radiology* 1990;177:619–626.

7. Levin DC et al. Training standards for physicians performing peripheral angioplasty and other percutaneous peripheral vascular interventions. *Circulation* 1992;86:1348–1350.

8. White RA et al. Endovascular surgery credentialing and training for vascular surgeons. *J Vasc Surg* 1993;17:1095–1102.

9. Spittell JA et al. Recommendations for peripheral transluminal angioplasty: Training and facilities. *J Am Coll Cardiol* 1993;21:546–548.

10. Rutherford RB. Popliteal issues in endovascular surgery. *Surg Clin North Am* 1992;72:757–765.

11. Abbott WM et al. Evaluation and performance standards for arterial prostheses. *J Vasc Surg* 1993;17:746–756.

Index